DOING REFLEXIVITY
An introduction

Jon Dean

First published in Great Britain in 2017 by

Policy Press
University of Bristol
1-9 Old Park Hill
Bristol
BS2 8BB
UK
t: +44 (0)117 954 5940
pp-info@bristol.ac.uk
www.policypress.co.uk

North America office:
Policy Press
c/o The University of Chicago Press
1427 East 60th Street
Chicago, IL 60637, USA
t: +1 773 702 7700
f: +1 773-702-9756
sales@press.uchicago.edu
www.press.uchicago.edu

© Policy Press 2017

British Library Cataloguing in Publication Data
A catalogue record for this book is available from the British Library

Library of Congress Cataloging-in-Publication Data
A catalog record for this book has been requested

ISBN 978-1-4473-3085-1 paperback
ISBN 978-1-4473-3084-4 hardcover
ISBN 978-1-4473-3086-8 ePub
ISBN 978-1-4473-3087-5 Mobi
ISBN 978-1-4473-3088-2 ePdf

Cover design by Andrew Corbett
Front cover image: Arthimedes/Shutterstock
Printed and bound in Great Britain by CPI Group (UK) Ltd, Croydon, CR0 4YY
Policy Press uses environmentally responsible print partners

For Jenny

Contents

List of tables

About the author

Jon Dean lectures in politics and sociology at Sheffield Hallam University. His research focuses on youth volunteering, inequalities within the charity sector, and how public participation is affected by social class. He has also written and published work on research methodology, using innovative tools such as drawing and soundscapes to investigate discrete aspects of society, and on the political culture of the USA in the 1960s. This is his first book.

Acknowledgements

In *Tintern Abbey*, Wordsworth writes of 'little, nameless, unremembered, acts of kindness and of love'. Research projects are the result of such acts: a myriad combination of personal support and collegial advice, mixed with fleeting moments of inspiration and reassurance. I have probably bored most of my colleagues at Sheffield Hallam to despair during the writing of this manuscript, so I thank them first for their good humour. The book was supported both by a sabbatical, and by the generosity of colleagues in giving their time to review chapters, and to go with my whims on the *Desert Island* research project discussed within. Special thanks go to Andy Price, Peter Thomas, Julia Hirst, Ian Woolsey, Bob Jeffery, Arash Heydarian Pashakhanlou, Diarmuid Verrier, Cinnamon Bennett, Penny Furness, Henry Lennon, Stephen Spencer, and Carissa Honeywell, Knut Roder, and Anjana Raghavan. I also thank our community of undergraduate and postgraduate students, for asking the awkward questions and for accepting the challenges.

Further back, the postgraduate community at the University of Kent was a constant source of support and ideas, as we made the often lonely academic journey together. I would like to extend my thanks to all my fellow postgraduate students but especially Dara Blumenthal, Jon Ward, Eugene Nulman, Jonah Rees, and Vicky Tedder. But especially, I want to thank my doctoral supervisors Iain Wilkinson and Tim Strangleman, and Beth Breeze at the Centre for Philanthropy, who all took a chance on someone with no knowledge of sociology and no experience of research. I didn't always know what you were talking about but I hope that the important bits went in.

The team at Policy Press has been fantastic: enthusiastic about the project, rigorous in their feedback on the text, and prompt at replying to my incessant queries. To my editor Victoria Pittman in particular, thank you for the opportunity and for providing a shoulder to whinge on.

My mum and dad, Helen and Alan, and my brother Andy, have, while not seeing much of me, managed to keep me going throughout. Whether it was cutting out bits of the newspaper, forwarding relevant emails, and just chatting on the phone, knowing that they are always there takes the pressure off. And to Vera Dean thank you for your continued inspiration. I love you all.

And finally, when I started writing this book Jenny Carr was Jenny Carr. She is now Jenny Dean. And being able to write that is the most satisfying bit of doing the book.

Prelude

Do not copy nature too much. Art is an abstraction. (Paul Gauguin)

A research project can come to envelop everything. Glance at a newspaper and the idea at the core of your project will be the only word in focus. Turn on the radio and the story you're hearing will be tangentially related to *exactly* the point you're trying to make in that chapter you're currently on. You dive for a pen, or rip that page out of the paper, or, increasingly in my case, take a photo of the page in question, saved for later. The roll of photos on my phone is an odd mix of selfies, landscapes, pages from social theory texts grabbed from the shelves of well-stocked book shops, and potentially relevant cartoons from satirical magazines.

It also happens in art galleries. In the spring of 2013 I took my dad to see an exhibition called Force of Nature: Picturing Ruskin's Landscapes at the Millennium Gallery in Sheffield (Museums Sheffield, 2012). A small but perfectly formed exhibition, it sought to frame new and old depictions of landscape through the thought of John Ruskin, the Victorian art critic and philanthropist, who, alongside William Morris and Matthew Arnold, was one of the most radical and dominant figures in nineteenth-century British culture. Ruskin was obsessed with landscape, believing that the close observation and honest depiction of nature would in turn 'lead to imaginative engagement, moral rightness and even God' (Yallop, 2012: 2).

Among the blend of cutting-edge photography and historic watercolour and oil paintings, my researcher spidey-sense was tingling as I looked at a painting from 1890 called *The moon is up, and yet it is not night* by the pre-Raphaelite painter John Everett Millais.[1] A rather intriguing oil landscape, the painting offers the viewer a Perthshire estate at dusk, with a stag and a hind just visible in the descending gloom. Painted in a very limited palate of oranges, browns, and dirty yellows, the title and the painting 'endow the remote Highland setting with the atmosphere of an exotic and romantic locale' (Virag, 2001). As the exhibition's curator wrote of it: 'It is a mist filled scene, full of shadows and flickering light, and it perfectly captures the current feel of late autumn with the chill of winter now pressing in' (Pullen, 2012). Liking it, but recognising its relative blandness, I usually would have just shrugged and moved on, but decided to read the small information panel next to the painting, more out of museum visitor diligence than any particular enthusiasm for finding out more about the composition.

Millais' most famous artistic endeavours were his fantastical depictions of biblical or romantic scenes from literature: his *Ophelia* (1852), dead in the water among the reeds, is probably his most recognisable work. But his landscapes,

---

[1] Viewable at: http://www.tate.org.uk/art/artworks/millais-the-moon-is-up-and-yet-it-is-not-night-n05632.

this small sign told me, were not universally popular, often criticised for being merely faithful reproductions of scenes, or naturalistic and overly detailed. A prestigious publication, *The Art Journal*, the most important Victorian magazine on art, wrote of *The moon is up* in 1890 that while it showed 'higher aspirations and more pathos' than Millais had previously exhibited in pure landscape (Virag, 2001), it was felt that his pre-Raphaelite roots discouraged him from generalising, unable in his landscapes to paint what wasn't there. 'The drawback is still that he reproduces rather than interprets nature', the *Journal* wrote (cited in Virag, 2001). As someone researching the nature of interpretation and subjectivity and the epistemological underpinnings of social research, my interest was piqued.

In that small gallery in Sheffield in 2013, there was also a piece by Turner; unsurprising, as it would be vital to represent the work of the man who Ruskin thought most 'stirringly and truthfully measure[d] the moods of nature' (Piper, 2004: 321). In contrast to Millais, the landscapes of Joseph Mallord William Turner, that most lauded of British painters, remain some of the most well-regarded and loved by the public. *Landscape with water* (1840–5) ostensibly depicts the River Aniene in Tivoli, Italy.[2] Painted late in Turner's life, it shows both his mastery of, and confidence in, playfully using light in natural scenes, as an almost ghostly nothingness dominates the frame. There is an intense concentration of white in the middle of the painting, representing the light of the sun reflected on the surface of the water (Tate, 2010).

Turner's impressionistic works were heralded as creative, emotional, and a forceful challenge to the art scene, a challenge represented in the award-winning 2014 film *Mr. Turner*. John Ruskin's views on landscapes and how to record and respond to them shifted during his lifetime to take in some of these radical new beliefs. He moved from 'initial belief in realistic, visually accurate representation' (Moss, 2012), where it was an artist's 'understanding of detail that allows them to express the enormity of landscape' (Pullen, 2012), to a wider appreciation of work like Turner's, whose inventive approach to watercolour elevated 'the importance of conveying our emotional response to the landscape' (Moss, 2012).

One of the criticisms of Millais' work made by *The Art Journal* was that he failed to combine 'the result of his observation with the sympathetic warmth and transforming power of his own emotion'. This was not a critique one could make of Turner's work, but Ruskin saw how the two approaches, the faithful representation and the imaginative and emotional portrayal, added up to something more:

> Ruskin's defence of Turner *and* the pre-Raphaelites was founded in his belief that their work brought together the act of seeing with an act of imagination to recreate landscape. While close observation was the starting point, Ruskin believed that *it was imagination that subsequently*

---

2   Viewable at: http://www.tate.org.uk/art/artworks/turner-landscape-with-water-n05513.

allowed a proper understanding, transforming truth to nature through the imaginative sight of the viewer. (Yallop, 2012: 4, emphasis added)

At the core of this book is the problem *The Art Journal* identified in Millais' work: how do researchers faithfully observe and report the social world, while recognising that we have powerful emotions, and are subjective, imaginative beings? Social research, particularly qualitative research, is in many ways based on an individual's or team of researchers' interpretation of the findings emanating from their study. To pretend these researchers are emotionless and detached from this process 'obscures more than it illuminates' (Kahn, 2011: 202). Therefore there is a role for emotion and attachment in social research, alongside the recognition that researchers, as social beings themselves, are always combining their observation with the 'transforming power' of their biographies and personalities. Such a conceit is central to the methodological problems this book wishes to unpick. As the arts journalist Jonathan Jones (2014) wrote recently: 'only part of the content of an image is determined by the artist. The rest is born in the mind of the person looking. What you see is not what you get – it is what you bring.' What the following text hopes to do is examine *how we think* about *what we bring*.

Jon Dean
Sheffield
July 2016

ONE

Introduction: a rationale for reflexivity

> I know a scrupulous adherence to rules of method will not lead to objective truth. Surely this is in part because being a social scientist does not preclude having strong opinions, values, or feelings. But here it demands a willingness to be public about the way they affect one's standards and the claims one makes. One of the great barriers to maintaining standards is the strong attachment one develops with one's subjects, which can lead to emotions that make the idea of social *science* less than realistic. Riding downtown on the subway with Ovie that morning, I was full of passion for the vendors and their sidewalk life. But I tried, with both success and failure during my ride, to remain detached. (Duneier, 1999: 79)

Social research requires us to account for our humanness. Indeed, as Steven Deutsch (1971) wrote nearly half a century ago, social research is too often the work of humans who have failed to account for their humanness while attempting to objectify other humans for study (Gouldner, 1970). Reflexivity offers us a route out. This book aims to help social science researchers to plot a course when operationalising (doing) reflexivity within their research. Building primarily on the theoretical and empirical contributions of Pierre Bourdieu, it addresses an issue all researchers face. While it has been the qualitative methods literature in which the importance of reflexivity has figured most strongly, through using a broad range of examples from eclectic disciplines and fields of study, I hope to show how vital reflexivity can be to all areas of (social) scientific enquiry. While reflexivity has become a widely highlighted issue in research practice, and openly tackled as a problem in research organisation, data collection, and the dissemination of findings, it still causes confusion, suspicion, and wariness. This book will help provide readers with some of the history of reflexivity and a rationale for its crucial role. It offers the reader a combination of theoretical analyses, interpretations of methodological choices, and a series of big and small case studies, drawing both on reflexivity-centred issues arising in recent research projects and on original empirical data from new projects conducted by myself and colleagues.

The central problem of reflexivity stems from the role of positionality and subjectivity in social research. By this we mean the macro and micro elements that make it difficult to conduct social research in the 'scientific' laboratory conditions of the physical sciences. These can be *methodological*, where we examine how the particular methods employed affected the data produced; or a matter of *theoretical* analysis, where using one theoretical framework above another may be likely to cause the researcher to draw different conclusions; or they may involve the need for *disciplinary* reflexivity, in which studying the history, prevailing literature, and common practices of a particular academic discipline may lead to a narrowing of the gaze; or they may be *practical* and perhaps mundane issues of how everyday constraints, such as money, time, and resources, affect the depth, scope, conduct, and outputs of a piece of research; and finally they may be about *personal* reflexivity, the most central factor to be examined in this book, where we have to think about how the researcher's personal characteristics (such as their 'race' and ethnic background, social class, gender, and their general habitus and social disposition), and their position in the field of research (their research supervisors and colleagues, career position, or similar), affects their research practice and their results.

Social science is not practised in a vacuum, an idea we haven't always been comfortable with. As C. Wright Mills (1940) argued three generations ago, many thinkers of his time failed to consider the relevance of asking epistemological questions of knowledge acquirement processes in examining the validity of truth claims. Over recent decades, however, such analyses have become an established principle of social research, with the idea that researchers need to 'leave room to explore the relevance of their position in producing (imperfect, partial) knowledge' (Finlay, 2002: 207) overwhelmingly accepted, both in the positivist and naturalist traditions (Hammersley and Atkinson, 2007). With the feminist and cultural turns recognising the power relations inherent in conducting social research, the need to find ways of controlling for these became pressing. Norman Denzin and Yvonne Lincoln (1998) have strongly argued that what we can call the 'reflexive turn' in qualitative social science, and its objection to the idea of objectivity, has created the space whereby it is now accepted and normal to write the researcher into the world they investigate. More than that, as this book argues, it is necessary. As we shall see, this reflexive turn is about power and risk because to ask such questions is to ask the social scientist to expose 'their origins, biography, locality and "intellectual bias"' (Blackman, 2007: 700). Such biases, whether intellectual, disciplinary, biographic or other, need to be thought about and examined in the same way a researcher thinks about their material, whether that comes from the literature they read or the empirical data they collect.

Overall, the text will be structured on answering the following questions:

- What is reflexivity and why is it important in social research?
- What are the different ways in which reflexivity has been conceptualised within the social sciences, and in research methodology?
- Which social theorists have put methodological reflexivity at the heart of their research, and why have they done this?
- How have researchers operationalised reflexivity in the past, and how should and can researchers do it in their own research?

As hopefully appears obvious, accounts of reflexivity usually require a degree of personal involvement, both from you as researcher or reader, and from me as author. It is no coincidence that the epigraphical quote to this introduction from Mitchell Duneier starts with 'I'. I (both the word and me) will be writ large throughout this book, and we will look at whether it is a useful word scientifically or just induces narcissistic navel-gazing.

The book and my interest in this subject stem from several experiences: first, as a doctoral researcher, researching a field (volunteering) in which I previously worked as a practitioner, and researching in local areas which I knew well. The problem of producing an 'objective' and 'scientific' report of this research troubled me, until following my interpretation of Bourdieusian reflexivity (Bourdieu and Wacquant, 1992; Bourdieu, 2003a, 2007), I decided to draw attention to these issues, thereby combating a perceived objectivity deficit with a clear articulation of the subjectivities contained within the project. This empirical problem is fully explored in chapter seven.

The second experience comes from teaching the theory and practice of research methods at both undergraduate and postgraduate level at universities in the UK for the past five years. This notion of subjectivity, and controlling for one's own impact as a researcher upon research findings, is one that, after many discussions with early career researchers, provokes continued angst and confusion. While researchers understand and can conceptualise the impact of their positionality and the potential power-deficits which can exist between researcher, participants, and their research site, they often struggle when asked to reflect on how these processes may have affected their research, and in writing up and incorporating such reflection. I saw this manifested most plainly when I presented initial findings of this research at the British Sociological Association conference in London in 2013 in a session entitled 'Reflexive research or the narcissism of biography?' I was used to presenting my work to rows of empty chairs, but there was a standing room only crowd for this talk and afterwards a stream of early career researchers came up, not to congratulate me on the quality of my output but to thank me for assuring them that other people were also struggling with this issue. Similarly, students whom I have taught in interdisciplinary research methods courses, especially those engaged primarily in the STEM (science, technology, engineering and mathematics) subjects, can express bafflement at the reflexive approach in qualitative methods: for example, I remember one accountancy student asking incredulously, 'You mean we're *allowed* to do this?!' This obviously raises issues about academic disciplines and what we can do to guard against taking, in Bourdieu's phrase, a 'scholastic point of view'. One of the problems is that the social science establishment increasingly instils within students the importance of *being* reflexive but has provided little structured guidance as to how to *do* such reflexivity: exhortations to be reflexive are common, but advice on managing it and accounting for it are rare (Taylor and White, 2000; Mauthner and Doucet, 2003). It is my hope that this text starts to fill that gap.

The problem of doing a social, subjective, and empathetic science

How to study people's character, actions, and their institutions? That is the establishing question of the social sciences. It stems from Auguste Comte's coining of the word 'sociology' in the 1830s, absorbing concepts from the tradition of thinking which emerged in post-revolutionary France, a selective borrowing of ideas from the Enlightenment, and the work of economist Adam Smith (Turner et al., 2012: 19–36). Philosophy, theory, and art go much further back, and the value of the insights into humankind of Shakespeare, Plato, Machiavelli, or Austen should not be forgotten (Chinoy, 1954), but the principle of applying organised and rigorous *scientific* method to the study of people is a relatively recent phenomenon. This desire to measure and predict the behaviour of people can lead us not only to understanding but also to the solution of practical problems which people face in their everyday lives. But, as Sandra Harding (1991: 15) writes, there is a long-established hierarchy of knowledge, with maths and physics at the top, followed by chemistry and biology, then the 'harder' social sciences of economics and cognitive psychology, with anthropology and sociology playing in the ball pit of science. In their teaching and public practice, Bourdieu posits, university professors are to be agents of their institutions and repositories of established knowledge, rather than of uncertain knowledge that is still being worked on. This ambiguity is 'particularly pronounced in a discipline such as sociology', which knows its place in the hierarchy of the sciences, 'with mathematics at the top and sociology at the bottom' (Bourdieu, 2014: 38). Yet, as the leading public astrophysicist Neil de Grasse Tyson (2016) recently put it: 'In science, when human behavior enters the equation, things go nonlinear. That's why Physics is easy and Sociology is hard.' There is no single 'human standpoint' because social and historical conditions and material circumstances vary wildly (Letherby et al., 2013). Here we find the *social* side of the social sciences.

The problem with trying to do a science of society is of course that people are confusing, inconsistent, and tricky little bleeders who will say one thing and do another (Jerolmack and Khan, 2014), avoid putting their thoughts into action, and care (often far too much) about what other inconsistent people think about them. The difficulties of measuring a potentially infinite set of variables that make up an individual and their views, understanding how this messy ball of emotion and action interacts with other people and institutions, and trying to discern some pattern to this madness, means conclusions in social science are almost always hamstrung by 'what about-ism' ('What about gender?' 'Couldn't location explain all this?'). As Howard Becker (2014) has said, 'Life does not consist of people responding to a limited number of variables.' Many research texts and the study of methodology itself exist to examine and minutely re-examine how best to get the right answers. Your local university library may have more textbooks, monographs, and specialist journals focused on precisely unpicking the issues of methodology than it does on any other subject: shelf after shelf of very similarly titled chunky books detailing the best ways to manage a focus group, or collect a representative sample of participants.

As Michael Pickering (1997: 11) has put it, 'there are many different ways for us to grab on to the world and many different ways for it to grab on to us'. If a research participant is a messy bundle of behaviour and thought, and their social networks consist of friends and family who are similarly messy and complex, and the institutions they interact with – such as the government or their place of work – are themselves designed by and staffed by other messy complex people, as well as being institutionally messy, we must remember that the social science researcher trying to make sense of this mess is themselves a collection of personality traits, experiences, and biases. They are as much a result of their social conditioning as their research participants and any question which aims, for example, to elicit how a participant felt can easily be turned inwards ("Well, how would *you* have felt?") – *and should be*. In sum, there are inherent problems with studying people while also being a person (Bull, 2015). It is the central argument of calls within the social sciences for methodological reflexivity that researchers understand their own positioning on an issue or research question in order to fully understand how they are collecting, interpreting, analysing, and disseminating the data they have collected. 'Only, if you like, by subjecting the practice of the researcher to the same critical and sceptical eye as the practice of the researched is it possible to aspire to conduct properly objective and "scientific" research' (Jenkins, 1992: 61). Our subjectivity is tangled in the world of others (Denzin, 1997) and, as researchers, it is reflexivity which can help us unpick it.

While interest in reflexivity has grown significantly in recent years (see Alvesson and Sköldberg, 2000; May, 2011; Lumsden and Winter, 2014), such a focus is still not always treated as a central part of scientific (or scientistic) inquiry. Such calls for reflexivity are often dismissed as a distraction, or a level of abstraction too great, or narcissistic navel-gazing, or 'benign introspection' (Taylor and White, 2000: 6). But since we would not accept such reasoning for not considering the full gamut of possibilities when critiquing our data, why create such artificial limits for our reflective gaze? Reflection is important because, as the pragmatist philosopher John Dewey (1910: 6) wrote, it gives us space to consider and amend erroneous beliefs or conclusions:

> Active, persistent, and careful consideration of any belief or supposed form of knowledge in the light of the grounds that support it, and the further conclusions to which it tends, constitutes reflective thought.... It is a conscious and voluntary effort to establish belief upon a firm basis of reasons.

Throughout this book there are several examples of where looking at social research data again, or differently, or through different eyes and experiences, frames it in a different way. That scientists, albeit scientists of society, would seek to limit their space for reflection or cast it as unnecessary, even if that reflection is ostensibly personal, seems to leave the job unfinished. Such a mindset is redolent of the supposedly hard sciences that conduct 'hygienic', objective research and the idea that such research is the gold standard. On this I have always been very taken by words of Shamus Khan (2011: 201–2), who writes that:

> To stand outside people, looking in at their lives as if they were in some laboratory or snow globe, is not to understand them.... The study of human relations is necessarily an embedded one; to pretend otherwise obscures more than it illuminates.

Khan's ethnographic research (discussed at length in chapter five) involved living among the school students who were his research participants 24/7 for a year, teaching them, supporting them, questioning and probing them in order to get the answers he was seeking for their behaviour. He, or any social researcher, cannot do their work in laboratory conditions, the 'mind-in-a-vat' of Latour's (1999: 12) description. Social science cannot seal the room, cut off all outside interactions and influences, and test a subject again and again to verify a result. It is a science which gathers its data through both establishing relationships and catching fleeting moments, through in-depth discussions and casual asides. But personal involvement is not necessarily 'dangerous bias', it is 'the condition under which people come to know each other and to admit others into their lives' (Oakley, 1981: 58). Therefore, it is very subjective, but in a good way.

The case for reflexivity

Reflexivity raises questions about the role of objectivity in social science. But the notion of objectivity has to be challenged head on: 'objectivity' is rarely, if ever, objective. Within my discipline of sociology, this often relates to concern with the disadvantaged and the appearance that we align with society's underdogs (Lumsden, 2013b), summed up by Becker's (1967) famous question 'Whose side are we on?' But as John Holmwood (2015) describes, we have to carefully unpick what is meant by taking sides:

> [Becker's] was not an argument for partisan social science, but rather involved the observation that any social science that took seriously the circumstances and attitudes of the disadvantaged would be seen as partisan, simply by virtue of accounting for their views. As Becker observed, a social science that addressed the interests of those in subordinate positions would also appear unrespectable and partisan, while that which addressed the powerful would appear respectable and cloaked in 'objectivity'. However, it was an 'objectivity' that derived simply from the naturalisation of power relations, not from being outside them.

Science has done much to exacerbate this problem. There is a scholastic illusion of neutrality nourished by 'the myth of the impartial spectator' as Simon Susen (2007) puts it. This myth emanates from the continued disregarding of the fact that such an 'impartial spectator' is nourished by partial social interests, and academics are complicit in keeping the game of the scholastic thinker going, as Bourdieu (1990d) sought to show in his book about the academic elite, *Homo Academicus*.

While traditionally research is thought of as the 'creation of true, objective knowledge, following a scientific method', no matter whether that research is into social facts or personal meanings (Alvesson and Sköldberg, 2000: 1), such a conceptualisation does not stand up to sustained analysis, and even those researching in the physical sciences have to engage in rhetorical transactions and socially and politically affected behaviours to fund, conduct, or present their 'neutral' research (Taylor and White, 2000: 30). The scientific world is the site of competition, prizes, and the desire for prestige and distinction just like any other profession, and its hagiography needs to be challenged accordingly (Bourdieu, 1993: 9). The Nobel Prize-winning economist Angus Deaton (2015) made similar comments about the supposed objectivity of statistics, and their use by politicians, in the *Financial Times*:

> Headline statistics often seem simple but typically have many moving parts. A clock has two hands and 12 numerals yet underneath there may be thousands of springs, cogs and wheels. Politics is not only about telling the time, or whether the clock is slow or fast, but also about how to design the cogs and wheels. Down in the works, even where the decisions are delegated to bureaucrats and statisticians, there is room for politics to masquerade as science. A veneer of apolitical objectivity can be an effective disguise for a political programme.

To quote the psychological behaviourist Charles Shimp (2007: 146) on the supposed neutrality of quantitative research fields, they are just as likely as qualitative methods to involve 'implicit and unevaluated assumptions, incomplete descriptions of empirical and theoretical methods, self-interest and conflicts of interest, strongly held opinion accepted as fact, and political conflicts and angry disputes'. Shimp argues that behaviourist analyses of the behavioural analysts themselves must take place to understand the disciplinary and intellectual processes (Fuller, 2005) which affect their research practice. There has to be recognition that all scientific knowledge is provisional, positioned and incomplete (Pauwels, 2012), something political actors, in their desire for headlines and simple, reductionist slogans, are rarely willing to do. Yet the enquiring scientific mind must explore the resources that individual brings to bear on their scientific inquiry, including their social location, social positioning, and motivations (Jenkins, 2006). 'All learning depends on the reflexive interpretation of one's experience together with the experience of others', as the psychologist Paul Lafitte (1957: 17) wrote over half a century ago. Researchers rely on the valid, careful, and reasonable findings of other researchers. If we are standing on the shoulders of giants, reflexivity is a tool we can use to understand our relation to those giants and the foundations on which we base our knowledge. As William Stoner, the titular character in John Williams' bestselling campus novel posits, we are all in some ways hindered by our past education.

Reflexivity is the way we analyse our positionality, the conditions of a given social situation. This is both our position in social structures and institutions, and the thinking through of how such a position arises, and the forces that can stabilise and distort that position. It is an exploration of the researcher's own placement within the many contexts, power structures, and identities and subjectivities of the viewpoint (England, 1994). Establishing positionality is important for all research contexts as our ethnicity, gender, sexuality, social class, educational experience, current role and other aspects of our self and lived experience continually form, shape, and redefine our identity, and therefore the ways in which we approach and conduct our research (Moore, 2012).

Some writers see such an undertaking as potentially problematic and personally stressful, both because reflexivity can unsettle previous ways of thinking (Taylor and White, 2000), but also because it can be a personally introspective and almost confessional experience:

> it is about making oneself vulnerable. It is exposing one's strengths, weaknesses, innermost thoughts, and opening it up for others to criticize. It's voluntarily standing up naked in front of your peers, colleagues, family, and the academy, which is a very bold decision! (Forber-Pratt, 2015: 1)

While it may not immediately seem to be the case that laying out subjectivities is a way of staying neutral, through examples from many different fields this book will hope to convince you it is better than the alternative. To not recognise subjectivities or deny subjective influences, or to not think about the choices made in research and the reasons behind these choices and the unmistakable consequences of them, will inevitably lead to substantially less scientifically useful insights (Pauwels, 2012: 261). It's not just that in research honesty is the best policy: it's that a lack of clarity and exposition ends up invalidating your work, and potentially the work of others who wish to make use of it:

> Like all observers, I have my subjectivities. I know that scrupulous adherence to rules of method will not lead necessarily to objective truth. I believe that what is most important is I try to help the reader recognize the lens through which the reality is refracted.... I endeavour to explain my procedures for selecting data and my own biases and uncertainties about the inferences I draw. (Duneier, 1999: 14)

Calls for honesty about positioning are obviously not confined to the world of research. The British current affairs journalist and presenter Jeremy Paxman, on leaving the BBC (British Broadcasting Corporation), revealed himself politically as a 'one-nation Tory'. When asked if his now public personal political standpoint would affect his ability to do his job and suitably hold politicians to account, Paxman (quoted in Sparrow, 2015) responded, 'I hope not … I just don't think it's got anything to do with it': 'I think it's terribly hard to achieve impartiality. I think fairness is important, but I don't know whether impartiality is every really truly achievable.'

Such debates about impartiality in journalism and broadcasting have become a white noise. In the United Kingdom for instance, when any politician or cultural figure is interviewed on the BBC, for example, you can guarantee that social media, admittedly not the surest barometer of sound judgement, will immediately be filled with the howls of 'Bias!' *from both sides*. The right see the BBC as an overly liberal, cosy metropolitan elite, and the left see it as a cowed and simpering tool of the establishment and neoliberal consensus. The BBC fall over themselves to dispel such notions in debates on Radio 4's *Today* programme, in which having two guests on, each taking a diametrically opposed view on a public issue, is seen as a way of countering accusations of impartiality, and, worryingly, as a decent way of producing an enlightening public debate.

These small examples seek to demonstrate how debates about on the one hand the need for neutrality, but on the other the impossibility of objectivity, arise in science and social science research, but also politics, economics, and journalism. While we await these professions' critical self-reflection on their positioning, it is in public services and the caring professions that reflective practice has been most developed and has the greatest cross-over with methodological reflexivity. There has been a huge increase in interest in subject in areas such as health and social care (Taylor and White, 2000), social work (White, 1997; Butler et al., 2007; D'Cruz et al., 2007), youth work (Emslie, 2009; Forrest, 2010), nursing (Moore, 2012), teaching (Brookfield, 1995), and similar areas of public service, seemingly as part of changing professional practice in an increasingly marketised society in which austerity and neoliberalism have driven the welfare state into retreat (Beresford, 2016).

In health and social care and welfare settings, this has involved practitioners being encouraged to apply a 'critical, learning perspective' (Barnes and Cotterall, 2012: 231), taking a step back to think about what they know about their work, and how they know it. Taylor and White (2000) argue that under a value system which encourages outcome measures and evidence-based practice, there is little consideration of how this evidence is gathered and how practitioners make and construct their knowledge. The situated inscriptions of a care home or an acute trauma ward, for instance, affect how patients are cared for, how conditions are diagnosed and labelled, and how treatments are decided. A hierarchical process-driven and *unquestioning* approach to practice, where a single reading of a patient is enough, can lead to incorrect decisions being made. Unreflective practice in this case, which ignores power structures and social conditioning, cannot make sense of the competing versions of the same set of circumstances that may be offered by clinicians, family members, or patients themselves. A reflexive thinking through of these issues can lead to more informed choices, and more humane and understanding care.

Similarly, in social work it has been argued that reflexive practice can provide a nourishing dose of creativity, imagination, and hope, while avoiding the pitfalls of 'naive objectivism and the nihilism of anarchic relativism' (White, 1997: 739). In their excellent overview of the field, D'Cruz and colleagues (2007) examine the variations within reflexivity in social work, arguing that it is an emancipatory process examining how life choices and social and political conditions can help in understanding disadvantage. In such a conceptualisation, being reflexive prioritises a critical awareness of self and sees knowledge as socially constructed with the social worker expected to acknowledge the influences of their subjective experience on how they create knowledge. These qualitative and interpretivist approaches to challenging evidence-based policy and practice encourage social workers to engage with service users differently, with an attention to individual experience and intersubjectivity (Butler et al., 2007), and to think through the relationship between their logical positivist education (Rogers, 1967) and professional training, and their own personal psychology and individuality. Such contemplative unpicking of how *work* is done is also increasing. Recently Taylor and colleagues (2016) have argued that reflexivity at work is concerned with the ability to reflect upon experiences, which in turn can reinforce shared values and a community of practice. Despite the deep structural inequalities of workplaces and the field of work in general (Rainbird et al., 2004), work-centred reflection can help make sense of one's own attitudes in order to change goals and future development.

So reflexive thinking increasingly spans professions, and it increasingly spans academic disciplines. Sociology, gender studies, and anthropology have long been the centres for this sort of methodological thinking, but subjects like criminology (see Lumsden and Winter, 2014) have recently seen a reflexive turn due to their focus on the relationship between the powerful and powerless. Likewise, as the journalist Stuart Jeffries (2014) wrote of cultural studies, it was 'never a smug academic activity, but one that often involved facing awkward truths about oneself and how one was deeply, painfully implicated in existing power structures', especially when seen through the research output of Stuart Hall and his colleagues at the Centre for Contemporary Cultural Studies at the University of Birmingham in the 1980s and 1990s. In research involving film and visual production, MacDougall (2011: 111; see also Pauwels, 2012) sees reflexivity as a way of contextualising the content by openly revealing aspects of its production, such as interactions between the filmmaker and the field, and in more implicit ways such as in the choices made in editing.

In all these fields we must reiterate that reflexive work cannot just be about the person doing the research. It is the examination of both the structural and personal conditions which help us understand the knowledge we create. As Derek Robbins (2007: 78, emphasis added) says, writing of Bourdieu's sociology: 'Objective analysis of the grounds of one's own subjectivity thereby becomes *one* analysis of objective conditions to be *set alongside others* within a community of participating perceptions.' Because science and knowledge will 'always be deeply permeated by the social relations through which they come into existence' (Harding, 1991: ix), taking both macro and micro views of the context in which research is produced is vital.

Punk it!

This brief overview and introduction has served to acquaint readers with the many fields in which reflexivity should be an important consideration. While I am ostensibly a sociologist, my undergraduate work was in politics and American history, my PhD was a critical social policy analysis, and I now teach both in sociology and politics and to postgraduate students from a wide variety of disciplines. One of the themes of this book is the benefit of thinking eclectically, about the fact that inspiration can come from anywhere, and that thinking and working in rigid disciplinary structures with their inherited reflexive strictures of knowledge can be debilitating. Dave Beer's recent book *Punk Sociology* (2014) is a vital piece of reading for any social science student or researcher who wants to break free from some of the shackles that disciplines, institutions, and policy agendas force us to operate in. A short intervention, written with a straightforward and humane warmth, it is an argument for a better, less stilted and strangled, more creative, less plodding, quicker social science. Engaged with a wide range of topics and endlessly quotable, it uses the ethos of punk – an ethos centred on 'questioning the prevailing modes of thought' (Beer, 2014: 23), the subversion of hierarchy, and of valuing one's independence – to challenge the myriad crises faced by the social sciences in the UK. Beer lists the ways in which sociology is under attack, from the threat of commercial and cultural forms of social inquiry, the opportunities and challenge of digital scholarship, and the position of such disciplines within an audit-driven neoliberal university culture. And he rightly highlights sociology's failure to provide a detailed answer to *how* things may improve:

> How do we reimagine the craft and promise of sociology? How do we find ways of being creative, inventive, and lively? How can we deploy the sociological imagination in inventive ways? How can we resist the restrictions of uncertainty, crisis, and measurement? (Beer, 2014: 12)

Beer cautions that being *too* self-aware and offering nothing but constant critique and negativity towards the discipline (a tendency of which anyone who follows social scientists on social media will be aware), and of talking of crises in sociology too frequently, we are demoralising undergraduate students and early career researchers. Instead he offers a hopeful manifesto, which should be music to the ears of any enquiring mind: we need to resist particular pressures to play it safe and think radically about the way forward.

Reflexivity plays a part in such a manifesto. Gane and Back (2012) reflect on the 'promise' and 'craft' of sociology as set out in the work of C. Wright Mills. They argue that 'the enduring relevance of Mills' legacy is his way of practicing intellectual life as an attentive and sensuous craft but also as a moral and political project' (Gane and Back, 2012: 404). Social science needs to recognise the important part it can play in moral and political debates, which, as Beer rightly highlights, may be contentious in disciplines where 'neutrality has become a central feature' (Beer, 2015: 8). This fear of the subjective has to be confronted, turned around, and made into a tool itself:

> A punk is not afraid of their own limitations and vulnerabilities. Nor do notions of legitimacy or authenticity inhibit them. Punk seeks to break down and transcend boundaries and obstacles and to erode the lines between the performer and the audience. (Beer, 2014: 28)

Thinking about 'the position of the researcher in the research process' from the position of a punk sociologist, Beer (2014: 40) argues, would be to sidestep any debate about the rights and wrongs of such an issue, to look to embrace one's part in the research process and play with distinctions between the researcher and the researched. In a self-critical section, where he laments his own writing for accepting the strictures of academia, Beer writes 'Sociologists are often trained to be neutral and passive.... I follow the dictum, which I assume is a product of the attempt to draw on an objectivist and scientific approach in order to legitimize the discipline, "be more neutral"' (Beer, 2014: 54–5). Perhaps open reflexive practice is part of the punk musicians' 'deliberate *un*learning' (Savage, 1991: 82), which the social sciences have to do if they are to 'play with and sometimes defy conventions' (Beer, 2014: 42) which suffocate and choke off the discipline's connection with the publics it is meant to be serving. We can be, as Bourdieu (1993) puts it, a science that makes trouble. Those who expose awkward truths are often dismissed as politically motivated and unscientific. But critically asking questions of other's truths, and questioning the science as we question ourselves, is the reflexive imperative.

Overview of the book

This book is structured to examine the gamut of reflexive issues briefly outlined above. It starts with a wide focus, looking at the development of social theory and the people behind it, moving onto epistemological debates surrounding reflexivity and the production of knowledge, before gradually moving into biographical, positional, and personal explorations of reflexive work in the context of social research. The book also tries to move from a focus on theoretical and methodological arguments, to a granular attention to specific empirical case studies, which make up the majority of the second half of the text. The text incorporates thinking on the doing of reflexivity regarding the five aforementioned areas – theoretical, disciplinary, methodological, personal, and practical – and broadly moves through these, but readers will find that these areas intersect or run in parallel as we examine various facets of reflexivity.

Chapter two serves to provide an overview of Pierre Bourdieu's sociological project – his focus on social and cultural inequality, his development of the theory of habitus as an explanation for the logic of practice, and his personal biography – and examines how these elements entwined throughout his career. The extent to which the focus of Bourdieu's academic work mirrored his personal experiences is fascinating and underexplored academically. This chapter provides the reader with an account of Bourdieu's theoretical work, which is key to the main methodological message of the book, and a clear case study example for the reader of the relationship between research and personal experience. It argues that, in turning theories like that of the habitus inwards, we learn more about the fields of science and academia and so have a better conception of the realities of knowledge production.

From his studies of marriage practices in Béarn, to his research into the landscape of higher education, Bourdieu 'continually turned the instruments of his science upon himself' (Bourdieu and Wacquant, 1992: 36). Bourdieu argues that through performing a reflexive sociology the social sciences give us the 'epistemic benefit' of bridging the gap between objectivism and social constructionism. Building on chapter two therefore, chapter three moves on to an extended examination of Pierre Bourdieu's reflexive sociology. It focuses on the methodological lessons we can take from the personalised research work he produced, offering the theoretical rationale and reasoning for the work outlined in the previous chapter. This chapter builds on this in detail, drawing on Bourdieu's key contributions to methodological debates (Bourdieu and Wacquant, 1992; Bourdieu, 1999, 2007), critiquing his development from largely structural reflection on the scientific method to more personal reflexivity, ultimately concluding that a thoughtfully and critically open subjectivity is more scientific than a closed pretence of assumed objectivity. This focus on Bourdieu is not to disavow other scholars who have written passionately of the need for reflexivity, especially Alvin Gouldner (1970), whose position was that no good theory can be formulated without expressing the basic sentiments and ideals of its author. Gouldner's work is certainly a touchstone in developing the idea that an author's morality and ethical standpoint pervades their theory, whether they like it or not. So by applying such a Gouldner-esque framework to Bourdieu's theory, method, *and* call for reflexive sociology, we can see how Bourdieu's call for reflexivity is both often inconsistent and absent from much of the literature aimed at helping researchers think and work reflexively.

Chapter four moves on from Bourdieu to examine other theoretical and methodological contributions to the understanding and practice of doing reflexivity. First, there is a focus on the developments under the banner of feminist research methods and standpoint theory which have become so entwined with qualitative research practice. Much of the need for reflexivity comes from the issues that can arise from a powerful researcher studying a less powerful population or context, and it is the work of Sandra Harding, Ann Oakley, Helen Roberts, and other researchers who have moved us from the unreflexive dynamics of the 1950s and 1960s to a position where we are better at seeing and working with such inequalities. After this, the chapter moves to critiquing the issue of academic disciplines, using David Graeber's anarchist anthropology to think through the issues for knowledge production of having such narrow boundaries for examining the social world. Finally, this chapter focuses on a discussion of the American sociologist C. Wright Mills and the spatial and biographical consideration that must be undertaken in reflexive inquiry. This builds on the work of Brewer (2004, 2005), who has argued that such a situational reading of the researcher doing the research is necessary to truly understand and ground their output.

In chapter five we examine four recent research projects and how the author in each case struggled with and tackled the issues of being reflexive. The four pieces of research, two from the UK and two from the US, are Mitch Duneier's *Sidewalk*, Lisa Mckenzie's *Getting By*, *Privilege* by Shamus Rahman Khan, and *Negotiating Cohesion, Inequality and Change* by Hannah Jones. In each of these books the authors grapple with negotiating personal biases and positions, alongside carrying out excellent academic research. The chapter examines how these researchers faced the issues of personal loyalties and positionality, and worked reflexively to minimise any issues these created, relating back to the theoretical concepts raised in previous chapters. This secondary analysis aims to show readers how different figures needed to adapt their approach and reflect on their positions as they carried out their fieldwork and undertook their analysis. In none of these pieces does the reflexive work dominate; in fact it generally merges seamlessly with the data, showing how reflexive research practice does not need to be an abstract add-on, but can be incorporated into research work fluently and naturally. They demonstrate how reflexivity operates in the field, and how social research can retain its scientific approach even when the researcher is far from detached.

While we are well aware that different researchers may look at the same data and get different results, it is a relatively under-reported phenomenon (Dean et al., 2015). Chapter six reports on empirical research which articulates many of the occasionally mundane and practical issues arising in doing reflexive work. It examines an original, qualitative research project I recently completed with a team of colleagues at Sheffield Hallam University. A group of six of us, from varying methodological, philosophical, and disciplinary backgrounds, as well as obviously having different biographies and personal experiences, each analysed three transcripts from the popular BBC radio programme *Desert Island Discs*. We completed this parallel analysis at the same time, but separately, and then came together to discuss our different interpretations of and approaches to the data. This involved asking the reflexive question 'Why do you think you have analysed the data in the way that you have?' This chapter draws heavily on our analyses and our discussions, which bring up issues such as the difference between being trained as a psychologist or a sociologist, the theoretical underpinning a researcher has to their previous work, and more personal issues, such as how an individual's age and gender affected their approach, and how the amount of time one has to devote to research can alter one's focus and conclusions.

The penultimate chapter focuses on me. It details the multiple reflexive tasks I undertook during my doctoral research, which drove me towards writing this book. As a researcher studying youth volunteering in two different areas of the UK, and as a young volunteer with strong links in both of the areas, it became apparent the research would have to consider the impacts of my own biography and individual subjectivities upon the research process and findings. This chapter provides some examples of how this reflexive turn was operationalised in the research project and reflection on their effectiveness and how other researchers could appropriate them. These include interviewing my parents about my upbringing and writing a substantial critical autobiographical analysis of my own class and political positioning as a result; writing reflexive autoethnographic fieldnotes, which critiqued my own practice and relationship with research participants, and presenting these unedited to the reader; and surveying fellow doctoral students to examine whether the conclusions my research was coming to were *as a result* of the pressures of being a PhD student having to finish within three taut years.

Finally a concluding chapter will draw the book together. At the centre of this conclusion is a detailed reading of Alice Goffman's *On the Run*, a recent social science publication in which the (perceived) lack of reflexivity has been one element in a string of controversies the book has garnered. Goffman's study of young black men in Philadelphia has become a touchstone twenty-first-century example of the difficulties of doing reflexive work, with Goffman's status as a privileged white woman heavily critiqued. This ongoing saga has served to vividly highlight the relationship between reflexivity and research ethics, and the thorny question of who gets to speak for whom. The final chapter also explores the presentation of social science research, how we build spaces for reflexivity in research dissemination, and the extent to which reflexive work has been labelled narcissistic and whether this is a valid worry for researchers. Finally a coda is offered on the knotty issue of how writing in the social sciences is a significant barrier to good reflexive practice.

Doing reflexivity: some conclusions and questions for reflexives

There is an apocryphal tale all early career researchers tell, of the fellow researcher who publishes a vital book or thesis *on exactly your topic* two weeks before your deadline. For me, finding out that Nina Eliasoph (2011, 2012) was publishing *two* books on the social class divisions and politics of volunteering two-thirds of the way through my doctoral research on that exact same issue was a real grind. However, as I found out when I sat down grumpily with the two texts, the problems associated with such a scenario are generally overblown. Eliasoph's work is excellent, and I have found it monumentally useful for understanding the trends within volunteering. There is a need to stay calm and remember there are always differences between two pieces of research. It is almost impossible that your fellow researchers will have been speaking to the same people as you, and they are probably researching in a different community with different local and state policies at play, for example. They will probably be bringing in different theories, literature, methods, and perhaps orienting their work to a different audience. Take it as a reassuring sign that other researchers see the field as important enough to be publishing extensively in. If you want to be super-critical, if you find yourself unduly troubled by a 'rival' publication, ask yourself who would not want their research to be as informed as possible by current thinking?

It also means you can cite them when they print what you want to say. As I was starting to write this book, Helen Kara (2015) published her own monograph on creative research methods, an introduction to the growing strands of innovative practice within research (Gauntlett, 2007; Jacobsen et al., 2014; Lury and Wakeford, 2014). It only includes a short section on reflexivity (Kara, 2015: 71–5), but within it is a list of key questions that methodological reflexivity requires the researcher to consider. Kara's list is an excellent starting point for our discussions over the following chapters:

• How do I define my identity? How does that affect my research practice?
• What are my values and beliefs, and how are they operating in my research work?
• Which of my biases and assumptions are relevant here, and how are they affecting my research?
• What impact do my emotional responses have on my research?
• How does the time at which I am working affect my research?
• What effect has this relationship had on my relationship with others? What effect, in turn, has this had on the research? What about relationships between other relevant people?
• Which institutions are relevant in my research? What effect have they had on the research? What effect has the research had on them?
• What are the political aspects of my research? How do they play out in practice?
• What are the relevant power balances and imbalances? Are they changing during the research process? If so, in what way? What effect do they have on my research?
• How do these considerations affect the choices I make in my research?
• How can I use these considerations to inform, enrich and develop my research?
• Am I being as honest and transparent as possible about all these factors in presenting my research?

Kara's questions provide us with a solid starting point; some are practical, some methodological, some theoretical. The job of this book is to discuss how we can start to answer them.

TWO

Pierre Bourdieu and the development of theory

> The goal of sociology is to uncover the most profoundly buried structures of the various social worlds which constitute the social universe, as well as the 'mechanisms' which tend to ensure their reproduction or their transformation. (Bourdieu, 1996: 1)

This chapter serves to provide an overview of Pierre Bourdieu's sociological project: his focus on social and cultural inequality, his development of habitus as an explanation for the logic of practice, and his personal biography, and examine how these elements entwined throughout his sociological career. It will give the reader an account of Bourdieu's theoretical and empirical work, and, in order to underscore the main methodological message of the book, provide a clear case study example to the reader of the relationship between research and personal experience. While overviews of Bourdieu's work are legion and varying in their approach and focus (see Harker et al., 1990; Jenkins, 1992; Fowler, 2000; Everett, 2002; Grenfell, 2004, 2008; Calhoun, 2010, Thatcher et al., 2016, among many others) the following section will briefly introduce several of Bourdieu's key concepts, specifically those that will aid us in understanding the development of his reflexive sociology. What this chapter and the next aim to add is a focus on the ways in which Bourdieu's academic work mirrored his personal experiences, a notion always slightly below the surface (for exceptions, see Jenkins, 2006; Frangie, 2009).

Bourdieu's studies of the Algerian war (in which he was a soldier), the social and family practices of rural France (in which he grew up and was socialised), the French elite (which he entered), the French university system (in which he came to dominate), the media (in which he came to be a frequent presence), and in other areas serve to foreground the often deep relationship between a researcher and their research. Can we be surprised that Bourdieu, a man who felt out of his comfort zone in the elite schools of the French academy and subjugated by his humble upbringing (Bourdieu, 2007), would devote his time to developing theoretical concepts like habitus and hysteresis (Bourdieu, 1977, 1990c) to explain the bourgeoisie's battle for cultural distinction (Bourdieu, 2010 [1984])? Bourdieu's sociological project was to uncover and highlight the invisible structures which govern our lives (Bourdieu and Wacquant, 1992: 7). Therefore, if all science, but particularly social science, exists as part of this larger social construction, the choice is not to be either part of this construction or not – a false dichotomy – but to be aware of the construction or not, and to raise awareness of it or not

(Bourdieu, 1999: 608). By looking at the link between the collection of data and the development of theory, in this chapter we can undertake a secondary reflexive analysis of one of the central social thinkers of the contemporary period.

'I don't like definitions much': Bourdieu's key ideas[1]

Pierre Bourdieu was born in 1930 and died in 2002. In that time he became the most celebrated public intellectual of the late-twentieth century, particularly in his native France, and since his death his ideas, theories, and contributions have percolated through Western social sciences to an at times unbelievable extent. He was the author of 37 books and over 400 journal articles. The range and scope of his research work, much of which he carried out himself alongside a team of researchers, was varied and influential. Of interest to us here is how his personal life, particularly his upbringing and formative experiences, can be read in tandem with his theoretical and empirical work. He was born in Denguin, a small rural town in the Béarn region of south-west France near the Pyrenees. His father was a postal worker, and this very modest upbringing stayed with Bourdieu his entire life, despite his rapid upward social mobility as he excelled academically. Educated at one of the leading secondary *lycées* in Paris (the Lycée Louis-le-Grand, the school attended by Hugo, Voltaire, Derrida, and Durkheim), he took his degree in philosophy at the École Normale Supérieure, one of the *grand écoles* of French higher education, similar to the Ivy League in the USA or Oxbridge in the UK. After becoming a teacher, he was conscripted to the French army and served in the Algerian war in 1955, staying in the country after his service to lecture and undertake research. This work, *Sociologie de l'Algérie* (Bourdieu, 1958) was to become a cornerstone of his contribution to anthropological and social theory, and, alongside his experiences in the grandest institutions of the French education system, as an out-of-place, working-class boy from a rural nowhere, gives us the best insight we can hope to generate about Bourdieu's bearing on his own work. He was a 'de-peasanted peasant', a 'man between two worlds' (Goodman and Silverstein, 2009; Reed-Danahay, 2009), and if we are to start thinking through his contribution to examining how the researcher affects the research, this context is vital.

What Pierre Bourdieu's contribution to social science offers us is a toolbox of ideas and approaches to challenge orthodoxy. Bourdieu's theoretical goals, which he himself felt he kept in the background out of both arrogance and modesty (Bourdieu and Wacquant, 1992: viii), can be brought under five broad headings. They speak to five false (as he saw it) dichotomous relationships, 'absurd oppositions' (Bourdieu, 1990a) and 'deep-seated antimonies' that 'rend social

---

[1]   Pierre Bourdieu quoted in Wacquant (1989: 5).

science asunder' (Bourdieu and Wacquant, 1992: 3), which Bourdieu sought to (re)connect. They are best summed up as divisions between:

- subjectivist and objectivist modes of knowledge
- analysis of the symbolic and the material
- theory and research
- structure or agency
- using the micro and the macro as the unit of research.

To this list, first formalised by Wacquant in *An Invitation to Reflexive Sociology* (Bourdieu and Wacquant, 1992: 3), we could add a sixth:

- the split between social researchers and activists.

Such splits are still common in social science. As the former US Secretary of State Henry Kissinger famously remarked, academic politics is usually vicious, because the stakes are so small. Today, despite the myriad exhortations regarding the value of mixed methods, we still see battle lines drawn between qualitative and quantitative researchers, and students being taught that they are opposed to and in competition with each other. One does not need to spend much time working in a UK university to see (and become part of) the sniping between subjects such as psychology, sociology, and criminology, which, if anyone in the real world cared, would look like the foolish and insufferable vanity of small differences that it is. Writing of his disdain for such artificial splits, and articulating his famous disregard for disciplinary boundaries, Bourdieu comments with de Saint Martin (1978: 7):

> how artificial the ordinary oppositions between theory and research, between quantitative and qualitative methods, between statistical recording and ethnographic observation, between the grasping of structures and the construction of individuals can be. These alternatives have no function other than to provide a justification for the vacuous and resounding abstractions of theoreticism and for the falsely rigorous observations of positivism, or, as the divisions between economists, anthropologists, historians and sociologists, to legitimize the limits of *competency*: this is to say that they function in the manner of a *social censorship*, liable to forbid us to grasp a truth which resides precisely in the *relations* between realms of practice thus arbitrarily separated.

This critique of the frequently elitist and undemocratic approach to knowledge does not always easily translate into applications of Bourdieu's own work though. Bourdieu and Wacquant (1992: 5) posit that one problem with the application of Bourdieu's sociological project is that it is deeply fragmented, with different groups of researchers taking the bits applicable to their work and ignoring the rest; twenty years later, though, Michèle Lamont (2012) suggests this pick-and-choose approach is perfectly reasonable (see Atkinson, 2013, for a critical take on this issue). In my experience social researchers who use Bourdieu tend to be *fans* (Bourdieuphiles, in Lamont's [2012: 229] terminology). This can be seen in the profusion of Bourdieu-inspired social science, particularly in the last few years. The British Sociological Association's Bourdieu Study Group has prospered with a new publication called *Bourdieu: The Next Generation* (Thatcher et al., 2016), which aims not just to present new research in the Bourdieusian mould, but for the authors to explain their growth *as Bourdieusians*, including reflection on why his work speaks to them and their own personal background. This desire to understand the researcher's cultural habitus (Hammersley, 1997) is Bourdieusian in itself.

Habitus, capital, field and hysteresis

Key to understanding Bourdieu is understanding social change, or the lack of it. Why, he makes us ask, at a time of immense social change – technological, emancipatory, political – are things seemingly destined to stay so static? Why do the educational elite (Bourdieu and Passeron, 1977) reproduce their advantage with such abandon; why, throughout history, have some tastes been given more prominence and value than others (Bourdieu, 2010 [1984]); and why, at a time of supposed increased freedom, do smaller and smaller numbers of large corporations have powerful monopolies (Bourdieu, 2005)? As Hawthorn (1997: 19) writes in review of Bourdieu's book *The State Nobility* (1996a):

> Other social theorists persist in asking how much of the social world we can make, how much we have to take. That, Wacquant tells us, is pointlessly scholastic. Bourdieu's achievement is to have shown that what we believe to be our acts of 'will' are determined by real divisions that our acts serve in turn to sustain. 'Tout se passe,' he has often said, 'comme si.' It always has and, as he has repeatedly insisted (even to striking students in Paris in 1968), it always will.

Key to his theory of social stasis is habitus. In order to explain the concept of habitus, I often ask students to think of an onion. Imagine a fully developed adult is an onion, with layer upon layer of experiences built up over time all coming together to make up the whole of the being. The external forces that act upon it such as warm, fertile ground, or a complete absence of sunlight, affect its growth and development at various stages. Some of these forces will have definite impacts on the onion's development, and others will be coped with as they are not vital to the final product. Any one layer of onion on its own is relatively inconsequential – soft, supple and easily malleable. But building layer on quality layer, or not, hardens the overall structure into a rock solid personality (or onion). This, at its most basic, is the theory of habitus. It is an embodied way of thinking about people's character, about how growth and development builds on previous growth and development; how external forces as varied as culture, economic welfare, stigmatisation, or social networks can affect one's strength, type, or stability of character; and how privilege and certainty, or precarity and doubt, can be reinforced through socialisation to become embodied ways of acting and thinking, such as how a person holds or sees themself. While every person in society is an individual, it is through thinking with theories like habitus that social scientists are able to generalise and classify, identifying trends and possibilities at a social level.

Habitus sought to explain how the social structures within which one is brought up affect later everyday practice: a 'socialized subjectivity' (Bourdieu and Wacquant, 1992: 126). It was Bourdieu's response to the structure–agency debate (Calhoun, 2011; Wacquant, 2016), a way of explaining social behaviour and the structure in which those behaviours occurred. A 'durable but generative set of dispositions' (Burawoy, 2008a: 4), which are created and change as structures and personal experience collide (Harker et al., 1990), habitus is a mediating construct where one's previous knowledge and experience combine to a greater or lesser extent to determine responses to situations. Through habitus, as Diane Reay (2004: 432; see also Kuhn, 1995) writes, we can see how bodies and the social world have a symbiotic relationship. As Robbins (2000: 16) puts it, habitus is a concept developed to explain how 'individuals internalise as a guide to their actions and attitudes, the practical structural explanations of their situations which impinge upon them partially as a consequence of those situations'. Similarly, the theory of capital sees society as the product of accumulated history. For sociologists and anthropologists trying to understand the impact of both structure and agency, it has been Bourdieu's study of social class which has become the paradigmatic intellectual framework for these analyses in the twenty-first century. Whereas traditional understandings saw social class as a primarily economic categorisation – classifying individuals through measures such as their employment or income – a Bourdieusian conceptualisation of social class puts social and cultural aspects of everyday life alongside the economic ones. It is the interplay between one's economic resources (or economic capital), one's friends and social networks (social capital), and education and understanding of cultural institutions (cultural capital) that truly make up one's class position. The increased prominence of such a class analysis moves social science on from the 'empty signifiers' of *what we have*, to the arguably more important but more value-laden *who we are* (Lawler, 2005: 804, 797). Such a model of class has become *de rigueur* in sociology, especially since the publication of the BBC's Great British Class Survey (Savage et al., 2013), although there are myriad recently published critiques of this specific approach (for overviews see Woodward et al., 2014; Skeggs, 2015).

Therefore in social situations people use personal experiences and resources, and their knowledge of unwritten social guidelines to manage their behaviour; consequently their actions are somewhat contained within a structural cycle. A person's identity is not shaped 'in opposition to the social world' but by the social world (Lawler, 2008: 7); it comprises their individual history, shaped by their social history (Bourdieu, 1990a, 1990b), with habitus stemming from the internalisation of experience. So the development of the habitus is a continual process, where layer upon layer of experience develops and determines how an individual reacts to situations. The 'primacy' layers, acquired early on in life in childhood, are the most vital because they may shape every action which is to come (Garnham and Williams, 1996: 61), but social analysis shows a certain level of similarity across experiences. For example, growing up in a poor neighbourhood is both an individual experience (which every individual will face slightly differently) but also a common experience (about which people can share familiar stories).

In a fascinating example of how these structural processes can become subsumed, Bourdieu asks why school timetables around the world are split as they are, broken up into hour-long periods without question. 'When you put this question to teachers and pupils, you discover that they find it absolutely natural, and that the very idea of doing anything different seems inconceivable to them' (Bourdieu, 2014: 171). Even though pupils may be in the middle of some creative activity or successfully getting on with their work they are instructed to stop and go to their next lesson; similarly, teachers have to design lessons which last one hour precisely. It is habitus and internalised rituality which means these 'deprivations are reproduced quite contentedly' (Bourdieu, 2014: 173).

Where this action takes place is theorised as a *field* of play, where social actors bring their habituated selves to 'compete', and their position is determined as a result of their interaction with the specific 'rules' of that arena, their habitus, and their capital. A field 'consists of a set of objective, historical relations between positions anchored in certain forms of power (or capital) … a *relational configuration endowed with a specific gravity* which it imposes on all the objects and agents which enter in it' (Bourdieu and Wacquant, 1992: 16–17, original emphasis). Any field presents potential rewards and failures, and contains considerable uncertainty and strategic interplay, whether it is education, the law, government bureaucracy, or sport. All these fields have particular social and cultural rules and actors are judged by their ability to adapt to the rules of the field:

> [Strategy] is the product of a practical sense, of a particular social game. This sense is acquired beginning in childhood, through participation in social activities.… The good player, who is as it were the embodiment of the game, is continually doing what needs to be done, what the game demands and requires. This presupposes a constant invention, an improvisation that is absolutely necessary in order for one to adapt to situations that are infinitely varied. This cannot be achieved by mechanical obedience to explicit, codified rules (when they exist). (Bourdieu, in Lamaison, 1986: 112–13)

Leading on from this, and key for our discussion of critically reflecting on research practice, is the concept of hysteresis. Hysteresis is a theoretical term popularised in Bourdieu's sociology and is used to identify discordance between habitus (the sense of one's self and cultural practices) and field (setting, place or institution). Often referred to as the 'fish out of water' syndrome, hysteresis arises in class terms when individuals enter unfamiliar social settings, or need to act outside of their comfort zone. As Bourdieu writes (1977: 78): 'practices are always liable to incur negative sanctions when the environment with which they are actually confronted is too distant from that in which they are objectively fitted'. These negative sanctions can be a sense of dislocation, unease or wariness, or the imposter syndrome, a favourite topic among early career researchers.

Classically applied in sociological studies of education, where, for example, working-class students struggle to fit in at elite universities (Reay, 2003; Reay et al., 2010), hysteresis is one of Sennett and Cobb's (1972; see also Hoggart, 1957) 'hidden injuries' of class. In culture, for instance, hysteresis is used frequently to dramatise the journey of characters. In modern British plays such as *The Pitmen Painters* by Lee Hall, Willie Russell's *Educating Rita*, and *The History Boys* by Alan Bennett, academically and artistically talented working-class characters face choices and challenges in entering the middle-class dominated fields of art, literature, and Oxbridge respectively. The feeling of dislocation and of leaving behind what they know contests with their fearful hope for social betterment, as they encounter educational institutions. In keeping with Bourdieusian critical analysis, we could reflect that middle-class sensibilities are never far away from drama ostensibly about the working-class experience.

In practice, habitus has been utilised by social researchers in 'contrasting the self-assurance of the middle class with the unease and discomfort of the working class' (Bottero, 2004: 993; Reay, 2005), with the theoretical frameworks of cultural capital and habitus notably applied in studies of education. For example, in *Privilege* (2011, discussed at length in chapter five), Shamus Khan explores the non-academic lessons that are taught to students at an elite American boarding school. Students learn the skills that will support them through their adult lives at the very heights of business, politics, and public life. Students buy the knowledge of how to be *at ease* in various social situations, expressing a 'radical egalitarianism' in taste, a cultural omnivorousness, while making it appear that they are successful and confident because of natural ability rather than having had the social advantages of an upbringing where such tuition was affordable. He dissects through a Bourdieusian framework how this elite habitus comes about:

> Being an elite is not a mere possession or something 'within' an actor (skills, talents, and human capital); it is an embodied performative act enabled by both possessions and the inscriptions that accompany experiences within elite institutions (schools, clubs, families, networks, etc.). Our bodily tastes, dispositions, and tendencies are not simply something we're born with; they are things that are produced through our experiences in the world. Not only do they occur in our minds, but they are things we enact repeatedly so that soon these performances

> look less and less like an artificial role we're playing – a role that might advantage us – and instead look more and more like just who we naturally are. (Khan, 2011: 136)

This is the knowledge of a new elite, which de-emphasises 'who you know' and emphasises 'what you know', with the 'what you know' focusing on behaviour and 'fitting in' to certain fields. Because the habitus is 'internalised as second nature and so forgotten as history' (Bourdieu, 1990c: 56), these elite students see their privilege as natural and earned. They would not be able to pinpoint a time in their history when they were told to act with this confidence and assuredness, and to know 'how to play the game'. Instead, habitus is built up over time. Khan witnessed the class differences within the school, as young people from disadvantaged backgrounds are given opportunities through scholarships, and taught the same formal lessons as students from wealthier more privileged backgrounds, but cannot cope in the same way. He writes about how poorer students valued and appreciated the opportunity much more, but were so deferential to their superiors they failed to make the same relationships with staff, one of being at ease and relaxed, which reinforced hierarchy and hindered their ability to embody the experience of the school and of the elite.

The symbolic

If Bourdieu's (1986) forms of capital were economic, cultural, and social resources, it is symbolic capital which enables their power. Symbolic capital is prestige and recognition, the badge of honour an individual receives because of their position. This can come in many forms and is often to do with perception: writers such as Skeggs (1997) and Mckenzie (2015) have written movingly of the ways in which working-class women are culturally dismissed because of their perceived lack of status. In his career, Bourdieu provided descriptions of the legitimation of symbolic power in art, taste, the education system, academia, and through masculine power, showing how there are some (generally hegemonic white, male, middle-class, and heteronormative) behaviours, tastes, and dispositions which become natural and legitimate over time, including in fields such as social research, science, and universities.

How is this symbolic capital operationalised? Bourdieu reaches for a term from Spinoza – *obsequium*, meaning respect paid to the state or the social order. We may have a uniformly negative understanding of what obsequious means today, but Bourdieu sees obsequiousness in even the most critical and anarchic person's response to the state, its institutions and its representatives. From the person humbly and fearfully applying for a mortgage, to the teachers and pupils dogmatically following a superior's timetable (Bourdieu, 2014: 13–16, 171–3), 'homage is paid not just to an individual who is the apparent object of respect, but to the social order that makes this person respectable' (Bourdieu, 2014: 35).

Bourdieu (2010 [1984]: 473) argues convincingly that the social order is reinforced by a dominant establishment who are able to impose their inherited views on social categorisation, so that social structures appear as objective necessities. The continued existence of an elite and unequal education system would be one (Bourdieu and Passeron, 1977), and a more recent example would be in the stigmatisation and abjection of welfare recipients and marginalised groups (Jones, 2012; Mckenzie, 2015; Shildrick and MacDonald, 2013; Tyler, 2013). People assume the structures that exist in society are natural and necessary, rather than reflexively seeing them as emanating from past struggles and the dominance of certain sections of society, and from inequalities in micro (class, gender, or ethnic) or macro (national, Western) power relations (Bourdieu and Wacquant, 1992: 14). Using the metaphor of social life as a 'game', Bourdieu's sociological project sought to expose how the elite 'players' have not only been heavily involved in the design of the games' rules but also have the power to decide what a winning hand looks like. The dominated 'always contribute to their own domination' (Bourdieu, 1996: 4) and this domination begets further domination as it is a disposition which takes root, stemming from the symbolic power of social positioning.

> Bourdieu forged this concept of symbolic violence to designate a kind of violence which is misrecognised as such, and therefore accepted by the dominated because they share with the dominant representations categories of thinking that are inculcated through the educational system and the media. (Sapiro, 2010: x)

This is how middle-class tastes and values come to be seen as inherently tasteful, knowledgeable, and *right* (Lawler, 2008). They are offered legitimacy by their symbolic cultural value (Skeggs, 2004a), whereas working-class values 'are [always] read as immoral' (Skeggs, 2004b: 91). Such acceptance in seen in the talk of people caught up in cycles of low pay and no pay: research has shown such individuals to be in denial of their poverty and willing to morally condemn 'the poor', wanting to dissociate themselves from such symbolically immoral categories (Shildrick and MacDonald, 2013). Such 'false consciousness', in Marxist terms, explains why workers are 'unable to grasp the "true" nature of their interests or their historical role as a subordinate class because their view of reality [is] filtered through their class position' (Morrison, 2006: 62).

The state

Bourdieu's (2014) work on the state is immortalised in a huge edited collection of a lecture series he delivered at the Collège de France in the early 1990s. Building on the classic definition of Max Weber, that the state has the 'monopoly of legitimate violence', Bourdieu argues that the state is that which possesses 'the monopoly of legitimate physical *and symbolic* violence' (Bourdieu, 2014: 4). This obviously ties in with the themes above, that powers and capitals have to be legitimated by dominant actors, and it is the state that ultimately holds the role of legitimator. Bourdieu used his lecture series to explain the how and why, through a litany of historical, political, and empirical examples. These vary from extremely detailed policy analyses, conducted either himself or by his team of researchers, to more anecdotal cultural instances, ranging from the emotional significance of the civic calendar (which sits 'at the very heart of our personal consciousness') (Bourdieu, 2014: 7), to the French spelling of water lily (and why those who write *nénuphar* possess state-sanctioned symbolic superiority over those who write the more common *nénufar*) (Bourdieu, 2014: 119–21).

The concept of field also plays an important role in Bourdieu's conceptualisation, with the state seen as a form of supra-field. It is both a field in itself, but, more significantly, occupies a position in the structure, conditioning, and functioning of other fields like universities, literature, religion, and employment. Bourdieu sought to move beyond what he saw as the traditional Marxist conceptualisation of the state's function (the maintenance of order for the benefit of the dominant) and that of the state as a neutral site where disagreements meet. Instead he poses the idea of the state as constituting 'the form of collective belief that structures the whole of social life' (Bourdieu, 2014: 381) within temporal and cultural contexts. The state and its ministries act as the guardians of doxa, with the ability to socially construct a position in which 'how things are' and 'how they should be' are the same. To reinforce and reproduce such a position, state institutions have to 'present the spectre of universality' in values and logic (Bourdieu, 2014: 28). In critiquing the state in this way, Bourdieu argues against the anti-democratic (and anti-populist) view of the emergence of the state, which sees institutions as growing from an organised population who delegate power to elected representatives. Instead he argues that a certain number of social agents and jurists gradually built up institutions, using them as specific resources which can be deployed to 'say what is good for the social world' and to proclaim the official in the form of orders (Bourdieu, 2014: 33). The state, he argues, is the product of the agents with the authority to do the state's work, and not the other way around.

He made use of the metaphor of the two-handed state: on one side, the left-hand, which 'safeguards the interests of the dominated, the culturally and economically (Bourdieu, 2003b: 34–5) and other marginalised groups, made up of ministries such as those of health, education, housing, and social security, in essence, those ministries which have been fought for in past struggle, and whose functions are generally thought of as the principal duties of the state by those on the political left. In contrast, Bourdieu positions the right-hand of the state as encompassing the duties of overseeing capitalism: that is, finance and business, as well as the repressive police, judiciary, and military. This is a metaphor which would spill into his work as a public sociologist (Burawoy, 2004, 2008b) and activist.

Politics and public engagement

> I have tried to be objective. I do not claim to be detached. (Mills, 1962: 11)

While there was always an activist element to his work (his early studies of Algeria [Bourdieu, 1979] were designed to affect the debate about colonialism and independence in France [Robbins, 2007: 80–1]), late in his life and career Bourdieu became more visible and active. In his obituary in January 2002, *The Times* newspaper would call him 'the most convincing embodiment of the politically active intellectual since Jean-Paul Sartre or Michel Foucault'. His causes were left-wing in nature, including an anti-market concern regarding inequality and the tragic dismantling of the welfare state. With 1980s neoliberalism he saw the dramatic return of soulless individualism and unquestioning acclaim for cold, unempathic 'responsibility', where proclamations of 'Let's return to the individual' mask little more than creating 'a creature who can be blamed when he is the victim, who can be attacked for the deficit in the social security system' (Bourdieu, 2014: 364). The social sciences, therefore, which see social life as relational, with people caught in a system of relationships, are well-placed to offer a guide out of the mess. *The Weight of the World* (Bourdieu, 1999) was written with his team of associates in order to document how the retrenchment of the state generated victims of neoliberalism, to promulgate the idea that these different instances of social suffering may have common cause, and hopefully to compel politicians to act on the abuses documented by the authors. A surprise success, selling over 120,000 copies in depressed early 1990s France, it showcased dozens of short case studies of differing yet themed individual narratives of suffering, presented as a series of transcript extracts alongside narrative presentations of the conditions of interviews. It does not draw on established theory directly, but the case studies are intercut with essays by Bourdieu, which seek to direct the reader to the grander themes under discussion.

Therefore, we add to the list of five dichotomies listed at the start of this chapter, presented in *An Invitation* (Bourdieu and Wacquant, 1992) as the central focus of Bourdieu's career, a sixth one, more pronounced in Bourdieu's final years, that of challenging the dichotomy between academic researcher and activist:

> It seems to me that the most urgent task is to find and mobilize the material, economic, and, above all, *organizational* means to encourage all competent researchers to unite their efforts with those of the responsible activists in order to collectively discuss and elaborate a set of analyses and proposals for progress … (Bourdieu, 2003b: 15)

This 'scholarship with commitment' must break free of dusty and unread (Remler, 2014) academic journals and books, and into the press and onto the streets in order to synergistically improve both scholarship and activism (Came et al., 2015; see also Dreger, 2016). It is no coincidence that in the documentary film *Sociology is a Martial Art*, in the first two scenes we see Bourdieu delivering a prestigious lecture by videoconference and attending a noisy and passionate demonstration against capitalism.

> For reasons no doubt relating to my own person and to the state of the world, I have come to believe that those who have the good fortune to be able to devote their lives to the study of the social world cannot stand aside, neutral and indifferent, from the struggles in which the future of that world is at stake. (Bourdieu, 2003b: 11)

The unreadiness of much of his theoretical work was challenged through a change in Bourdieu's writing style, the use of a 'simplified and less-specialized discourse' (Sapiro, 2010: x), leading both to the massive sales of *The Weight of the World*, and of Bourdieu's most successful work, *On Television* (1998), which sold more than 200,000 copies. Concerned with television's ability to produce and reproduce representations and social categorisations, which led to symbolic violence and the stigmatisation and marginalisation of disadvantaged groups, and the medium's ability to depoliticise society, Bourdieu saw a concern with image and ratings as a roadblock to debate, reason, and attempts to move past 'common sense' understandings of the world. He also railed against the failure of the scientific and academic communities to engage in public debates, especially their arrogant failure to stymie the 'prattling and incompetent' (Bourdieu, 2003b: 13) figures who fill newspaper columns and television panel shows with empty and ill-informed nonsense:

> I am aware that by calling on researchers to mobilize to defend their autonomy and to impose the values at the core of their profession, as I do here, I run the risk of shocking those among them who, opting for the cozy virtuousness of confinement within their ivory tower, see intervention outside the academic sphere as a dangerous failing of that famous 'axiological neutrality' which is wrongly equated with scientific objectivity. (Bourdieu, 2003b: 12)

Bourdieu is here positioning the traditional academic concept of value neutrality as a concept designed not to preserve academic rigour but rather the safety and privilege of *homo academicus*: a form of scientific escapism rather than scientific objectivity (Bourdieu, 2003b: 18). It is a challenge which argues 'You do not stay out of public debate in the best interests of your pursuit of knowledge, but because you are too secure to try anything dangerous', to become a troublemaker (Bourdieu, 1993). This 'sacred boundary' (Bourdieu, 2003b: 24) is inscribed or habituated in the minds of academics, but needs breaking through, because researchers are perfectly placed to cut through the distortions of public debate and 'give a *visible and sensible* form to the *invisible but scientifically predictable* consequences of political measures inspired by neoliberal ideology' (Bourdieu, 2003b: 25, original emphasis). Bourdieu (1990e) argued that it was important to resist developing a 'scholastic point of view' on issues like social class. Such a view is overly intellectualist and theoretical, a way of looking at social life detached from the situation it aims to describe. Instead, it is vital that researchers engage with how class is played out in reality, through the lived experience of class, including its hidden injuries. There was some reflexive realisation that he was failing in his aim to replicate sociology in his image, which led to his political activism and engagement.

For balance, it should be noted, before we all rush to the barricades, that one problem with Bourdieu's political writings, many of which emanate from his later public speaking, is that they are more slapdash than his more precise theoretical and empirical work. For example, in *Firing Back* (2003b: 35) he claims that life expectancy in Britain and Russia fell by a decade in the 1990s. This is just not accurate: according to the World Bank, life expectancy in Russia did fall in that period, but by 3.6 years, and in Britain life expectancy actually *rose* in the period by just under one year.[2] This does not mean that investment in public services was strong at this period (famously in Britain at the time the National Health Service was chronically underfunded with waiting times for operations often extending to 18 months) but does show the perils of competing with the media commentariat Bourdieu so deplores. Academic rigour and citation can easily be jettisoned in favour of impact and soundbite. The noble aspirations of public sociology are always weighed against the agenda of public political life: the careful and considered habitus of the academic is perhaps out of place in the field of competitive one-upmanship that is the media sphere.

Conclusion

In response to scholars of the 1990s, such as Anthony Giddens and Ulrich Beck, for whom the significance of class diminished against the dominance of the individual, there has been a renewed movement to understand how social inequalities are lived (Reay, 1998), and how structural and individual inequalities are borne out by everyday choices and actions. Bourdieu's theories have been central to this. Under such a conceptualisation, individuals 'may well regard themselves as free agents making their own, individual ways in the world', but due to the continued impact of structural forces 'continue to derive from their family, class backgrounds particular sorts of social and cultural capital rooted in local economic history and conditions' (MacDonald et al., 2005: 886; see also Roberts, 1997; Lawler, 2008).

Pierre Bourdieu produced the following rudimentary equation in *Distinction* (2010 [1984]: 95), which, while he felt it over-simplified his ideas, in that a

---

[2]   These figures are available at: http://tinyurl.com/WorldBankUKRusFrDeath.

mathematical value cannot be attached to the concepts we are addressing, proves a useful tool to explain the processes of structurally informed agency:

$$(Habitus \times Capital) + Field = Practice$$

To break it down, we can see this as:

$$(Who\ we\ are \times What\ we've\ got) + Where\ we\ are = What\ we\ do$$

While we should take the use of mathematical equations in exploring social experiences with a pinch of salt (one plus one always equals two, but ultimately you cannot predict with certainty how uncomfortable a newcomer will feel at the opera), we can use this one as a general model to explain how Bourdieu's theories, *in sum*, explain why social practice is relatively regulated, consistent and reproduced.

And for our purposes moving forwards, if we move into focusing on reflexivity and we apply these principles to social research, we are given a very broad schema for understanding why reflexive consideration is vital:

$$(Personal\ biography/position \times Research\ skills/resources) + Site = \\ Research\ practice$$

Ergo our research practice is made up of the complex interplay between our personal biographies and position in the social world, our resources as researchers, our disciplinary knowledge and space within the research hierarchy, and the specific nature of the research site we intervene in. How do we go about understanding and assessing how these things come to affect our practice? Well, biography has a significant place in the reception and generation of social experience, and Bourdieu turned to invoking his biography to expound his ideas. In his analysis of Bourdieu's Béarnais research, which was conducted in his home town of Denguin and principally focused on the marriage strategies of peasant families, Tim Jenkins (2006: 45) argues that the principles and practice behind such social enquiry give us 'privileged access to the link between biography and theory, as well as a means of grasping what is at stake in a reflexive sociology'. This desire to unpick what is at stake in reflexive sociology underlies the next chapter, which will document Bourdieu's attempts to start to fill in the blanks of this equation.

In conclusion, social structures exist as both material and symbolic entities: 'objectivity of the first and second order' in Bourdieu's terminology. Structures are made up of both the distribution of amounts of sometimes scarce capitals but also of the worth of those capitals, which exist as symbolic templates for the practical knowledge and ordinary activity of social agents (Bourdieu and Wacquant, 1992: 7, 9). Research methods adept at handling both first and second order structures (i.e. the quantitative distribution of money *and* the qualitative lived experience of inequality) must be combined to make best use of the epistemological benefits of each, while smoothing out each other's drawbacks. This is ultimately a combination of focusing on *social physics* and *social phenomenology*.

Bourdieu and Wacquant artfully express the problems of only exploring one or other of these foci: to only address social physics is to reduce the social action of agents to the mere carrying out of preordained duties, 'passive supports of forces that mechanically work out their independent logic' (Bourdieu and Wacquant, 1992: 8). Conversely, a purely phenomenological approach is too fluid, and inadequately explains why things stay the same and are *reproduced* with such regularity and force: 'social agents construct social reality, both individually and collectively, [but] we must take care not to forget ... that they have not constructed the categories that they implement in this construction' (Bourdieu, 1996: 29). Threading the needle between an objectivist-positivist quantitative reading and a constructionist-interpretive qualitative reading of the social world is hard, especially when 'epistemological priority is granted to objectivist rupture over subjectivist understanding', and 'epistemic primacy' (Bourdieu and Wacquant, 1992: 11, 35) is granted to theory – in other words there is a tyranny of numbers and theory is privileged over experience. This demonstrates the need, therefore, for a reflexive sociology which openly and honestly lays on the table the inherent subjectivity and limitations of any method. The 'graphic documentation' of methodological procedures is required to properly undertake the 'methodological balancing [and] constant juxtaposing of the general and the particular' (Robbins, 2007: 82) between statistics and ethnography. To argue that conducting research is a process of detached engagement rather than a highly involved and political act is to obscure rather than illuminate, to deny awkward truths, and to miss the 'social' in social science. Bourdieu writes of a sociological schizophrenia, where the researcher has to speak of context, of historicity, and of relativity, but is condemned to use a discourse of universality and objectivity (Bourdieu, 2000b: 93; McNay, 2014). Such a double bind can only be overcome through taking a reflexive approach.

Doing reflexivity: theories and theorists

Think about the theories and thinkers you like or are most comfortable working with, and those whose ideas you are looking to apply and develop in your work:

- Why do you like them?
- Who inspired you to read them, and in what context?
- What critical assessment can be made of that introduction or your current application of them?

You may also want to ask if there other theorists, theories, or philosophical frameworks which would provide a very similar model or solution to your research problem, or would significantly reorient your findings. If so, why have you chosen one above the other?

The equation in the previous section can help us think about locating our own research practice. Start to fill in the blanks, considering your personal biography, the research skills you possess and feel comfortable using, and the site in which you are conducting your research (both the institutional environment and the field of study). How do these interact in your practice? But also critically consider the value of thinking about research and researchers' subjectivities in this potentially formulaic way.

THREE

Putting yourself in? Bourdieu's reflexive project

Bourdieusian reflexivity can be read first as the requirement for researchers to be aware of their own habitus, such as their own predispositions, knowledges, and competences while undertaking research, in order to produce if not objective, then honest and open research. This adherence to or belief in epistemic reflexivity is presented as a regulative idea which should undergird intellectual and methodological practice. For example, in *The Weight of the World* Bourdieu and colleagues (1999) argued that understanding and taking account of the nature of the interview–interviewee relationship was of key importance in conducting an interview and eliciting a meaningful response. This reflexive approach is central to being able to evaluate the findings of the research, and is best served through what is called 'active and methodical listening'. This apparently contradictory process requires an empathic, supportive, and in some cases imitative relationship, allied with ensuring that the interviewee feels that they are in control of the interaction. Such a recommendation is about ensuring that research never becomes unthinking and complacent.

The obsession with reflexivity, obvious in the latter half of Bourdieu's career, is neither an obsession with himself (or the self of the researcher), nor an obsession with words and theory, but an obsession with doing science right:

> It fastens not upon the private person of the sociologist in her idiosyncratic intimacy but on the concatenations of acts and operations she effectuates as part of her work and on the collective unconscious inscribed in them. Far from encouraging narcissism and solipsism, epistemic reflexivity invites intellectuals to recognize and to work to neutralize the specific determinisms to which their innermost thoughts are subjected and it informs a conception of the craft of research designed to strengthen its epistemological moorings. (Bourdieu and Wacquant, 1992: 46)

This chapter will present a detailed examination of Bourdieu (and Loïc Wacquant's) invitation to reflexive sociology, navigating through the output of the latter half of Bourdieu's career. It examines what we mean by doing reflexive sociology, why it was considered vital, and how Bourdieu did it himself. It is made clear that Bourdieu's research and theoretical philosophy is not meant to be absolute or complete, and certainly not unchallengeable: instead we are presented with 'an invitation to think with Bourdieu [which] is of necessity an invitation to think beyond Bourdieu, and against him whenever required' (Bourdieu and Wacquant, 1992: xiv). It is a call to reject the 'magic rituals' (Bourdieu, 1988) of formulaic methodologies, and embrace mosaic and eclecticism (Barrett, 2015). The purpose of this chapter is to take advantage of such an invitation: to present Bourdieu's reflexive project to you, and then address what I see as its two key flaws for research practice, the failure to fully examine the role of the personal in social research, and the lack of any practical guide as to *how to do* such reflexive work.

Accepting the invitation

In his preface to *An Invitation to Reflexive Sociology* (Bourdieu and Wacquant, 1992), Loïc Wacquant clarifies that the book is not a basic manual to Bourdieu's thought; instead it is an attempt to explicate the principles that underwrote his scientific practice. I like to see the book as the archetypal Bourdieusian analysis of Bourdieu. It just so happens to be written by Bourdieu and his closest *protégé*, offering a guide to Bourdieu's way and method of doing social research. It is a didactic, pedagogic dialogue which invites the reader to '(re)think Bourdieu by thinking along with him' (Bourdieu and Wacquant, 1992: xi): showing how Bourdieu is good to think with as both Jenkins (1992) and Lamont (2012) put it.

The most useful overview of Bourdieu's stance towards reflexivity comes in the section on epistemic reflexivity. In it, Wacquant posits that it is Bourdieu's preoccupation with the issue that most makes him stand out in modern social theory. While this is true to some extent (methodological reflexivity is rarely an issue explored by the 'great' social theorists [and we should be wary of the term 'great' in this context]), the issue is far more foregrounded in the social sciences today than it was at the time of writing of *An Invitation* in the early 1990s.

The book argues for an inclusion in social research of a *theory of intellectual practice*, centred on the presence of three main elements (Bourdieu and Wacquant, 1992: 36):

- an examination of the 'social and intellectual unconscious embedded in analytic tools and operations' in enquiry as a whole, rather than focusing on the individual researcher;
- a 'collective enterprise' undertaken by the whole academic community;
- a process whose principal aim was to reinforce and solidify the 'epistemological security' of the social sciences, not undermine them.

While Bourdieu was a methodological polytheist, the first point underlines that Bourdieu's methodological reflexivity comes from the position that not only must the methods, the 'analytic tools and operations', fit appropriately the phenomena or situation under study, but the use and impact of such methods must constantly be reflected upon in the doing of that research, as 'one cannot disassociate the construction of the object from the instruments of construction of the object and their critique' (Bourdieu and Wacquant, 1992: 30). Research is produced and methods are applied in a world affected by the same structural forces as those acting upon the subjects of that research and therefore to consider one's research as produced in a hermetically sealed bubble of science is to fail to learn the lessons of that *social* science. That Bourdieu and Wacquant stipulate that focus should *not* be on the individual researcher, but on the way in which that researcher is embedded in wider systems, is an occasionally tautological problem, but one we will seek to solve.

The second point makes clear that critical reflection must be a collective endeavour, that we should make best use of others' critiques of the disciplinary hegemonies which affect how we do our work. But it is the final point especially that summarises Bourdieu's, and my, reasoning in support of reflexivity. It is not important because we want to undermine the idea of the objective researcher, but to solidify and buttress the knowledge which they produce. This 'epistemic benefit' addresses the perceived imbalance between the positivism of quantitative methods, the 'privileged epistemological authority accorded to objectivity' as Jenkins (1992: 49) puts it, and the more subjective interpretive method. There is a *social relationship* present in all research, quantitative or qualitative, which we must recognise as rendering impossible the 'positivist dream of an epistemological state of perfect innocence' (Bourdieu, 1999: 608). This issue of whether objectivity is possible is well queried (see, for example, Myrdal, 1970; Letherby et al., 2013). Khan (2011: 201–2) writes that objectivity is 'often a false mask that researchers hide behind in order to assert their scientific authority'. Rather than ignoring this issue, reflexivity helps us tackle it head on.

Kenway and McLeod (2004) write that while the process of the researcher reflecting on the impact of their presence and interpretation is an important part of the reflexive turn, it is a 'milder and more limited' form of reflexivity than that promulgated by Bourdieu. Instead, to fully realise Bourdieu's project, one must undertake a reflexive analysis of the academic field itself, contextualising (in space and history) the position of oneself both within the realm of scholarship and as a scholar (see Burke et al., 2013). Bourdieu (1990c: 14) saw this problem as the necessary 'objectification of objectification', where researchers must 'objectify the objectifying distance and the social conditions that make it possible, such as the externality of the observer, the objectifying techniques that he [sic] uses, etc.' As Jenkins (1992: 61) explains the concept:

> Only, if you like, by subjecting the practice of the researcher to the same critical and sceptical eye as the practice of the researched is it possible to aspire to conduct properly objective and 'scientific' research. Only by doing this is it possible to hope to understand social reality properly.

Bourdieu wanted researchers to take two steps back. First, to go beyond the descriptive, and analyse, using theory, the data collected from research participants. At this point the researcher must 'objectify' the data, that is, categorise it, find commonalities, and identify themes. The second step is to be aware of the distortion that was created in the data by the presence and subjectivities of the researcher. This awareness must be acted upon, through subjecting the researcher to the same analysis as the data collected from participants. This serves two purposes. It enables the researcher to perform 'an imaginative leap into the shoes of the objects of study' (Jenkins, 1992: 50), and is a strategy to overcome the antimony of objectivism and subjectivism – social physics and social phenomenology. This is what we can perhaps call 'creative objectivity' (Jenkins, 1992: 49–50) – one clear practical step a researcher can take to understand their bearing on their own work.

Bourdieu criticises authors like Bennett Berger and Anthony Giddens for failing to conceptualise reflexivity as a key element and requirement of social science practice. And he goes on to critique the tendency of sociologists to limit the reflexive gaze to the individual researcher's class, gender, race, and so on – 'the most obvious bias' (Bourdieu and Wacquant, 1992: 39). Presenting such a focus as limited and somewhat simple, Bourdieu and Wacquant state that while such an analysis is important, it ignores the researcher's position in the academic field. Alongside these personal biases, they add two more that they see as more important and much less discussed. First, there is the *individual researcher's position in the academic field*, in which social scientists, the poor deluded cousins of mathematicians and physical scientists, are much closer to dominated than dominant, inheritors of a relatively elite social position but, within academia, the lowest of the low. And finally the *intellectualist bias*, which causes researchers to see 'the world as a *spectacle*, as a set of significations to be interpreted rather than as concrete problems to be solved practically' (Bourdieu and Wacquant, 1992: 40). Here the authors have in their sights approaches like Rational Actor Theory, which are so caught up in the beauty and simplicity of their theory they fail to see the people inside it, with their own practical logics for action. They argue that there has to be an analysis of the social scientific field *in toto*, because of the embedded scientific unconscious (Bourdieu and Wacquant, 1992: 40; Bourdieu, 1993).

Recognising personal positioning

This is where I feel Bourdieu and Wacquant split hairs and fail to fully explain how they set themselves apart from other philosophies of reflexivity, such as the feminist approach (discussed in the next chapter). Of the three biases they list above – personal, position in field, intellectual field as a whole – they downplay the importance of the first, in order to differentiate their critique and promote the latter two. Wacquant terms Bourdieu a 'merciless critic' of after-the-fact 'reflections on fieldwork'-style reflexive work, and even disdains the use of the first person as a (fake) way of emphasising empathy (Bourdieu and Wacquant, 1992: 43), which seems both incorrect and illogical. 'It is not the individual unconscious of the researcher but the epistemological unconscious of his discipline what must be unearthed' (Bourdieu and Wacquant, 1992: 41). For example,

Bourdieu heavily criticises the use of the term 'modernisation', seeing it as a euphemistic terms used by American social scientists to impose an 'ethnocentric evolutionary model according to which the different societies of the world are classified in terms of their distance from the most economically advanced society, that is, US society, instigated as the endpoint and end goal of all human history' (Bourdieu, 2003b: 85–6). Such a failure to empathise and to see the world in any other way than one's own shows a complete lack of understanding of one's own position. While he is right to hold such terminology to account, this focus on reflexively critiquing the academic field and academic trajectory does assume that all researchers are fully enmeshed in their, or any, discipline. Many researchers only come to understand the practical workings and structure of their disciplinary fields in advanced postgraduate study, or even later. (Some of us are still working it out). Such a formulation of reflexivity risks making it the private realm of the elite, those with the experience, privilege, and confidence to critique whole schools of thought. Such a conceptualisation of reflexivity is not practically useful to the undergraduate testing the water, or the contract researcher not grounded in the academic terrain. Independent researchers, individuals doing research for charities, or think tanks, or in governmental organisations, are excluded from such an institutional definition.

It also tells only a partial story about *how* this is to be done. We can agree that avoiding 'spurious primitivist participation' (Bourdieu, 1990c: 14) is a good thing: ethnocentric *faux*-insider research has both ethical and scientific issues. But Bourdieu and Wacquant (1992: 41–2) present their clarion call to reflexivity – a call to 'objectivize [the] objectivizing distance [of social research] and the social conditions which make it possible' – through the examples of focusing on 'the externality of the researcher' and the 'techniques of observation he uses'. These two examples are exactly the sort of personal and individual areas for reflexive critique that were dismissed only a page or two earlier in *An Invitation …*, and gaps which Bourdieu sought later to somewhat fill. Indeed ten years later, as Bourdieu (2003a: 287) writes in an article on 'participant objectivation', there is a more personal shift: 'Nothing is more false, in my view, than the maxim almost universally accepted in the social sciences according to which the researcher must put nothing of himself [sic] into the research', alongside writing of the importance of reflexivity as a way of neutralising the researcher's innermost thoughts (Bourdieu and Wacquant, 1992: 46). As Kim (2010) puts it, Bourdieu's attempt to distinguish his epistemic reflexivity from the more postmodern, personal, and intersubjective reflexivity does not feel like a convincing distinction.

The research self comes to play a larger part in Bourdieu's sociology. He drew on examples from his studies in Algeria and his home village in Béarn to demonstrate how '[i]diosyncratic personal experiences methodically subjected to sociological control constitute irreplaceable analytic resources, and that mobilizing one's social past through self-socio-analysis can and does produce epistemic as well as existential benefits' (Bourdieu, 2003a: 281). As Wacquant highlights (Bourdieu and Wacquant, 1992: 44), one of the key criticisms on the release of *Homo Academicus* (1990d) is that Bourdieu failed to adequately explain his own story.

Wacquant labels this Bourdieu's failure to be sufficiently narcissistic. The trend in methodological reflexivity since its publication, however, would suggest that this articulation is out of date, and feels like an over-protective politician's defence, denying being something you were never accused of. Discussing oneself and narcissism are not the same thing. If Bourdieu and Wacquant fear the narcissism of personal analysis, then why does this not apply as strongly to disciplinary analysis? Who wants a discipline to spend its entire time discussing itself? Bourdieu argues that he does not need to go into 'intimist confession' because, as his sociology aims to bring to life how the social world exists in the individual, it is enough to present the 'generic features of his most formative of social experiences' (Bourdieu and Wacquant, 1992: 44). In layman's terms, this is a bit of a cop out. No ethnographer would consider a group of participants' 'general formative experiences' enough to draw patterns or conclusions from. Also, given the publication of *Sketch for a Self-analysis* ten years later (in English, 2007; discussed below), alongside the greater use of interviews (see, for example, Lamaison, 1986; Wacquant, 1989; Bourdieu, 1993: 8–19, 2010a, 2010b, 2010c), the transcription of workshops within *An Invitation* (Bourdieu and Wacquant, 1992: 60–215), and in allowing a documentary film about him to be made, Bourdieu realised that there was some need to make 'resounding private revelations' in order to truly do reflexive social science (Bourdieu and Wacquant, 1992: 44).

What this section has tried to do is to provide the reader with an overview of Bourdieu and Wacquant's approach to reflexive sociology, particularly that which emerged at the start of the 1990s. However the section has also served to indicate how there is some inconsistency or work still to explicate in *An Invitation*, which seems to scholastically split hairs as to whether reflexivity requires a focus on the individual development of habitus (both as a researcher but also as a person) or not. What the following section shows is that, in one reading, perhaps as a result of the reaction to *Homo Academicus*, which encouraged Bourdieu to be *more* personal, there was a, perhaps grudging increase in inward focus. This is most obvious with the publication of *Sketch for a Self-analysis* (2007).

Undertaking a sketch of self-analysis

> To understand is first to understand the field with which and against which one has been formed. (Bourdieu, 2007: 4)

I hope to have a long career working in sociology. I want to be able to teach students, complete interesting and useful research projects, and collaborate with colleagues, for a long time. At the end I want to look back on an eclectic body of work which is either academically stimulating, or socially useful, or both, with pride. I am currently 30 years old, and with an ever-ageing population, and thus an ever-increasing pension age in the UK, I expect to be doing this for another 40 years at least.

This rather depressing (and morbid) thought often strikes me when I reread Bourdieu's *Sketch for a Self-analysis* (2007). Famously, Bourdieu's professorial lecture on entering the Collège de France was the 'Lecture on the Lecture' (Bourdieu, 1990a: 177–98), in which he argued that a reflexive sociology would better control for biases through its ability to unhinge the 'rites of institution' (Wacquant, 2002: 549) in the quasi-aristocratic French university system (Calhoun, 2002), and deconstructed the issues he faced in giving a public performance in such an esteemed setting, in front of an audience of the most acclaimed academics in French society. In his final lectures, entitled 'Sketch for a self-analysis', he subjected himself to the exercise of personal reflexivity for which he had been a semi-proponent, with a more (auto)biographical edge than his previous work had deemed necessary. Republished as the book of the same name, in German in 2002, French in 2004, and English in 2007, *Sketch* is his effort to codify his feelings on his own habitus and, consequently, explain his work's trajectory. While many issues should pique our interest in *Sketch*, the issue of *when* it was written, 'as if as a final challenge' (Publisher's Note, in Bourdieu, 2007: x), at the very end of his career, and just before his untimely death from cancer, is fascinating. As Robbins (2002: 113) writes, in this period Bourdieu was 'acutely aware that he was running out of time', and *Sketch* was completed one month before he died, in January 2002. Therefore it may be best to understand *Sketch* as a post-event map to events, an autobiographical manual to investigate Bourdieu's interpretation of his own academic journey, and the key personal events which he felt shaped that journey. It is the manual Bourdieu and Wacquant did not provide a decade previously, and performs the task of balancing structural and personal reflexive analyses.

The first half of the book is academically situated, continuing Bourdieu's assertion that the contextual detail required for sociologists to produce sociology is the academic construct in which they find themselves: he termed *Homo Academicus*, for example, a 'very self-conscious "epistemological experiment"' (Bourdieu and Wacquant, 1992: 67). He positions himself against authors such as Sartre, whom Bourdieu dismisses with quiet anger as someone too comfortable in the established academic elite and someone who refused to 'call the intellectual world into question' in the same way that intellectuals called the world into question (Bourdieu, 2007: 23).[1] There is a sense of Bourdieu's repugnance

---

[1] In a fascinatingly scathing article in the *London Review of Books*, published after Sartre's death in 1980, Bourdieu (1980: 11) asks the 'anti-Sartrian questions' of whether this massive totalising force in French intellectual life was actually 'dominated by what he dominated', whether the self-determination of being a free academic spirit was actually an illusion? He labels Sartre's work arrogant through its attempt to establish Sartre as the 'unchallengeable' and 'ultimate' authority in French intellectualism, whose 'transcendental consciousness' could reveal the truth to individuals and institutions which they themselves could not see (Bourdieu, 1980: 11–12). Through a logical process of accumulation, Sartre undertook a 'capital-concentrating operation' in order to rise to the top of his field. Bourdieu reasons that Sartre's failure to question how this happened was a significant disservice to intellectual critique.

towards exercises in theoretical exhibitionism, dismissing 'grand' theory and 'grand' discourse on epistemological issues (Bourdieu and Wacquant, 1992: viii), rejecting both methodology for methodology's sake and audacity without the rigour of abstract theorising. Part of this bashing of social theory and philosophy is due to the intellectual climate from which Bourdieu emerged, that is, mid-century France, which 'rewarded philosophical and theoretical proficiency while nourishing strong resistance to empiricism' (Bourdieu and Wacquant, 1992: 31). Such a field needed critique and understanding in order to create a 'sociologistic interpretation of the sociological description of the intellectual world' (Bourdieu, 2007: 25) – the sociology of sociology, which considers the social circumstances in which theory is produced.

We can have no doubt that this is important. Speaking from personal experience, my intellectual world is shaped quite clearly by the sociology department at the University of Kent where I undertook my doctoral work and, most dramatically, by my supervisory panel. Being young and impressionable, when they suggested reading something or applying a theory, I was more than likely to accept their advice. To be painfully honest, I cannot pretend that I knew who Foucault was before I started my doctoral work. One supervisor suggested I look at Foucault's work, particularly on 'the conduct of conduct' (Foucault, 1991), which shaped my analysis of volunteering policy as part of a long process of governmentality (Dean, 2013). Had I been at a different university or had different sources of supervision and inspiration, the same empirical data would have been analysed differently; I would have ventured down different avenues and would have amassed different skills and knowledges and assessed them according to different standards. This is a very localised example, but, as Bourdieu expands on his own academic journey and key relationships in *Sketch* we can see how the implanting of intellectual ideas in such a way has a massive bearing on academic conduct and output. As with Nietzsche's perspectivism, there is a biography and history to the development of theory that must not be overlooked (Robbins, 2007), which requires a socio-genetic understanding of intellectual works (Bourdieu, 1993).

When looked at in totality, these conditions had a large impact on my future and an impact on my suitability for employment in different (academic) fields once the thesis was complete. Bourdieu acknowledges this, describing how his relations with some of France's academic elite altered his relationship to others. His choice of academic field and direction is a reflection of his inhabited behaviours and experience, the rebellion against and discomfort with the elite and the abstract that had influenced his military career:

> I had entered into sociology and ethnology in part through a deep refusal of the scholastic point of view which is the principle of loftiness, a social distance, in which I could never feel at home, and to which the relationship to the social world associated with certain social origins no doubt predisposes. (Bourdieu, 2007: 41)

This unease at the presence of social distance between research practitioner and research object is attributed directly to the manifestation of Bourdieu's habitus. To explain this, he fulfils his sociological project, and gives the reader an analysis of himself and his life growing up, and asks himself how his early experiences developed his dispositions. Several stories he tells give some clues.

Bourdieu was a man who struggled with class division all his life (Calhoun, 2010). When serving in the Algerian war, he held back from becoming an officer because, while intelligent and a highly suitable candidate, he felt a profound discomfort with the heavily stratified nature of military hierarchy:

> I had refused to enter the reserve officers' college, no doubt partly because I could not bear the idea of dissociating myself from the rank-and-file soldiers, and also because of my lack of affinity with the candidates ... with whom I felt little common ground. (Bourdieu, 2007: 37)

But his displacement was furthered by his obsessively socialistic organising of the regular soldiers, who could not understand why this academic was serving beside them, nor why he was determined to get them into trouble through arguing with and protesting against his superiors. Later, Bourdieu offers an emotionally charged confessional passage, in which he asserts his own habitus, which is worth quoting at length:

> I discovered little by little, mainly through the gaze of others, the particularities of my habitus which, like a certain propensity to masculine pride and ostentation, a marked taste for disputation, most often somewhat put on, or the propensity to indignation over 'trifles', now appear to me to be linked to the cultural particularities of my region of origin, which I perceived and understood more clearly by analogy with what I read about the 'temperament' of cultural or linguistic minorities such as the Irish. Only slowly did I understand that if some of my most banal reactions were often misinterpreted, it was often because the manner – tone, voice, gestures, facial expressions, etc. – in which I sometimes manifested them, a mixture of aggressive shyness and a growling, even furious, bluntness, might be taken at face value, in other words, in a sense too seriously, and that it contrasted so much with the distant assurance of well-born Parisians that it always threatened to give the appearance of uncontrolled, querulous violence to reflex and sometimes purely ritual transgressions of the conventions and commonplaces of academic or intellectual routine. (Bourdieu, 2007: 89)

Bourdieu explains how he hid all his initial theoretical work, the interventions in which he critiqued the work of the grander names of French sociology, doing so in order to avoid 'seeking the rhetoric of importance' (Bourdieu, 2007: 103–5). As this is immediately preceded by a detailed account of how his habitus developed, one should not be surprised that Bourdieu would come to that conclusion, or should conduct his academic conduct in this way. The habit(us), born in Bourdieu's case on the rugby fields of boarding school, of 'getting stuck in' in order to cover up your differences (Bourdieu, 2007: 101), diffused into his academic work. As Calhoun (2010: 280) argues, it was his 'insertion into an intensely competitive social world' that was one of the inspirations for applying habitus and for wanting to understand social doxa. Given his monumental output in terms of books and articles, it has often been noted how Bourdieu is perhaps the best example of Bourdieusian social theory applied to class we could find.

Bourdieu fears that the reader will assume he is 'darkening the picture' (Bourdieu, 2007: 93) of his childhood, and that memories written down as an adult are inadequate substitutes for hard data. He also recounts the difficulties Foucault had, as, in revealing his homosexuality, his criticism of the prison system was shrouded by objections to his personal life on the part of his critics, who claimed 'epistemological privilege' over him (Halperin, 1996). Yet Bourdieu (2007: 81) praises Foucault's 'reconciliation of scholarship and commitment', similar to his own challenge to the academic/activist dichotomy, in opposition to the previous shared notion that separation of the two was sacrosanct. The connection between scholarship and commitment, research and activism, is, and should be considered, unbreakable. The researcher must understand 'the hidden interests that are invested in [research]' (Bourdieu, in Bourdieu and Wacquant, 1992: 68), which includes not only grasping the interests of outside agents, but the interests of the researchers themselves.

To summarise, in his later, more personal work, Bourdieu offers the incomplete idea that this participant objectification is not about the narcissistic researcher, but is concerned with explaining the conditions in which the research intervention takes place. More specifically, he highlights the idea that what truly creates the research situation is the academic background of the researcher – their institution, their methods, their supervisors and colleagues. It is possible that Bourdieu is advocating this approach because he became so disillusioned with structuralism, which he felt pushed into at the start of his academic career under Lévi-Strauss (Lemert, 1991; Jenkins, 1992: 17–18), and because of his reaction against the pretensions of Sartre (Bourdieu, 2007: 23).[2] Burawoy (2008b: 11) made efforts to 'turn Bourdieu on Bourdieu', but fails to do so substantially. Bourdieu's account in *Sketch* follows the guide he had previously set out, merely resting on his own academic trajectory and his place within the sociological discourse, that is, the site of his knowledge and not the personal circumstances of the creation of his

---

[2]   Echoes can be seen in Mills' reaction against pragmatist philosophy, on the analysis of which his early career was almost entirely based, because it lacked the rigorous empirical investigation sociology could provide (Geary, 2009: 20).

knowledge.[3] Bourdieu was a sociologist who believed that the layers of life that shaped action were built up over time through habitus, and that 'the ethno-sociologist is a kind of organic intellectual of humanity' (Bourdieu, 2000a: 10), yet he frequently restricted discussion of the habitus of his academic output to his academic world. But this must be juxtaposed to all we know of the social and biographical origins of Bourdieu's output: Algeria, Béarn, the education system, the academic elite – Bourdieu's life runs through his work, often subtly, sometimes more dominant.

Doing reflexivity with Bourdieu

Whereas Bourdieu (2007: 1) starts *Sketch* by stating that he does not conceal his apprehensions in conducting a socio-analysis of the self, there is a clear argument that researchers have some duty to do so. To reiterate, in the process of researching and writing, potential accusations and real doubts run through your head. Can such an exercise actually be described as scientific? Does this detract from the insights about the social world drawn from the empirical research and analysis? I found it deeply comforting as a postgraduate that Bourdieu faced similar problems, and set out these agonies, as he feared his work being decried under the label 'simplistic relativism':

> '[A]fter all, this is only the opinion of so-and-so, of the daughter of a teacher, etc., inspired by resentment, jealousy, etc.' … people are interested in my background or on my tastes insofar as it may give them weapons against what worries them in what I write about class and taste. (Bourdieu and Wacquant, 1992: 203)

'This is not an autobiography' runs the epigraph of the book (Bourdieu, 2007: v). Well, *Sketch* is part autobiography, part sociological analysis of the self. For 83 pages it is an academic autobiography, expanding upon how Bourdieu's sociological project developed and was shaped by the academic landscape around him, particularly his research philosophy and design. It is not until the final section of the book (Bourdieu, 2007: 84–110) that Bourdieu reflects on his own personal biography and journey.

He begins the section: 'This sketch for a self-analysis *cannot avoid* giving some space to the formation of the dispositions' of the author (Bourdieu, 2007: 84, emphasis added). Bourdieu's endemic humility, which again we can tie to habitus, was perhaps his reason for prevaricating on producing biographic work. My argument is that 'cannot avoid' presents socio-analysis of himself as a negative imposition; instead we can reframe this statement to read '*should* give some space to the formation of dispositions'. Let us embrace reflexive biographical work as a

---

[3]   Burawoy (2008b) does however focus on Bourdieu's dissemination as a public sociologist and the founding of this in his rejection of much of the French intellectual tradition.

necessity to be thought of positively, rather than a duty to be thought of negatively. 'Evidently reflexivity or reflexive action does not imply a liberation from a rigid and explicit methodology, but rather a necessary and demanding expansion of it' (Pauwels, 2012: 261). Despite Bourdieu's protestations, he knew that such a self-analysis 'was inseparable from his quest for objective science' (Robbins, 2007: 78).

Perhaps the easiest argument against an unachievable objectivity is that, with any dataset, quantitative or qualitative, if someone else studies it their analysis may result in significantly different conclusions (discussed at length in chapter six). As Blumer (1999) perceptively notes, the social sciences are sensitising rather than definitive. Accusations of subjectivity in social research can be used to undermine it as evidence, its validity and accuracy, to posit that findings are not 'true' reflections of social processes. Yet Bourdieu is arguing that for a researcher to pretend they are an objective outsider, unaffected by their habitus and by the experience of data collection, is a *double untruth*, misleading both about the methods of data collection and blind to subjectivities which may have affected one's findings. Being aware of one's subjectivities, and making them clear to the reader, is, he argues, preferable to pretending they do not exist.

Sketch for a Self-analysis is not, as Bourdieu feared, an arrogant or narcissistic work, concerned only with the 'facile delights of self-exploration' (Bourdieu, 2003a: 282). It is best to think of it as a guide book, a tour around the habits and practices of the man who had stimulated so much academic and public discussion. It is also, in my opinion, what readers of his work desperately needed, a methodological tool through which we can frame and interpret his sociological output. To produce such material was not without risk, especially for someone so apparently humble about his position:

> [Bourdieu] knew that to take himself as his object exposed him to the risk of not only being accused of self-indulgence, but also of giving weapons to all those who only wait for an opportunity to deny the scientific character of his sociology. (Publisher's Note, in Bourdieu, 2007: x)

But the argument for such an approach is democratic, ethical, and scientific. It is the researcher opening up to the reader and saying 'Here I am, here is my research, make your own minds up': an approach which draws an audience 'into a collective experience in which a version of truth is demonstrated for the collective to judge' (Butler, 1997: 928). Jenkins' (1992) earlier conceptualisation of this as 'creative objectivity' needs a little reworking. This use of 'creative' may merely be a disguise for its antonym; perhaps it is to be read as 'thoughtful subjectivity' rather than 'assumed objectivity'. The goal of reflexivity, when applied in this way, is not to make research objective, it is to make clear the subjectivities and to understand how they may have affected both the collection and interpretation of data.

It is not always easy. In an interview[4] with Wacquant (1989) concerning the publication of *Homo Academicus*, Bourdieu is clearly ill at ease with his own research. He did not want the book, dealing with the relational nature of the academic field in France and the student radicalism of 1968, to be seen as a pamphlet advocating self-flagellation on the part of academics, but as an effort to objectify the subject of objectivation, a study of the studiers and of the tools they use for study. The book's reception caused emotional pain for Bourdieu in that it separated him from friends and colleagues who, in part, assumed he was critiquing their positon without critiquing himself, yet, as he maintained, 'of course I was doing [that] all the time' (Bourdieu, in Wacquant, 1989:3). Alongside his increasingly political work, his own personal story would frequently feature more and more in his academic work until his death.

Conclusion

'Bourdieu forces us to critically re-examine not only the institutional conditions of our professional conduct, but also the *scientific unconscious* which regulates our daily practice as symbolic producers' (Wacquant, 1989: 2). Bourdieu argues persuasively that every intellectual can and must submit themselves to reflexive critique before engaging in any political action. He attacks the 'unrealistic impulse' of the 'campus radicalism' of his generation's support of the Communist Party, which, critics would argue, still resides in the student politics of today. It would be foolish to believe that holding debates at academic conferences or writing a blistering critique of neoliberalism in a journal article contribute in any way to make a credible and useful intervention in the affairs of the political sphere (Bourdieu, 2003b: 19–20):

> The intellectual world must engage in a permanent critique of all the abuses of power or authority committed in the name of intellectual authority or, if you prefer, in a relentless critique of the use of intellectual authority as a political weapon within the intellectual field. Every scholar must also submit himself or herself to the critique of the *scholastic bias*, whose most perverse form is the propensity to a kind of 'paper revolutionism' devoid of genuine target or effect. (Bourdieu, 2003b: 19, original emphasis)

In other words: get real. If we refuse to understand this scientific unconscious which regulates our behaviours as symbolic producers we will only be doing half of the job of research.

---

[4] Interestingly, in *An Invitation* (Bourdieu and Wacquant, 1992), Bourdieu asks the reader's forgiveness for the necessary arrogance of the interview form. Whether one reads this as modesty or false modesty is down to personal preference.

Being reflexive, which this book takes to be the practice of openness and honesty about the impact that the researcher and research conditions and environment have on the conduct and results of their research, should not be something to fear. This chapter has aimed to demonstrate that any criticisms stemming from undertaking such an approach are misguided. Instead, it is the research that does not fully understand the position of the researcher that is unscientific, as it denies the presence of social actors in the active social landscape that is field research:

> It is an attempt to provide an experimental demonstration for the necessity and potency of a genuinely reflexive sociology: Bourdieu's aim is to show that sociologists can overcome the antimony of objectivist explanation and subjectivist understanding and account for the very world within which they live on condition of turning upon themselves the scientific tools for objectivation that they routinely employ upon others so as to neutralise the biases inscribed both in the contemplative relation between the social observer and her object and in the fact of occupying a particular location in the universe under investigation. (Wacquant, 1989: 1–2)

It is hard not to read Bourdieu's life-long research project as that of someone trying to understand themselves. Perhaps this is a modern condition, where we reduce the theory to the individual, but given Bourdieu's insistence on analysis of where knowledge comes from and the structures and processes in which it is created, it would be an impolite refusal of the invitation to reflexive sociology to draw any other conclusion. While there are occasional problems with the applicability of Bourdieu's reflexive project, and it frequently fails to break free of the scholastic shackles of academia, in thinking of reflexive sociology as a tool of vigilance against one's research self (Bourdieu, 1990a) we are given a weapon to break free of the self-imposed constraints of research practice.

Doing reflexivity: research as problematic

Bourdieu was wary of researchers becoming guilty of scholastic bias: focused too much on seeing social problems as intellectual puzzles to be solved, and not enough on ameliorating them. Alice Dreger's (2016) excellent book on the role of scientific research and evidence within activism clearly demonstrates the often complicated relationship that exists between documenting and explaining a social problem and advocating for change. Therefore consider:

- What are the inherent privileges of being a social science researcher?
- What are the problems associated with approaching social research *as a researcher*, rather than as a policy practitioner or activist? Think about how we currently draw these

boundaries in social research, and how we can redraw them for a better, perhaps more symbiotic relationship.

In the previous chapter, we have also seen how Bourdieu struggled with the idea of being seen as self-obsessed or partial in his later focus on personal reflexivity. In my experience this is a concern many early-career researchers have:

• Do you have worries about conducting work which is introspective, and somewhat confessional and self-critical? Why?

Consider where such concerns come from, both personally and professionally and remember to share stories with friends and colleagues about managing such worries. Assuage such worries by asking colleagues and friends to read your work with this very question in mind.

FOUR

Standpoints, disciplines, spaces

In 2015, I published a piece of research on how potential charity donors see homeless people (Dean, 2015). Utilising a creative visual method of drawing, I gave participants pens and paper and asked them to 'draw what homelessness looks like'. Their images overwhelmingly showed dishevelled men, sleeping rough or begging on the streets: stereotypical depictions of scenes of homelessness which we know represent only a small element of the huge and growing problem that is homelessness in the UK and around the world. The project aimed to explore the common perceptions of the problem of homelessness in the minds of potential donors, stemming from other research (Breeze and Dean, 2012, 2013) exploring the representation of homeless people in fundraising literature. I like to think of it as a simple and yet interesting project, where a creative method was justified in exploring a problem which would not work through purely verbal or textual methods. But the story of where the idea came from does say something about the individuality of researchers and the randomness of doing research.

I presented our initial research findings on fundraising literature at a large non-profit and voluntary sector research conference in Toronto in 2011. While there, I got very annoyed at what I felt were an unbelievably boring set of oddly repetitive and characterless conference presentations. To compensate for this (and because I was an over-privileged, know-it-all British PhD student), I got a bit drunk and complained loudly about the rather lousy conference to someone I'd just met, who must have thought I was rather terrible. I said we needed to do more inventive presentations. He politely asked for an example. I said perhaps in a presentation about homelessness you could ask the audience to close their eyes or lie on the floor and imagine sleeping rough, probably thinking I was being very inventive in bringing in this embodied element to research dissemination. He said this was really distasteful and stupid, a stunningly insightful critique of my nonsense. Stunned, I quickly said, 'Well, yes, but how about you give out paper and ask the audience to draw what they think homelessness looks like, and then see if it matches the fundraising adverts, and if they look the same examine why?' He thought about it, nodded, and said 'Yeah, that might work.'

So there I was, a bit drunk, in an awful Toronto bar inside a shopping mall, haranguing a quite senior academic from a prestigious US university I'd never met before, blurting out the précis of a journal paper which would be published three and a half years later. It's funny how things work out. Dave Beer (2014: 37), reporting on Howard Becker's assertion that good sociological ideas can come as much from art and drama as from what one is 'supposed' to be reading, writes: 'Perhaps we need to cast the net even wider and to find sociology in an even broader range of places and maybe in even less predictable forms … consider the value of all sorts of resources.'

This anecdote serves not only to embarrass me, but to point out the varied, subjective, and at-times odd nature of being a researcher. If, as Umberto Eco said, an intellectual is someone who is creatively producing new knowledge, we have to recognise that these ideas can come from nowhere, but are liable to be heavily influenced by the surrounding structures or chaos you find yourself in. How creative these structures are requires examination. Therefore this chapter wants to move on from Bourdieu to examine other theoretical and methodological contributions to the understanding and practice of reflexivity, particularly those that examine and critique the space within which academic knowledge is produced.

First, there will be a focus on feminist research. Much of the need for reflexivity comes from the issues which can arise from a powerful researcher studying a less powerful population or context. The large social surveys of 1940s and 1950s American sociology were rightly criticised for focusing on a patriarchal, 'head-of-the-household' reading of family life (Waring, 1990; Presser, 1998). In the research relationship, social scientists usually have authority over what gets said and done, and earn prestige and power from their research (Ellis, 2007). Feminist researchers, making more use of qualitative methods such as interviews, sought to reduce the power of the researcher and encourage an emancipatory methodology, much studied and utilised today. This analysis of one's privilege (whether through 'race', gender, social class, or other privileging social construct or resource) is allied to recent popular exhortations to 'check your privilege' when discussing social issues, a stance which sees cis, straight, white, middle-class men as experiencing the fewest layers of marginalisation in society (Connell, 2005) and who therefore have most difficulty in recognising and understanding it. Recognising the practice of research as an unequal act is an important step in reflexive work. These ideas are particularly important here given the valid criticism of the thinness of Bourdieu's discussion of gender.[1] The chapter will then move to discuss two other distinct elements of reflexive work: the necessity of reflexively critiquing the notion of disciplines within academic study; and the spatial nature of social research, using the legendary mid-twentieth-century American sociologist C. Wright Mills as a case study. Therefore this chapter aims to add to our previous examination of Bourdieu, to highlight other ways of thinking about reflexivity in social research, both why it is done and how it is done.

---

[1] Bourdieu's main intervention in gender theory was *Masculine Domination* (2001), a highly contentious work which one reviewer labelled quite damningly 'a brisk treatment of a subject that does not have Bourdieu's full attention' (Wallace, 2003). While many feminist scholars (such as Bev Skeggs, Lisa Mckenzie, Diane Reay, and many others) have taken Bourdieu's main theoretical contributions and reoriented them to research on gender, this gap is still obvious. For a critical feminist reading of Bourdieu, see Lovell (2002) and Adkins and Skeggs (2004).

Feminist research methods

> [O]ne could easily come to the conclusion that the concepts of women and of knowledge – socially legitimated knowledge – had been constructed in opposition to each other in modern Western societies. (Harding, 1991: 106)

The framework developed by feminist researchers in requiring a commitment to collective ways of knowing (Welch, 2006) provides a structure through which to analyse the importance of reflexivity and researcher biography in social research. At its core is the guiding principle that existing social theory and research is structured around male experience, and instead an epistemology should be built against a traditional Enlightenment model and from a female 'standpoint', centring on an explicit awareness of the gendered character of all human activity (Hartsock, 1983; Harding, 1986; Smith, 1990; for an overview, see Roberts, 1981a; Letherby et al., 2013: 38–42). Such a conceptualisation must take women and their patriarchal oppression as a starting point for research (Brayton, 1997), with 'a reflexive notion of knowledge … [that questions] what we know, how we know it and what difference this makes both to the type of research we do and who participates in it with us' (McDowell, 1992: 399–400). Qualitative methods such as interviewing, life histories, and ethnography have proven themselves to be central to feminist research, and, while some have argued that feminist research has yet to coalesce around one particular method (Maguire, 1987; DeVault, 1996), others write that the interview in particular became the paradigmatic feminist method (Kelly et al., 1994), with Ann Oakley's (1981, 2016) work on interviewing women being fundamental. It is perhaps best to think of feminist research as a way of seeing – an approach or mindset – rather than a method per se.

To preface the supposedly objective term 'research' with any political ideology (such as feminist or Marxist) is at first glance to pose more complicated epistemological questions, or questions of good research practice, than prefacing it with theoretical or technical terms (social, realist, or anthropological for instance). As will be demonstrated throughout this chapter, the point is that none of these terms are neutral, and unpicking the differences inherent within supposedly neutral theoretical stances is as important as unpicking them in allegedly biased ideologies. Research produced from a feminist standpoint should be critiqued in the same way as enquiry that is not, with both judged by their rigour and contribution, without one being dismissed as opinion or ideology. As Sandra Harding's (1986, 1991) ground-breaking critical examinations of sciences from a feminist perspective argued, the modern West possesses an androcentric, colonial, and bourgeois science and notion of knowledge. Following the emergence of second-wave feminism in the 1960s, there began a battle across the 'hard' and 'soft' sciences to include women and gender in the existing bodies of knowledge in their fields.[2] 'The conceptual schemes in these fields and the dominant notions of objectivity, rationality, and scientific method were too weak, or too distorted in some way or another, to be competent even for identifying – let alone eliminating – sexist and androcentric assumptions and beliefs' (Harding, 1991: 105).

Helen Roberts' pioneering collection *Doing Feminist Research* (1981a) sought to tackle two key oversights: first, that little work had been done within the social sciences to examine how taking a feminist perspective or even taking account of women affects the research process; and, second, that too many accounts of social research appear sanitised, devoid of conflict or complexity, as if guidance from textbooks can be operationalised without the messiness of life getting in the way (see chapters six and seven; see also Burawoy, 1991; Mauthner and Doucet, 2003; Blackman, 2007). In her own contribution to the collection, Roberts (1981b: 27) calls out social scientists who feel that until a matter can be measured scientifically it must be ignored: instead she argues that 'feminist sociologists, in arguing that gender should be taken into account in theory and in practice, are arguing for more and not less vigorous methods'. This can be seen as one of the earliest calls for personal reflexivity in social research, with Roberts positing that it is better to think through inequalities (both structural and personal) in research relationships than ignore what is too difficult to quantify.

In the same collection Ann Oakley (1981) writes that due to an overly masculine way of thinking about the interview, there is a lack of fit between theory and practice in research methods.[3] At the time, while some aspects of interview methodology (how many, how long, is there a standardised interview schedule?) were treated as legitimate concerns to be recorded, others, such as 'social/personal characteristics of those doing the interviewing; interviewees' feelings about being interviewed and about the interview; interviewer's feelings about interviewees' (Oakley, 1981: 31) and more, were considered illegitimate. This is bad science, because to sideline these aspects is to fail to examine the social relationship at the heart of research.

The interview is perhaps the most commonly utilised qualitative research method, especially in the UK. Halsey's (2004) research showed that the vast majority of qualitative articles published in British sociology journals in the year 2000 used interviews, increasing from around half in the early 1960s (see also Savage and Burrows, 2007). Interviews are especially useful when 'the goal of a piece of research is to explore people's experiences, practices, values and attitudes

---

[2] When confronted with the phrases 'hard' and 'soft' sciences (or being 'hard' or 'soft' on immigration or welfare), Pauline Bart (1974) observes that it comes as no surprise that we live in a world driven by male sexual metaphors, and perhaps we should replace them with female sexual metaphors in research, such as 'wet' and 'dry' data.

[3] Oakley's intervention was the subject of much debate at the time, and continues to hold a significant place in the social science canon, especially in the UK (even though Oakley [2016] herself remains wary of its paradigmatic status). A fuller exploration of this debate is not possible here, but see Oakley's (1979) *Becoming a Mother* for the research project at the centre of the methodological issue, and Oakley (2016: 196-9) for an overview and response to the responses.

in depth and to establish their meaning for those concerned' (Devine, 2002: 207). They are less time-consuming and all-encompassing that an ethnography or participant observation, but more in-depth than questionnaires or surveys, and more personal than focus groups. They 'generate data which give an authentic insight into people's experiences' (Silverman, 1993: 91), rather than necessarily finding out the 'objective facts' (Crouch and McKenzie, 2006: 485) which surround these experiences. The qualitative interview offers an opportunity to appraise the validity of respondents' answers with the interviewer 'in a position to observe not only *what* the respondent says but also *how* he [sic] says it' (Selltiz et al., 1964: 242, original emphasis).[4] Bourdieu was changeably sceptical about the ability of interviews to indicate participants' intentions because future social actions are dominated by individual habitus (Byrne, 2005), and for the rather prosaic reason that when people are asked questions they have a tendency to answer them, whether they have an answer or not. Ergo interviews, as with any research method, are not neutral and can invent perspectives rather than reveal them.

Therefore this is why Silverman and Oakley contend that interviews have to be about more than words, because they are concerned with the unsaid and the symbolic and the structural:

> Interviews are used as means of bringing to the surface underlying patterns submerged in a respondent's talk. Such talk is never heard *in itself* but as representing or corresponding to some reality routinely available in the world.... In hearing interview-talk, the surface appearances (the words used by the subject) are only important for the glimpses which they give of the patterns which purportedly underlie them. (Silverman, 1993: 33)

By talking to people about how they see their role in relation to others, we can see how personal stories are organised (Coffey and Atkinson, 1996). We can think of interviews as social events, which the interviewer and interviewee are both participating in and observing (Hammersley and Atkinson, 2007), with the contextual detail surrounding the encounter itself the necessary subject of objectification.

To read Oakley's (1981) framing of the interview as method, though, is to read how difficult it is in research to thread the needle of the relationship between occasionally contradictory advice, between necessary rapport and necessary detachment, and between answering an interviewee's questions or not. Teaching

---

[4] It is telling to reread Oakley's (1981: 31–41) deconstruction of interviewing as a 'masculine paradigm' and, from her review of the mid-century research methods literature, come to understand how gendered the language is. The majority of the guidance she highlights assumes the social researcher to be male, demonstrating to a small but important extent both the terribly unequal low base feminist researchers were working from over a generation ago, and how much impact they have made.

the doing of qualitative research is hard because it is impossible to give students an accurate and holistic experience of what they will encounter when they go out and ask the questions they have designed to interviewees whom they have selected. Ultimately the best way to learn the doing is to do it. This was what Oakley found when, as a feminist interviewer, she sought to speak to women. She found that:

- prescribing interviewing practice is 'indefensible'
- advice from methods texts was contradictory and weak
- the best data about people were collected when the research relationship was non-hierarchical and 'when the interviewer is prepared to invest his or her own personal identity in the relationship' (Oakley, 1981: 41).

In her research on pregnancy and transitions to motherhood for example, Oakley writes of how she would be asked a great many questions by the expectant mothers she was interviewing longitudinally. These questions ranged from enquiries about the book she was writing, to biological and medical ones about childbirth, and personal questions to Oakley about her own children and advice on looking after a child. Whereas the methods texts she had read (see Oakley, 1981: 31–41) advised researchers to avoid interviewees' questions, shrugging them off in order to retain neutrality, Oakley quickly came to the perfectly reasonable conclusion that to do so would be both stupid and uncaring and inhumane: she was asking a great deal of her participants in terms of time and cooperation, so how could she not act both as researcher *and* as a reassuring friend and source of useful information and care? In fact, Oakley (1981: 50) asked her participants whether doing the research had affected their experience of becoming a mother, and three-quarters said it had, with a quarter saying it was reassuring and a relief to talk.

In essence Oakley's argument is not only that a 'proper' interview is unattainable, but also that methods texts often pretend it is while knowing that it isn't. In the 35 years since her original intervention was published, it is clear that advances have been made in respect to thinking through the researcher–researched relationship, especially, as Oakley (2016) has recently suggested, regarding the role of intersectionality (Phoenix, 1994), and researchers being willing to discuss ethics and confront the practical realities of social research. But a more thorough examination of the role of 'friendship' and 'altruism' in research relationships (Tillman-Healy, 2003; Owton and Allen-Collinson, 2013) is required in order to truly navigate the path between producing authoritative scientific statements about social life and the task of 'living those lives and developing consistent narratives about them' (Oakley, 2016: 209).

Feminism is a political and social ideology that aims to counteract inherent biases in society which are doubly corrosive because they are presented as neutral (Benhabib, 1992: 242). For example, in her research with policy practitioners (discussed in the next chapter), Hannah Jones (2013: 140) argues that the feminist approach to method has become such an obvious piece of societal 'common sense' within social logics of practice, that her interviewees would reference it, yet, ironically, once they had explained their biases they would still go on to *frame their view as the neutral one*. Overall, the lessons of the work of Oakley, Roberts, and other feminist researchers in the 1970s and 1980s have been largely incorporated into the (qualitative) methods canon, and the way the subject is taught in research methods classes. But, as Oakley (2014) has recently put it, the demasculation of social science is a long-drawn-out and as yet unfinished business. In challenging the pretence of the possibility of detached, objective knowledge, the canon of work from a feminist standpoint is a bulwark against accusations of bias in doing reflexive work. Further, it has made the accusation of bias easier to turn round the other way. If one is 'biased' for being a feminist researcher, so be it. But feminism is the belief that men and women are equal and should be treated equally, judged and rewarded not for their gender but for the content of their character. So it is reasonable, if somewhat childishly simple, to argue that if you are *not* approaching your research from a feminist research perspective, it is you who are biased.

Disciplines as social censorship

> Sociology is sexist ... (Oakley, 1974: 2)

Continuing this focus on the structures of knowledge, We Need to Talk About Disciplines. The history of what counts as 'truth' is far from neutral (Foucault, 2013). Such an assertion rests on the idea of truth as being hidden, as having a concealed character until it is 'revealed' by science or philosophy. Such an approach is, of course, dripping with epistemological questions of legitimate power, as such a way of thinking bestows great validity on the practitioners of such subjects: 'such an approach to "truth" affords great power for those who are qualified to "see" it and construct it' (Burgum, 2015: 318). As Sandra Harding (1991: ix) writes:

> we need a more complex understanding of how the development of Western sciences and models of knowledge are embedded in and have advanced the development of Western society and culture but have also led to the simultaneous de-development and continual re-creation of 'others' – third world peoples, women, the poor, nature.

Hierarchies of knowledge are a complicated challenge for reflexive researchers as trying to understand where one sits in the hierarchy and how that hierarchy came into being may not be fundamental areas of research (or even interest) for many individuals who may nonetheless feel a reflexive imperative. For example, it would be unbecoming and unfair to expect every doctoral student to obsessively document the construction of political science as a discipline, and their place within it. Thankfully, that groundwork has been done elsewhere and can be incorporated through limited literature reviews and contemplation rather than further study which may distract from one's central empirical project.[5]

For example, the role of 'race' in determining what the academy elevates as knowledge has been discussed and critiqued at length. Sarah Burton (2015) argues that there is an obsession with the 'white theory boy' or 'dead white man' (Bancroft and Fevre, 2016) in much social science: an arrogant, unreflexive figure, unaware of his own privileges. This perpetuates the dominance of whiteness and patriarchy in academic study and 'ingrains institutional and epistemological racism and sexism through selectively showing a very particular version of knowledge and deeming that version as truthful' (Burton, 2015). Back and Tate (2015) complement this view, positing that there has been a complete failure to incorporate (female) black voices, where academics and writers hide behind an 'It's not my area' defence, as if race is something that only happens to black people. Allied to such debates are concerns within the student body about the lack of wider representation of diverse voices, brought to light so pointedly through the 'Why is my curriculum so white?' campaign.[6] The point is made strikingly by Bhatt's (2016: 399) assertion that not only is the academic mainstream white but also that, since the 1980s, cultural studies, a formatively 'black' discipline, has been disparaged and replaced by an allegedly more 'methodologically robust and empirically informed' white sociology, whose prime focus, and indeed habitus, is whiteness itself. Similar critical worries have been voiced regarding political science (Achen, 2014).

This lack of representation extends from gendered and racial biases, to political biases and failing to challenge hegemonic practice. The American anthropologist and activist David Graeber (2004), who was a leading figure of the Occupy movement in 2011 and was the man who coined the globally resonant phrase 'We are the 99%', sought to unpick the role of anthropology in promulgating dominant ideas in his excellent polemic *Fragments of an Anarchist Anthropology*. Arguing that anthropologists, as one of the few groups of scholars who know anything about stateless societies, should involve themselves much more in encouraging less (or no) governmental involvement in people's lives, he sees a conservative Western discipline unwilling to support the anarchist practices they see successfully implemented in less prominent areas of the world:

---

[5] Of course reflexivity should not just be undertaken in written publications or theses. It is a social and intellectual pursuit in itself. Some reflexive questions to consider about the nature of knowledge in your own discipline to consider are: who are the most cited authors? Which departments are the most highly regarded and why? What is the make-up of the leadership of the professional organisational (the British Sociological Association, or the Political Studies Association for example)? Who gets invited to give keynote addresses at prestigious conferences? Thinking through these issues will help you consider whether the 'elite' of your discipline is being drawn from a relatively shallow pool of expertise and experience, or not.

[6] For an overview of the campaign run within University College London see https://www.youtube.com/watch?v=Dscx4h2l-Pk. For a defence of the current curriculum see Williams (2014).

[I]f nothing else, [anthropologists] are keenly aware that the most commonplace assumptions about what would happen in the absence of a state ('but people would just kill each other!') are factually untrue. (Graeber, 2004: 95)

Sensing that his disciplinary colleagues are stymied by their 'squalid colonial history' (2004: 94), with their liberal guilt stemming from the discipline's history of white men going round the world to study noble savages, made possible by horrific scenes of conflict, colonisation, and mass murder (2004: 96), Graeber writes that the discipline has reflexively agonised over its history. Such prominent agonising has led to two conclusions, he suggests: non-anthropologists can dismiss the findings of the discipline as projecting anthropologists' sense of Otherness; and anthropologists see the vast amount of knowledge they have built up as something to be ashamed of and under-sold. Graeber sees this agonising as a convenient tool to protect academic knowledge, to stay safe and away from the real world: he sees anthropology as a discipline full of populist practitioners, desperate to be on the side of the little guy who is finding ways to successfully resist capitalism, but without participating in that resistance themselves.[7]

Not everyone will accept Graeber's position, or his politics. His argument, which positioned anthropology as a tool of academic hegemony and of standard capitalist practice, touched a lot of nerves when it was published. He was infamously denied tenure at Yale, as he sees it, because his writings and activism challenged his staid discipline to move from talking radically to acting radically. He has more recently argued that whereas academia used to be a refuge for the brilliant and eccentric, it now serves, through its peer review systems and reliance on endless applications for funding, to crush originality (Graeber, 2015: 133–5), subservient to metrics. In this vein, in his recent analysis of the impact of case studies submitted as part of the 2015 Research Excellence Framework unit of assessment for sociology, Les Back (2015a) has argued that much of this 'impact' seeks to reinforce government agendas (policy-based evidence if you will) rather than challenge them: 'radical ambition is being dwarfed by a conservative and timid version of the discipline'.

In being reflexive about the academic structures in which we operate, we are doing what Bourdieu (2000b: 5) claims is the job of the social scientist: to break 'the enchanted circle of collective denial'. He was himself, for example, aware of the institutionalised ethnocentricity of much university anthropology (Robbins, 2007: 92), and argued, as referenced in a previous chapter, that disciplines serve as a form of social censorship (Bourdieu and de Saint Martin, 1979; Bourdieu,

---

[7]   Such conversations also take place in the humanities. Historians like Eric Hazan (in Warren, 2014) have written that while the idea of 'historical objectivity' is long dead, and that in writing history 'you are also saying something about yourself', this is only true if you have the *right* subjectivity. Hazan argues that if one is offering ideas which rub against the 'there is no alternative' mainstream, your work is easily classed as 'shockingly one-sided'.

1993). Anthropology is not my discipline, and accepting or rejecting Graeber's position is not my point here. Rather it is to highlight how critical assessment of disciplinary knowledge (institutions, structures, methods, practitioners) must take place as part of comprehensive reflexive practice. 'Unthinking approval or uncritical applause is of little use' (Back, 2007: 182): for as Bourdieu puts it in the documentary film *Sociology is a Martial Art*, 'truth isn't measured in clapometers'. 'That's the way we've always done it' is an unacceptable answer in most walks of life: so should it be permitted in the assumedly critical field of social research. We must ask 'Why are we doing this?' and, resultantly, 'How did that affect what I've done?' As Stephen Turner (2014) writes, quite depressingly, of the orthodoxies that strangle disciplines and academia:

> academic life is clientelistic, and advancement and influence depends on finding friends and followers; it is caste-like in most disciplines, and this is especially true of sociology; opportunities to publish theory are limited, especially in prestigious journals, and reviewing is generally hostile unless one is in a club; stepping outside the boundaries is risky and rarely rewarded; feeding the audience what it wants, and in easily digestible pieces that have the appearance of originality, is the best way to get an audience; violating the norms of political orthodoxy or responding to criticism from those beneath you, violating the norms of caste, is the easiest way to lose one's caste status and the automatic audience that goes with caste membership. (Turner, 2014: 149)

Allied to Turner's critique is a consideration of the role of 'big names' in academia (Bartmanski, 2012): are we too ready to put authors and their work on a pedestal without a thorough examination of how it/they got there? For example, Lamont (1987) has sought to explain the contrasting legitimation of Jacques Derrida's work in the USA and France as a high-status cultural good as stemming from institutional support or exposure in public cultural journals. Similarly, Clegg (1992) looks at the profusion of texts on Anthony Giddens in the early 1990s and asks why his work took hold to such an extent (which in hindsight looks crazy as Giddens's work is often downplayed in social theory today).

I disagree with some of what Turner (2014) writes: changes in academic processes and the possibilities of the internet can advance our ability to be original and reach new audiences over the heads of established thinkers, and I would argue that innovative methodological work is harder to publish than innovative theoretical work. But the key is that, as long as we keep questioning the very foundations of how our knowledge is produced and disseminated, and remind ourselves that the ways we've always done it may not be the best ways to do it, there will always be room for critique and change. The key to being a good student of the social sciences is to develop a critical attitude towards societal processes: to achieve sufficient mastery of theoretical, methodological, and analytical skills to be able to see when established or 'common sense' ideas have become unthinking or incorrect orthodoxies. Critique is the 'solvent of doxa', as Wacquant (2004) has put it. We have an opportunity both to join civic debate and to question the very frames of civic debate itself. In critiquing disciplines in this way, we can practise reflexivity regarding the very pedagogic structures that taught us how to think and who to think with, and regarding the right way to *be* a researcher or academic.

Spatial considerations: the case of C. Wright Mills

> But you must not expect me to provide A Balanced View. I'm not a
> sociological book-keeper. (Mills, quoted in Summers, 2008: 6)

The growth and development of feminist research methodology demonstrates the extent to which researchers in the latter half of the twentieth century started to understand how the standpoint of the individual *in* society shapes how they learn lessons *about* society. In trying to understand the history of knowledge and how this history is shaped by certain disciplines, we can see how knowledge claims can be seen to be ideological, political, and permeated with values (Schwandt, 2000). Now we move on to seeing how the geographic and temporal, alongside a rather unique personality within the academic space of a particular time, can shape the research one produces.

C. Wright Mills' (1959) famous dictum about the sociological imagination, that it is social science which helps us to connect our own biography and experience with the bigger picture of history and to connect our lives with the lives of others, is a powerful message for those endeavouring to be reflexive. Politically, he also directed intellectuals not only to absorb themselves in efforts to 'know what is real and what is unreal' but also to be concerned with the politics of truth and publicly intervene in debate, repudiating what they know to be false. Mills saw a general abdication of democratic responsibility as a key factor in US society's failure to uphold knowledge as socially relevant (and one reason why political debate in the West today seems so detached from reality). He lays a significant proportion of the blame for this at the door of social science practice. In much the same way as the aforementioned feminist critics of the men-in-white-coats, 'Can I talk to the head of the household?'-style social survey, Mills challenged his discipline to adopt a more pluralistic and tolerant sensibility. He confronted those whom he saw as the dominant American social scientists of the time (Robert Merton, Paul Lazarsfeld, Talcott Parsons) as being apologists for the powerful and, to use Summers' (2008: 7) great phrase, of 'establishing a sort of ecclesiastical guardianship over social knowledge'. Mills (2008) wrote that these American intellectuals were failing to reinforce civilising tendencies and viewed them as ensconced in an elitist bubble through their small-c conservative instincts, thus sullying and distorting the social relevance and political applicability of knowledge. I think he would have got on with David Graeber.

Yet I want to pick up here a facet of Mills' work that has recently been reconsidered, that of applying the private/public frame to the obviously symbiotic relationship between the man and his work. In one charming anecdotal example, in John Brewer's (2005) analysis of Mills' sociology, written in light of the publication of Mills et al's personal letters and autobiographical writings (2000), he posits that *spatial* considerations need to be taken into account regarding Mills' output. Brewer recounts one story where Mills was asked why he wrote one of his books, and Mills replied 'Because I am Texan' (Brewer, 2005: 673). Brewer demonstrates how the 'outlander mentality' resonated with and resided within Mills, a mentality which he allowed to spill into his work and his public performances.[8] He was allowed to be cantankerous in his public attempts to reformulate sociology because he had humble Texan roots, a strategic spatialisation of his intellectual biography. While Bourdieu's humility forever seemed to weigh him down, shaping his discomfort in the elite academic arena where he always felt he was going in the opposite direction to the dominant tendencies in the field (Bourdieu, 2007; Frangie, 2009), Mills made use of his origins. Confident in his talent, he utilised his difference to say what he wanted to say, and mould how the ways he was construed.

Interestingly, this cantankerousness sits uncomfortably with Mills' commitment to what we have later come to think of as public sociology (or at least with the idea of Mills as a public intellectual). Tröger (2012: 175) has argued that Mills used his written work to come to terms with himself, and invites authors to use Mills to contemplate their own place within social theory: 'C. Wright Mills never pretended academia wasn't personal.' Like Burawoy's (2004, 2005) call for a social science which grapples with new audiences outside of the professional academic elite, Mills' work calls for sociology to be both accessible and egalitarian in the conduct of research and its dissemination, perhaps best demonstrated through the belief that private troubles could be understood and communicated as public issues, and that an articulate and knowledgeable public is required for the continued strengthening of democracy. There is a contradiction at work here, for Mills refused to sign or initiate petitions or protests (Burawoy, 2008b: 9), never joined any political party or took part in a demonstration (Geary, 2009), and remained physically inaccessible to his readers. Perhaps ironically, or even hypocritically, he rarely became an active part of his public or professional world, and reflexive personal accounts remain largely absent from his publications. This physical absence was countered by Mills' literary presence, both through popular

---

[8] Some have debated how much this 'outsider' status was an accurate portrayal of Mills' character, and how much was a media construct which Mills played up to, with the reality 'obscured by caricature' (Geary, 2009). For instance, one of the most famous images of Mills is of him riding a motorcycle, helmetless, foreshadowing the 'easy rider', Route 66 pioneer spirit of mid-century American cinematic rebelliousness. But the truth, as with most things, is more prosaic. Mills took to riding his infamous motorcycle, not because he wished to exude a buccaneering persona, but because there were limited car parking spaces at Columbia University (Geary, 2009: 2) (although it certainly aided the look he wanted to promote).

publications – he took to writing in popular magazines such as *The Saturday Review* (Brewer, 2004: 326) – but also through making his academic work highly readable and accessible to lay audiences.

Mills' biography, his personal story, the man behind the method, was hidden when he was alive, and has only been brought to life in the last decade through publication of his letters and autobiographical writings, edited by his daughters (Mills et al., 2000).[9] His aloofness mirrored that of those academics against whom Bourdieu was agitating in France, yet Mills' early career was centred on his methodological assertion that the production of knowledge is in itself socially situated (Mills, 1939, 1940), indicating an awareness of the hierarchical doxa of academic output. As already outlined, this is an argument reprised in Bourdieu's reflexive sociology: that researchers must be aware of the conditions of production of their knowledge and how these can lead to narrow ways of thinking, and must subject themselves to the same analysis they use to examine data. By doing so the sociological public, and through egalitarian dissemination the general public, have greater access both to the knowledge and the individual conducting the research. To leave the researcher absent, as was often Mills' practice, is to close off access to the full extent of the research, the values behind it and the conclusions it draws. Therefore, while Mills provides an interesting case study to think through the relationship between space, biography, and academic practice, it is difficult to argue that he was a particularly reflexive researcher, especially in his most famous works.

While Burawoy (2008b: 2) posits that Mills was 'Bourdieu draped in 1950s American colors', this is a comparison based in their struggles with and reformations of Marxism, and their focus on domination: a comment on content, not conduct. Burawoy (2008b: 12) picks up that Mills kept his distance from the 'duped robots' of the masses, and practised a more traditional sociology, at odds with his stated politics: 'He stood aloof from the organic public sociology that would have brought him into dialogue with the very people he was writing about'.[10] This is in comparison to Bourdieu, who: 'crosses over from traditional to organic public sociology when representing the voices of the dominated in *The Weight of the World*. He can no longer remain aloof from the plight of the subaltern' (Burawoy, 2012). Burawoy is keen to label both Mills and Bourdieu as reflexive thinkers 'as they dissected the academic and political fields in which they operated' (Burawoy, 2008b: 3). However, looking to practise within the academic milieu is not enough for Mills to pass the test which Bourdieu attempts (and often

---

[9] For analysis of these, particularly Mills' Letters to Tovarich (Mills et al., 2000), see Brewer (2004, 2005) and Merrifield (2001).

[10] Tom Hayden (2006) was critical of Mills for his lack of interest in the very poor, concentrating his 'working-class study', *The New Men of Power* (Mills, 1948), on the union bosses who held sway in mid-century America (see also Metzgar, 2000). Geary (2009: 8) expands on this point, positing that: '[a]lthough Mills was committed to challenging oppression, he ignored institutionalized racism and patriarchy as crucial sources of hierarchical power in the modern world'. Failing to focus his attention on oppressed African Americans or women were pretty major blind spots, where he greatly failed vital sociological publics (Tröger, 2012).

fails) to spell out. To be truly reflexive, not merely only the academic conditions of knowledge but also the biographical conditions of knowledge must be assessed.

Conclusions

This chapter has moved with and beyond Bourdieu to provide readers with considerations of other reflexive paradigms deployed within the social sciences, and how issues of subjectivity and position are dealt with within different frameworks. It has used three cases to illustrate how structural and individual inequality within the field of knowledge production can distort the types of questions one asks and limit the methodological analyses one is willing to undertake. We have seen how the paradigmatic shift of the feminist approach to research sought to make method more real and equitable. We have examined how disciplines, through storing knowledge in silos, serve intellectual censorship, and seen the stultifying effect this can have on the political engagement of academic work. And, in focusing briefly on C. Wright Mills, we have seen how certain forms of public engagement, geographic roots, and personal characteristics can intersect to affect intellectual output. The following chapters move from the theory to the practice: how do the issues we have discussed so far get operationalised in practical research projects? Through a close reading of several recent research projects we can see how issues of subjectivity, knowing and caring for the people you are researching, and your own personal characteristics, can affect the data a researcher collects and the conclusions he or she draws.

Doing reflexivity: citation and building a diverse knowledge

Despite being considered two of the founding thinkers of sociology and both working and writing prodigiously in the late nineteenth century, Emile Durkheim and Max Weber never cited each other's work. In his work to ascertain this fact and figure out what it means for academic work, Edward Tiryakian (1966: 336) considers whether researchers and thinkers are good enough at using information from outside of frequently narrowly intellectual horizons, asking what criteria are used to determine which external stimuli, such as different cultures or perspectives, are 'cognized by a writer or a school as being relevant for their own creative development'.

Undertake an audit of your citation practice:

• What literature is being privileged?
• Are most of your references contemporary, and if so, is the wheel being reinvented? Has this thought been thought before?
• Whose knowledge and ideas are being built upon?

If you are a teacher, then be honest – is your curriculum too white? Are you only taking your ideas from dead white men or white theory boys? And is your work dominated by work from Europe or North America? (These are both valid criticisms of this book.) What about thinkers from the global South? Look at sources like http://globalsocialtheory.org, which aims to provide engaging and accessible overviews of how central social and political concepts, such as civil society, feminism, and human rights have been conceptualised from a more diverse range of cultures and positions.

FIVE

Reflexivity in the field: four case studies

So far, our examination of reflexivity has stayed largely theoretical and structural. In focusing on Bourdieu, the feminist contribution to method, and various other examples, the previous chapters have sought to provide the reader with a concrete rationale for doing reflexivity, to highlight how it is a potentially political process within research, and to introduce some of the myriad ways it can emerge as a research issue. This chapter, however, moves on to more empirical material. It draws on recent in-depth social science research to demonstrate how reflexive issues can arise in social research and how different researchers negotiate these issues. As proposed in Hammersley's (2013) and Dixon and Singleton's (2013) recent explanatory work, one of the best ways to communicate methodological issues and approaches is to use well-rounded and fully fleshed out examples to show how problems and opportunities arise in the research process and are dealt with.

Therefore this chapter presents four recent social science research projects and discusses how, in each case, the author struggled with and tackled the issues raised by being reflexive, while managing potential biases and subjectivities. The four pieces of research, two by British academics and two by American academics, are:

- Mitchell Duneier, *Sidewalk*
- Hannah Jones, *Negotiating Cohesion, Inequality and Change*
- Lisa Mckenzie, *Getting By*
- Shamus Rahman Khan, *Privilege*

Just as in *Homo Academicus*, where Bourdieu's inherent cognizance of the universe under study was both a research asset and an obstacle (Wacquant, 1989), in each of these books the author grapples with negotiating their personal position, and their knowledges and absences, while carrying out excellent academic research. In Duneier's text, the author grapples with the problem of being middle-class and white, and studying the lives of poor black Americans. In the case of Khan, the problem is working as a teacher and studying privilege in the elite US boarding school he himself attended as a teenager. While the works of Jones and Mckenzie take different methodological approaches (interviews and document analysis in the former, deep ethnographic work in the latter), both authors recognise and are required to account reflexively for their positioning. Jones, similar to myself, used to work in the field she was researching and lived in the same local area; Mckenzie's study of St Ann's in Nottingham and the precarious lives of local residents in essence reflected her own story of life on a council estate, and entails reflection on the politics of such research.

Mitchell Duneier and the ethics of the reflexive

> I hope my own uncertainty rings out loud and clear ... (Duneier, 1999: 344)

Sidewalk, Mitchell Duneier's (1999) ethnographic account of street magazine vendors in New York's Greenwich Village, shows what can happen through slow, contemplative study. Off and on over an eight-year period in the 1990s, Duneier documents the lives of the ethnic minority men and one woman who sell second-hand books and magazines, and those who panhandle on the streets of this culturally rich and cosmopolitan area. In his wide-ranging book, which explores both the complexities of race and class in America, and the implementation and amendment of local laws, Duneier's aim is to understand the changes that have taken place on the pavements of a wealthy neighbourhood of one of the world's premier cities. Through asking *how* the informal economy of the sidewalk works in practice, Duneier looks in minute detail at how a certain strata of black men end up in such a position, and how they manage the situation among themselves: the relationships they build and the innovations they make in order to cope with their precarious state. After 'hanging around' the vendors for a significant period of time he eventually worked as a general assistant, running errands, watching the tables as the vendors went to the lavatory, assisting on scavenging missions, and ultimately working on the tables full-time (Duneier, 1999: 11). His immersion generated a large amount of data, and *Sidewalk* presents both huge driving narratives, and small, focused anecdotal moments emblematic of the larger issues at stake.

Duneier however is fully aware of the positional problems at the centre of his massive research project:

> When I began, I knew that I would have to bridge many gaps between myself and the people I hope to understand. This involved thinking carefully about who they are and who I am.... (1999: 20)

And:

> As an upper middle-class white male academic writing about poor black men and women, who are some of the most disadvantaged and stigmatized members of my own society, I have documented lives very different from my own. (1999: 352)

Quickly establishing his fear of romanticising the resistance of these vendors towards the traditional capitalist system, the problem he documents and tries to assuage is particularly important for this chapter. Duneier is the one author of the four discussed here who conducts research almost exclusively outside of his own social sphere. Wanting to 'maximize the advantages that come from being in that position' (Duneier, 1999: 353), Duneier is able to use his academic contacts to get the research checked and consult on possible interpretations of the findings with leading black scholars; he can also enlist a leading photographer from the *Chicago Tribune* to document the life of the sidewalk and can afford to pay a share of the royalties from the book to the people described in it. Duneier also sees himself as a sort of 'control group', who can test whether social interactions are equal, or whether the vendors are treated differently by society.

Race is the dominant social cleavage in *Sidewalk*, alongside its intersection with class, and this leads Duneier to dwell on how another researcher, from a different social position, could have generated different findings. Reasoning that wider studies have shown that black people and white people in the United States often speak differently, depending on the race of the person or people they are speaking to, he sensibly reasons that 'As a white person, it would be naïve for me to believe that the things blacks will say to me are the same as they would be to a black researcher' (Duneier, 1999: 352). Through this he (post)rationalises his use of participant observation rather than interview as the primary data collection method. This line of thought also helps determine the ways research questions regarding specific issues within the wider sidewalk ecology arise, and the reasons they do so. For example, Duneier focuses on the role of public urination and defecation in the lives of the magazine vendors. In his first summer working for the magazine vendors, Duneier would regularly go to local restaurants and fast food outlets to use the bathroom, thinking little of it, even though he rarely saw the (black, lower social class) vendors doing the same:

> I think the reason the issue didn't register on my radar is that my privileges made it a non-issue for me personally. Had the researcher been a poor black, he or she might have been excluded from local bathrooms enough times to say, 'This is a process that needs to be understood.' (Duneier, 1999: 353)

Interestingly, Duneier puts this down to a flaw in his reflexive outlook: while he obsessed about the extent to which his position may have affected what he saw, he failed to immediately recognise and manage the fact that his social position also affected *what he didn't see and didn't know*. This example of using the toilets of local restaurants is one illustration of this phenomenon, as is how dog walkers would be much more wary of talking to a panhandler than to Duneier himself. Similar to Khan's sofa intervention (discussed below), instances where the researcher purposefully imposes him or herself on the narrative to see what happens are significant strategic moments for reflexive learning. In *Sidewalk*, the most obvious of these occurs when Duneier has fully developed his confident researcher habitus.

Over the Christmas period in 1996, Duneier reports a vendor called Ishmael 'raising hell' (Duneier, 1999: 253), angry that the police had recently come and taken his table of wares away, he felt, illegally. Ishmael felt he was being punished because other men on the block had placed their goods for sale on the ground, in contravention of new laws, and, in a fit of spite, the police had come and thrown everything for sale on the street away. On Christmas Day itself, a police officer approaches Ishmael, who has scavenged for more goods to sell, and tells him to 'break down' (take his table down and move on). There is no legal requirement for him to do so, no specific Christmas Day ordinance, but the officer firmly tells Ishmael he is following orders from his captain. The conversation is quite respectful, but Ishmael, relatively uneducated about the local by-laws and powerless to do anything about it ('Ishmael does not know the law, and so has no confidence that he is correct' [Duneier, 1999: 271]), has to give way.

But Duneier (1999: 271), who has 'spent years studying these laws and spoken to experts on the codes', decides to intervene. Merging the instincts of the ethnographic social scientist testing theory and the human rights protester pushing the legal establishment, he takes a set of magazines and a small table and challenges the police to treat him (an upper middle-class white academic with a copy of the municipal ordinances in his pocket) the same way they have just treated a poor black homeless magazine vendor. The vendors on the street that day take up viewing positions eager to see the results.

While recognising that this spur-of-the-moment test is not perfect, both in that Duneier reasons a black police officer would not allow a white vendor to continue in his sales minutes after stopping a black vendor doing the same, and that he is clearly wearing a microphone recording the conversation, the results are clear. Duneier, informed of the law, articulate in expressing his concerns, confident in his arguments, frustrates and counters the police in a way Ishmael could not. Eventually a police captain arrives and relents over the issue of sales that day, largely because it wasn't worth the fuss. While Duneier reflects he would have preferred to see the vendors 'win or lose the battle without any interference or intervention on my part ... it seemed that my encounter with the police might have analytic value' (Duneier, 1999: 277). While the counter-factual is impossible to prove, as unlike in laboratory conditions the exact same scenario cannot be recreated, we know that 'white middle-class people are more able to mobilize the law than poor people of color' (Duneier, 1999: 278; see also Matthews and Hastings, 2013; Hastings and Matthews, 2015), and can therefore assume that race and/or class played a hugely significant role here. Hakim (another vendor, discussed below) who had opted out of his professional background due to the structural racism he witnessed and suffered in the corporate world, later had a similar struggle with the police, and used his detailed knowledge of the local laws to 'win':

> Because I am generally regarded as a Nigger, many white folks, even
> well-meaning white folks, think I am stupid. Stupid means: The

inability to achieve the tactical intelligence of a white person. (Hakim, quoted in Duneier, 1999: 278)

Hakim here demonstrates that it is race and class which operate in tandem in the sidewalk experience. To opt out of the formal economy is to be stupid. It is not that a working-class white person looks down on a middle-class black person: in Hakim's view, white people assume that to be black is to be excluded from being middle-class.

Working with participants

If there is a research study in which the author and researcher has worked harder to stay within the boundaries of good ethical practice and demonstrate their intense feelings of responsibility towards the people they are representing than in *Sidewalk*, I would love to read it. While he only expresses it plainly towards the end of the book, it is clear throughout that Duneier suffered from the overwhelming fear of exploiting his research subjects. Therefore it is pleasing that Duneier's ethic of care towards this group of lower-class, ethnic minority individuals, their families, and their livelihoods, never weakens, and goes above and beyond what is reasonably expected in most social research currently conducted. His desire to get it right sees him use research tactics which most would consider beyond their capabilities. These include the aforementioned commitment to paying a share of the royalties from the book to all of the people featured in it, and the scrupulous attention he pays to explaining precisely when he is quoting directly, or when the presence of a tape-recorder may have affected a participants' answers. There is no anonymisation because 'I am committed to the idea that the voices of the people on Sixth Avenue need to be heard' (Duneier, 1999: 13). Other authors (Sinha and Back, 2014) have argued that anonymisation has become too oppressive in the social sciences.

Methodologies like visual ethnography entail difficult choices about ethical and moral practice in research projects such as Duneier's, but should be seen as an opportunity to reflect on and critique current practices. Duneier, like Bourgois and Schonberg (2009), decided it was vital for his research to include the faces of participants, and accounts for this by referring to a journalistic standard of evidence, as opposed to an academic sociological standard, which often relies on the 'increasingly popular practice of creating composite characters, and combining events and quotations sometimes occurring months or years apart' (Duneier, 1999: 13). Critical questions like this suggest that academic insight has, in some ways, become stymied by the conservatism of research ethics committees and cautious disciplinary standards. Sinha and Back (2014) argue that, in its most recognisable and formal state, social science research is becoming a little detached, erecting the *faux* barriers of the scientific, conducting research 'on' rather than 'with' participants. This manifests itself in practices such as automatically offering anonymisation to participants, as if they don't matter, rather than talking to them about whether they want or need to be anonymous or not. We 'need to break down the barriers and enter more of a dialogue with those we are researching' (Beer, 2014: 40). As Duneier (1999) asserts, anonymity is often a way to protect the researcher rather than the research subjects.

The two most striking examples of his commitment to methodological and research democracy are that Duneier asked his central participant, Hakim Hasan, to write a lengthy and critical afterword to the book, and, more extraordinarily, the fact that Duneier completely reframed his research three years into it, after organising a series of teaching and reading seminars at the University of California-Santa Barbara with Hakim, also visited by two other vendors, Alice and Marvin. In these sessions, Duneier, Hakim, and a group of students explored the ethnographic data in forensic detail, alongside reading classic urban studies texts, and the 'black books' Hakim sold at his table. During this ten-week seminar series Hakim was paid a lecturer's salary and held regular individual seminars with students.

The result of this innovative research-led teaching, and the advice he received from all quarters, was that Duneier came to realise his focus was too much on Hakim, the most 'respectable' of the vendors in Greenwich Village, who concentrated on selling books and lived in an apartment, and not enough about the magazine vendors, who scavenged for material to sell, often slept on the streets, were more likely to drink or take drugs, and on the whole lived more precarious lives. Duneier's original research, a fully completed manuscript accepted by a publisher, was an incomplete view of the street. He had focused his attention on the most singular, most middle-class, most academic individual engaged in this area of the informal economy. Looking at it now, this original research may have been interesting, but held little wider public value. Duneier, through reframing and widening his research project, provides evidence as to the legitimacy of the vendors' actions, even though they appear illegitimate in the eyes of law enforcement and prevailing public opinion. Through the depth of study, he is able to show how people faced with dispiriting social conditions not only persevere but have developed strategies to make their lives better, which they share with each other. In reaction to a crime prevention mood, which posits that anything that *looks* as if it may engender crime must be stopped, Duneier (1999: 315) writes:

> Only by understanding the rich social organization of the sidewalk, in all its complexity, might citizens and politicians appreciate how much is lost when we accept the idea that the presence of a few broken windows justifies tearing down the whole informal structure.... Some behavior that appears disorderly to the casual observer is actually bringing about community controls, rather than leading to their breakdown.

Some of the weaker moments of the book are when Duneier presents overly long transcripts of the conversations, which can cover many pages. But even these serve as democratic reflexive moments, where Duneier's clear aim to avoid misinterpretation, heightened because of the elevated social position he holds in relation to his participants, is demonstrated through his refusal to 'quote pull'. Whereas many researchers may illustrate a scene, feeling, or research moment through one or two short quotes extracted from a longer conversation, Duneier overwhelmingly provides the lengthier context for such 'gotcha' quotes. While this may increase the amount of unnecessary verbiage, displaying the ambiguity and mundanity of conversation writ large, to do otherwise would be to potentially exploit one's participants, to draw conclusions from the abstracted position of an upper middle-class white academic. As he says of this decision:

> When a scholar is writing about people who occupy race and class positions widely divergent from his or her own, the inner meanings and logics embodied in language that is distinctive to those positions can easily be misunderstood and misinterpreted if not accurately reproduced. (Duneier, 1999: 13)

This continued commitment is exemplified by Duneier's insistence on reading the relevant sections of the book to each of the individuals contained within it. He expresses his fear and nervousness as he approaches 'passages in the manuscript that they [participants] might interpret as negative or disrespectful' (Duneier, 1999: 351), but has learnt to put up with the awkwardness (Lareau, 2000), working within the moral framework that he would never want to publish something about someone that he wouldn't be prepared to say to their face. In his methodological appendix, Duneier provides the transcript of one of these encounters, where he tries to explain to a homeless panhandler called Keith about the consent issues around his involvement in the book, and that he will be getting a portion of the royalties. Taking place in a small hotel room on Christmas Day, it is a highly amusing scene, where an academic tries to seriously convey a legal contract to a joyful (and inebriated) participant who is both over-excited to be quoted in book ('Oh my God! Oh my God. I've never been quoted before. My words is in print. That means it's law' [Duneier, 1999: 351]), and not fully able to grasp the importance *to Duneier* of going through his representation line-by-line ('Yo! It's all good, man. Far as I'm concerned, you're family.... Just give me the contract Mitch. I told you. I'm signing' [Duneier, 1999: 348–9]).

While Duneier's unstinting commitment to both reflexive ethics and piercingly accurate representations may be beyond the reasonable patience or ability of many researchers, in *Sidewalk* we can see an author put their heart and soul into trying to do the right thing. Kara (2015: 72) posits that reflexivity should not become a burdensome task. This is true, but what we can learn from Duneier's research process is that reflexivity is not something to be treated lightly, a jolly add-on. It has serious ethical implications but when done well can be an inspired element of meaningful social research.

Hannah Jones and being uncomfortable

> Yet this speaking out was the 'rant' that she felt the need to 'monitor'
> in order to be 'objective'. In the same sentence in which she asserted
> the need for objectivity, Emma recognised its impossibility. (Jones,
> 2013: 152)

On first hearing of Hannah Jones' (2013) award-winning book *Negotiating Cohesion, Inequality and Change* it could sound quite dry: an exploration of how middle-ranking practitioners in local government design and implement community policy is just not as sexy a topic as homelessness, or drug use, or council estates. But the subtitle, *Uncomfortable Positions in Local Government* hints at something more difficult and troubling, yet everyday.

One of the best book titles that exists in social science is *The Limits of Rationality* by Rogers Brubaker (1984). Occasionally I have to teach my political science students about rational choice theory (RCT), a theory often used to explain voting in elections, or decision-making and resource allocation in economics, where ideology and principle often go out the window for more individualised benefit (e.g. it is *rational* to vote for party x, because they have promised to give me y tax break and I will be better off as a result). Of the many problems with RCT, one of the most significant is that actors have unequal access to information, and the information they have may not be accurate (Cook and Levi, 1990). What Brubaker argues in *Limits* is that a morally worthy life, in Max Weber's terms, is liveable, but values are ultimately the product of a non-rational decision. Rationality cannot justify the ultimate values and purposes that render existence purposeful and meaningful (Seidman, 1985). Assuming rationality can only take analysis of social modernity so far.

Such an analysis resonates through Jones' work. For example she recounts the story of Hackney Council being ordered in 2007 by the UK government's Department for Communities and Local Government (DCLG) to implement the Preventing Violent Extremism (PVE) programme to tackle extremism – an obvious example of policy as heat not light (Jones, 2013: 59–65). The Council were undemocratically forced to take money they did not want, to deliver a policy they did not think would help, to tackle a problem there was no evidence existed in the borough. Even though the locally embedded policy practitioners thought it would mess up much of their cohesion work and alienate large sections of the community, they were forced to find ways to bend it to their current agendas, and navigate a way of working within PVE which they were comfortable with. Policy practitioners are not neutral or impartial as Paul Du Gay (2000) hopes, with separate personas of bureaucrat and individual. Instead, this 'useful fiction' is an ideal type rather than 'what actually happens' (Jones, 2013: 19).

In my own research on volunteering policy (see Dean, 2013), my theoretical analysis, which sees increased government engagement with volunteering as an example of Foucauldian governmentality, is hampered by the realities of policy delivery, where local discrepancies, the *actual* behaviour of young volunteers and recruiters, and the fact that policy is not delivered in a bubble or direct from the mind of a put-upon civil servant in Whitehall serves to make everything a bit more messy than hoped. 'The problem', as I once put it to one of my supervisors, 'is that policies are delivered by people, and people can be a bit crap.' It is this crapness that makes life more interesting and fun certainly, but researchers doing qualitative policy analyses are primed to explore and point out that crapness, to identify the messiness and unintended consequences of (hopefully) good policy intentions.

Jones does this with aplomb. Merging in-depth qualitative interviews with media and document analysis, policy discussions and autobiographical reflection, Jones examines recent developments such as gentrification, and policy programmes such as community cohesion, and equality and diversity at the local government level to see how such workers are subject to governmentality themselves, and hence forced into uncomfortable positions in managing professional, personal, and political commitments. She interviews many of her former colleagues and merges the interview data, publicly available documents, and *her own experience of doing the work at the time* to explore the disorderliness of doing policy at this level. This insider status gives us so much more of the story than social policy analysis usually provides. The use of 'uncomfortable' in the subtitle is our clue here. Jones is interested in the vagaries and effectiveness of community cohesion policy, but she is also examining the implementation of that policy, how words on a page and instructions from higher up filter through the policy practitioners of Hackney, Peterborough, Oldham and elsewhere, mingling *emotion* with *power* to see how one can lead the other.

Our interest in Jones' work as a useful text for any discussion of doing reflexivity is clear from the first lines on the first page, an extract from an interview:

Hannah: Do you think your background or identity affects how you
              think about cohesion?
Rachel: God it must do. It must do!

Jones goes on to write of the unequal power relations that often exist in policy work: one is usually in 'a relatively privileged position compared to many of the people for whom one is working', yet balancing 'one's own personal, political and ethical commitments with organisational and democratically agreed priorities' (Jones, 2013: 1, 152). While some policy workers saw themselves as 'neutral' in debates over equality and diversity *because* they were heterosexual, white men, others reflected to Jones on the impossibility of neutrality in policy work and the discomfort this could cause as a bureaucrat. It was considered 'common sense' that one's particular position affected one's practice, and that it was 'impossible to have a completely objective or neutral view' (Jones, 2013: 141), yet some still felt that their 'particular' view was 'the neutral one': these interviewees, out of a position of privilege, reincorporated reflexivity to reassert a view from a supposed nowhere (Skeggs, 2004a: 131; Jones, 2013: 144).

Jones' study is slightly different from many other interview-based projects in that she uses her interviews as an opportunity for interviewees to practise self-reflection. By questioning 'how ... [their] own identity, background or experiences informed thinking about community cohesion' (Jones, 2013: 225), she is asking her participants to explore their own biases, contradictions, and hypocrisies. One interviewee called Emma says that:

> And in terms of working for local government ... that's actually very difficult, because the whole culture of the organisation is that you need to repress that view and you need to be totally objective but you can't be. (Jones, 2013: 151)

Discussing such themes as the impossibility of impartiality is a challenge and produces a range of complex and emotional responses, particularly from a participant anonymised as Jack, a man from Barking. The day he talks to Jones, he says he is putting his house up for sale, moving out of the area where he's always lived because the 'town has completely and utterly and totally changed.... Doesn't look the same, smell the same, feel the same ...' (Jones, 2013: 176). He worries about becoming part of the white minority, which Jones (2013: 179) puts down to a loss of a feeling of cultural superiority and security: now his identity was one of many, and it made him feel uncomfortable. This feeling rubs up against his professional practice, as someone encouraging community cohesion, 'celebrating difference' as the local government literature may put it.

Knowing the field

Jones uses the Bourdieusian concept of 'feel for the game' (Bourdieu, 1990c) to explain her position as a researcher with a great deal of insider credibility. She understood policy practice and the organisational life of local government and was therefore both practically well-placed to talk about issues with professionals to a certain level of detail to generate accurate information, but also emotionally attuned to the pressures such workers would be facing. She sees her role as being to tease out the contradictions between policy practitioners' 'taken-for-granted understandings of the world and their empirical experiences' (Jones, 2013: 25).

In reflecting on the role of bias in her research, Jones points out that she had existing relationships with many of the research participants, and 'perceptions' about how the policy process worked. Realising that this gives her credentials for gaining access and doing the research, she also mentions the 'risk that these connections could lead to over-familiarity or lack of questioning of norms and practices' (Jones, 2013: 25). In particular, Jones (2013: 26) worries when interviewees put forward analyses which exactly matched her own. Rather than being delighted that an interviewee was expressing and confirming exactly what she wished to argue, Jones was concerned that this 'convergence' showed she 'was too close to the material and participants'. This issue is an important one to think about. Every researcher who hears an interviewee provide a sentence that *perfectly sums up an argument they wished to make* wants to listen back to the recording immediately, to transcribe it, and use it as the title of a chapter or article. While the usual criticism of 'quote pulling', prioritising one quote above all the others *because it is so good*, is one of representativeness ('Is this quote an accurate representation of what all the research participants said?'), here Jones is highlighting a further concern: do we think enough about why we like a quote in the first place? In asking such questions, reflexive practice should be thought of as a personal project of building a barrier to counteract confirmation bias.

Jones is also strong on the role of reflexivity as a methodological and academic duty:

> But by being *clear* about what research was done and how it was analysed, I hope to leave this work open to challenge from others.... [I]t is hoped [that] with this *transparency* about how the knowledge was produced, it is possible to develop academic insights ... (Jones, 2013: 27, emphasis added)

In this extract Jones is extolling the methodological rationale for reflexivity. It is about being clear and transparent, not in order to absolve the researcher from mistakes but to make the knowledge useful for other people to use. This is the reason we expect journalists with conflicts of interest to say so in their stories. It is a necessary addition to the prism through which we understand research findings. Jones (2013: 165) cautions that processes of governmentality, which seek to control and keep the policy practitioner 'neutral', work against attempts to open up complexities, discuss sore points, and generally be a bit of a nuisance. In complying with such processes, practitioners can be prevented from challenging power inequalities that exist in their localities and underlie their work. There is a parallel with research practice here. Imagining the neutral researcher blindly reciting quotes and statistics, is similar to thinking about the modern-day, clickbait-generating journalist, topping and tailing press releases and corporate puff pieces. Is it any wonder that 'neutral' and 'neutered' have a similar etymology?

Lisa Mckenzie and telling your own story

> This book is filled with stories like my own – fortunately not all of my own. (Mckenzie, 2015: 4)

UK sociology was hit by a storm in early 2015, as *Getting By: Estates, Class and Culture in Austerity Britain* by Lisa Mckenzie was published. Such phenomena are generally ignored in academia, where getting excited about something is often held up as a weakness, but it is fair to say that *Getting By* caused a serious stir. I joked online about British sociologists being 'Mckenzied', with noses everywhere pressed into its 200-odd pages, and constantly being asked by colleagues 'Have you read it yet?' That it caused such a stir is unsurprising. The book is a powerful and important contribution to a wide range of issues in social science, and local and national politics and economics. Based on nine years' ethnographic research in the St Ann's council estate in Nottingham, *Getting By* details the continual attacks suffered by the community as they deal with poor quality housing, a lack of available employment, high levels of deprivation, and, most vividly, the complete lack of respect they are afforded because of being St Ann's people. This symbolic violence is seen in the constant belittling they suffer at the hands of both institutions and government authorities, and residents of Nottingham who live in wealthier areas. The people of St Ann's are made to feel worthless or like 'fish out of water' in the posh shops of the city centre. Despite this, Mckenzie extensively documents the local value experienced by the people of the estate. They have cultural, social, and symbolic capital *in St Ann's*, which can be traded locally but becomes worthless outside of the estate. Their skills and knowledges have less value elsewhere: such capital cannot be traded on equal terms in different territories. 'Being "someone" on the estate is always preferable to being "no one" on the outside, so being part of the neighbourhood, being known and fitting in are elements to becoming a person of value on the estate' (Mckenzie, 2015: 114). This concept of local value has formed a central tenet of feminist research after Bourdieu, to examine the intersection between class and gender (Skeggs, 2004a, 2004b).

A huge part of what makes Mckenzie's work so vital, and what made so many people want to read it and generated so much coverage (such as articles in the *Guardian*, Mckenzie's appearance on BBC Radio 4's *The Moral Maze*, the fact that Danny Dorling and Owen Jones, respectively, wrote a glowing Foreword and Afterword for the book), was that it was Mckenzie telling this story. Mckenzie had grown up on a Nottingham council estate, the daughter of a mining family who were among the most ardent strikers in the mid 1980s. Raised on a diet of George Orwell, Mckenzie moved to St Ann's, and worked and raised her family there. A resident of the estate at the centre of her research for over 20 years, Mckenzie 'wanted to tell my story of council estate life from the position of both a working-class woman and a resident of the estate' (Mckenzie, 2015: 52). Such an aim requires her to ask the obvious critical question: is this little more than nostalgic sentimentalism or a highly subjective over-dramatisation of the destruction of working-class life in Britain? The question is probably unanswerable – different readers will make such judgements for themselves, locating the description within their own experiences, knowledges, and viewpoint. Yet despite this, the singularity of Mckenzie's research *and her position within it* has much to offer about how we can operationalise reflexivity.

Even though Mckenzie had lived on the estate for 20 years, it was still not automatic that she would be trusted by the local women she wished to speak to. There was initial scepticism, due to an embedded wariness as to the motivations of those who asked questions. Mckenzie writes of the importance of making connections in council estates, a 'network practice' of finding out who you went to school with, who your parents were, which pubs you frequented. While you could argue that such practices are characteristic of any community, perhaps differently directed (towards communities of common interest perhaps, rather than historical connection), Mckenzie highlights this practice as a specific skill she had developed – the natural consequence of being a resident of St Ann's first and an academic researcher second. She highlights how she made use of the family relations she had to make that common connection, an applied knowledge not available to the research outsider. Similarly, she examines at length the role of gossip and chat, particularly in relation to communicating in group settings, such as at the barber's in St Ann's. 'Chatting business' is explained as a common local custom or pastime, as it was considered important to be up to date with 'who is doing what with whom' (Mckenzie, 2015: 83), and also to show a willingness to contribute and participate.

The barber's shop was a 'black barber's', owned and run by black men and mostly patronised by black and mixed-race men, and mothers taking their sons for a haircut after school. It was an important research site for Mckenzie; alongside the local gym it was one of the few places where she was able to talk to the men of St Ann's. The barber's informal style – no appointments meant sometimes a customer could wait for hours – gave all present in the shop the opportunity to chat business at length. Sometimes this chat would centre on football and footballers (their performances, their clothes, hairstyles, and girlfriends), but, more usefully for Mckenzie, sometimes it would focus on the life of the estate, such as who was going out with whom, who had gone to or been released from prison, or who had 'beef' (conflict) with who. These long conversations were vital for Mckenzie's understanding of the local social ecology, how networks developed and knowledges were spread, and how people lived their daily lives.

But let us think about this from a practical research perspective. This identifies two skills or knowledges required to do the research that Mckenzie has done. First, a personal connection to the local community, a way of gaining access through being able to talk to participants about personal family connections, and being able to fit in without explanation or justification. Second, a skill of gossip and banter, of being able to join in in a way which keeps people at ease and keeps the conversation natural and informal. Being honest, not everyone has these skills. I certainly don't. I could talk to anyone about football for hours, but I am the worst gossip in the world. I am shy and awkward, much more comfortable in the semi-formal, policy-centred interviews I conducted for my research (see chapter seven) than these fluid conversations.

It is strange that in methods books and research training we often overlook a key aspect of the reality of research practice: the personality of the researcher. We often assume students to be blank canvases onto which research skills can be painted, forgetting that every canvas has already had a subjective and personal journey. Some people are awkward and clumsy, some are gregarious and loud. Neither is necessarily right or wrong for an ethnographer or researcher, but a constant re-examination of context and appropriateness is vital. This is what Carmel (2011: 553) terms the required 'flexibility' of ethnography, where 'playing it by ear' is an inevitable component of the negotiations, with the researcher frequently having to make instant decisions and think on his or her feet (Hornsby-Smith, 1993: 54–5). Different researchers need different skills in different scenarios but rarely is any analytical thought given to the effect that such differences and deficits may cause.

For example, Alex Rhys-Taylor is an urban sociologist who studies multiculturalism and globalisation through what is known as 'sensory sociology'. He has studied the role of taste (both physical and emotional) in exploring the disgust people display towards eating jellied eels (Rhys-Taylor, 2013a), and the role of smell in understanding the globalisation of East London markets (Rhys-Taylor, 2013b). This 'sensory turn', aiming to democratise the senses (because, especially in academia, sound and sight are prioritised [see Dean, 2016b]), is vital for Rhys-Taylor (2013b: 394) because '[s]ound, touch and vision each add something slightly different to social processes'. But lacking from Rhys-Taylor's work so far is methodological reflection on his own role as a smeller and a taster. Some people have a poor or no sense of smell or taste, either due to a medical condition like anosmia or hypogeusia, or due to having a very limited palate; or they may lack the vocabulary to adequately explain the differences between foodstuffs. Rhys-Taylor, as a young, cosmopolitan man embedded in the diversity of an area rich in emerging cultural capital (Prieur and Savage, 2013), may well have a more refined palate than someone who mainlines burger and chips, just as the research in one recent paper on wine tasting events (Vannini et al., 2010) was probably improved by the authors' interest in wine.

Mckenzie's knowledge as a connected local in St Ann's, and her skill as a gossip who can 'chat business' with ease, and Rhys-Taylor's developed senses of taste and smell, are part of the *personal audit* in which all researchers must take part. Being reflexively aware of one's competences and the gaps in one's knowledge is vital. Such reflexive work may be performed formally prior to research, through an internal 'What am I good at? What am I bad at?' conversation, or arise during the writing up of fieldnotes, when you may reflect on a missed opportunity. But being honest and frank enough to recognise these gaps and constructing a plan to fill them, and avoiding the overly humble or self-critical 'But I'm no good at anything' refrain, is an underplayed step in thinking about one's position as a researcher.

Class and representation as an insider

Mckenzie details how a research participant, a school secretary, welcomes her research, particularly into the lives of white mothers with mixed-race children. Talking in a demeaning manner of this 'problem', the secretary tells Mckenzie that these pupils are unbalanced, and the patterns of local relationships would lead to inbreeding. Mckenzie (2015: 69–70) does not detail how she reacted to this hatred, or how it made her feel, merely commenting that it was 'one of those situations where I heard first-hand what others thought about my community, not realising that I am part of that estate and my family and friends are those people they are passing judgement upon'. Mckenzie demonstrates a heightened awareness of the public reception of the messages she is putting across. She writes of *Getting By* causing her sleepless nights, in part because of the uneasiness and responsibility she felt in representing the lives of the people she knew so well and the community she lived in, but also because of a working-class value system which rejects 'washing your dirty linen in public' (Mckenzie, 2015: 107–10). Mckenzie notes the problem with insider research, that the communication and dissemination of that research becomes harder emotionally than if a detached outsider, potentially without the same responsibility, presents the same story. Wary of stories being taken out of context, and (purposefully) misunderstood and used against the people of St Ann's and similar places elsewhere, Mckenzie has to go to great lengths to explain why what could be read as irresponsible behaviour is actually logical, reasonable, and, frankly, normal.

She recounts how one young mother on the estate called Ayesha, who had talked to Mckenzie about feeling low and depressed due to not being able to afford more than cereal for her child's dinner, blaming herself as a 'bad mum' as a result, spent £25 on a pair of sunglasses after she had been paid. In her heightened awareness and anxiety, Mckenzie sees this story as dangerous to recount because it fits into popular narratives (i.e. myths; see Baptist Union of Great Britain et al., 2013]) of the lavish spending habits of people on low incomes, and particularly into a narrative of tabloid headlines screaming about the presence of flat-screen TVs on council estates. She worries about the story 'play[ing] into the hands of those who think living on benefits is an easy option, or a lifestyle choice' (Mckenzie, 2015: 110). But she saw what those sunglasses meant for Ayesha: she 'looked really good in them', had 'lots of compliments when she wore them', and 'for months recounted the stories of her friends commenting on her good taste' (Mckenzie, 2015: 110). Mckenzie refers to this as 'a little bit of sugar', a drop of happiness and normality brought into what was otherwise a hard and frequently colourless life.

Mckenzie's reflexive practice regarding possible negative consequences for her research participants (her remit for protection spreading to council estates as a whole, rather than just one person in this case, as Ayesha is a pseudonym), raises interesting questions about what researchers choose to include or exclude from their work. This is the only place in *Getting By* where Mckenzie details her worry at telling the story: are there other similar anecdotes and occasions, or details which she chose to leave out? If these examples could be interpreted as negative about St Ann's itself or its residents, then is this ethical protection, or political framing of research? She raises the valid criticism that much working-class literature can be sanitised, with clear narratives of the heroic overcoming adversity, but Mckenzie does not dwell on the local drug trade for instance, because she felt St Ann's and similar areas had already been kicked enough for such problems.

Later in the book Mckenzie reflects on the local phrase 'Don't watch that', usually used when participating in illicit activity and you want people not to pay attention to your behaviour or ask questions. On the face of it, this sounds bad for an ethnographer to hear, 'Hey, don't pay attention to this interesting thing I'm doing.' But, as Mckenzie (105: 148) writes:

> I am trusted because I don't judge. I accept how things are, and I understand that in 'getting by', hard choices and decisions are often made within families. And as long as I respect this code my 'watching' is tolerated.

Reflexivity is about recognising the reality of one's position as a researcher and thinking about how that is managed within the field and in post-fieldwork analysis and writing up. There are political and ethical concerns to be considered, and compromises to be made. Mckenzie worked hard to avoid further stigmatising the neighbourhood, *her* neighbourhood. When she recounts her own stories of growing up poor, such as how her was mother unable to justify spending money on the expensive brands advertised on television, it is a powerful piece of the research armoury:

> My own social position is important to the research that I undertake.... My stories link me with the people represented in this book – I would not have been allowed to collect them and represent them here without my relationships with these people, and the mutual respect and knowledge that I have built up over many years. (Mckenzie, 2015: 4)

Is it possible to understand St Ann's, or council estates in general, if you have not grown up on one? If you have lived a life away from council estates, either surrounded by or drip-fed the media portrayal of estates such as the one Mckenzie documents, is it possible to research them and their inhabitants adequately? The insight Mckenzie provides into the life of St Ann's is different from the one I would be able to give, just as the conclusions Mckenzie would draw from my research encounters would be different from mine. These themes will be discussed at length in the next three chapters, with the conclusion arguing that, as recent research by Alice Goffman (2014) leads us to ask similar questions about 'who can speak for who?', it is reflexivity which is our most powerful research tool in enabling those potentially strangulating insider/outsider boundaries to be broken down, and ensuring that all researchers can at least consider the research project they desire to undertake.

Shamus Khan and knowing your intervention

> Here I was again. Only now my motives were far more complicated.
> I was here to mold these young men and women, but I was also here
> to study them. (Khan, 2011: 12)

Shamus Khan's (2011) *Privilege: The Making of an Adolescent Elite at St. Paul's School*
is my favourite academic book.[1] I read it as a doctoral student, mostly in one
sitting, in the window of a greasy spoon café in Canterbury, where I ended up
ordering breakfast, lunch, and tea, so I didn't have to put it down. Drawing on
data from a one-year ethnographic study of St. Paul's, one of the United States'
most prestigious private schools, it details the lives, loves, and studies of the next
generation of the American elite. Khan teaches at the school for a year, becoming
a respected and well-liked member of staff, whose research role requires him
both to teach final-year students in moral philosophy and provide pastoral care
for the young students, who are bewildered and lost the minute they arrive in
the sumptuous, rarefied atmosphere. It is a dense relationship between students
and faculty with myriad contradictory and complex interactions. Faculty, Khan
included, live in student dorms and 'are expected to teach, advise, parent, coach,
discipline, watch, comfort, and console students' (Khan, 2011: 64). They work
from 7:30 a.m. till 11:00 p.m. and are always on call if something happens. It is
both a dense student–faculty relationship, and, in this case, a dense researcher–
participant relationship.

Khan had attended St. Paul's himself: his parents, a Pakistani surgeon father and
a Irish nurse mother, had both grown up in poor, rural towns, but ambition led
them to the US in the 1970s. His father's skill as a surgeon led to a comfortable
life, with luxury European cars, a home in the rich Boston suburbs, and culturally
enriching trips to institutions such as the New England Conservatory of Music: as
Khan (2011: 2) put it, 'they played cultural catch-up … we became cosmopolitan'.
Allied to this wealthy cosmopolitanism was attendance at one of the country's
foremost private boarding schools. Costing $50,000 a year to attend, St. Paul's
alumni include US Secretary of State John Kerry, former director of the FBI
Robert Mueller, and an assortment of politicians, sports stars, and artists. With
over 150 years of history, and a school where the heritage of attending families
is prominently displayed, we may expect Khan's ethnography to tell a tale of
unending snobbery, entitlement, and classed (but classless) superiority. But the
story is far more complex than that, revealing how the interplay between the
intersections of race, gender, and class with the school's liberal, forward-looking
ethos and curriculum leads to a tangled network of relationships between students,
staff, parents, and between them and education in general.

---

[1] We should recognise that the texts we like, and even more basically the ones we have read, are
the ones most likely to appear as key texts in our research projects, not necessarily the ones that
are most relevant or pertinent. The unknown unknowns of the literature review if you will.

Khan is literally, if not always methodologically, up-front about his position, and his own importance in *Privilege*. The book starts with a short autobiographical essay, detailing the terror and confusion he felt on his first day at St. Paul's, an ethnic minority student surrounded by other non-white students, in a sequestered minority dorm. The fears of entering the new he felt as a student are repeated in his role as a teacher. He is an object of interest for the students he is teaching: rumours swirl about him, about his supposed majesty on the squash court and mastery of the violin (both untrue). In research terms, Khan is quite up-front about his assumptions going in to research the school and its students:

> Upon first imagining this project I was pretty sure I knew what I would find. I would return to the world of my first day of school. I would enter a campus a campus populated by rich, entitled students and observe a few poor, black, and Latino kids sequestered in their own dorm. I would note the social and cultural advantages of the students who arrived at school already primed to be the next generation of elites. And I would see how advantages were protected and maintained. (Khan, 2011: 10)

He also writes of expecting students 'with insider or family knowledge of the place and previous experience at elite institutions' to be the most successful at the school (Khan, 2011: 51). In fact these students – from historic families such as Rockefeller and Vanderbilt – are somewhat sidelined at St. Paul's, shunted to their own dormitory, because the main student body, from the *new* elite, see them as representing an undeserving class of inheritors, rather than a deserving hard-working one.

Khan's personal politics and personal experiences are at the fore here. He notes how he finds 'too much inequality both immoral and inefficient' (Khan, 2011: 4), and writes of how he was discombobulated as a teenager, unready for the world of a prestigious boarding school, and how fellow minority students, from poorer neighbourhoods than he, fared worse. Here, Khan is doing what all researchers do, thinking about what he might possibly encounter, the research issues that might arise, the questions he will need to ask. There is only so much that can prepare a researcher for the field, and that preparation has to be built on what the researcher can reasonably know. Personal experience, anecdotes and tales, feelings and ideas, are the only things to go on if no previous research exists on a specific locale. This shapes the research process, and these initial steps can be entirely unique to the researcher.

Khan is central to the narrative of *Privilege*, the pivot around which the data emerges. There are occasions where he has to move the story along using provocation as a research method (Pangrazio, 2016), not just through the researcher's traditional method of asking questions, but in purposefully acting out of turn to see how participants, in this case young students, react. Khan tells the story of sitting on a sofa situated in the school Common Room that was usually the preserve of final-year students. The sofa was seen as a signifier of prestige and respect at the school, something that younger students would aim for as a goal to attain, indicating they had worked hard to make it through the tough academic environs of the school (Khan, 2011: 48). Khan and a colleague felt that such 'consecrated hierarchies' were a problem at St. Paul's, and so decided intentionally to break the hierarchies and sit on the couch, inviting a younger student to do as well. The young student is made to feel uncomfortable in this instance, and Khan reflects that 'what we had asked him to do was unfair' (Khan, 2011: 43). I read this story as one of Khan making data happen, intentionally stirring things up to generate action, pushing his research participants to see how they react, beyond the usual manner of asking awkward questions in interviews. Is this ethical? Khan reports that the young student who was forced to sit down 'looked terrified in his sunken posture'. A researcher should feel deep unease at causing research participants to be 'uncomfortable' and 'look terrified', especially if they are 14 years old. But as a teacher and mentor, Khan had an absolute right to challenge his students, especially in the St. Paul's educational environment, where learning outside of the classroom seems as, if not more, important than that which took place in the classroom. Is it that as a teacher he is allowed to teach his students a lesson, but as a researcher he isn't? How do we draw that line?

As in the example from Duneier earlier, we can see how researchers have a role in pushing the story. It is the researcher saying 'I am going to do something that upsets the equilibrium. It is an experiment to see what happens. It is not objective, but the results of my experiment will be more valuable than merely observing and reporting what happens ad infinitum.' It is the approach to research of a human being who is interested in the actions of the people around them, testing the boundaries of what acceptable behaviour is, or what boundaries are easily transgressed and which cause problems. This breach is complex and fluid, and deeply context-dependent, but, as Hannah Jones has shown, being and feeling uncomfortable is a deeply common issue, and cannot be absent in research. While finding out about research participants and sites can often take place unobtrusively, challenging and affecting them is also a rational practice, within reason.

Reflecting on gaining access

Khan is prominent throughout his book, but the nuanced realities of data collection and the politics of reporting such findings with minors in a named institution, are mainly dealt with in a five-page note, entitled 'Methodological and Theoretical Reflections' (Khan, 2011: 201–5). This section centres on the issues of gaining access and data sensitivity, but it overlooks asking some key reflexive questions of the study.

Khan says of the world of St. Paul's that as a student he 'had learned to fit into [it] but [it was not] one that I was … particularly happy in' (2011: 4). This unhappiness stemmed from his increasing awareness of inequality, that is, the realisation that he, and St. Paul's, are results of the promulgation of the mirage of meritocracy, leading him to study not at an Ivy League university but at a less prestigious (although still immensely successful) leading liberal arts college. He writes that his main aim in doing a sociology of elites was to contribute to our understanding of inequality, which is obviously and necessarily tilted towards a focus on the poor (see Savage, 2015). But in his book Khan doesn't, or doesn't feel the need to, address the fact that it is his position as an alumnus of the school, researching at a top-ranked sociology department at the University of Wisconsin, which plays a huge part in his ability to gain access and make best use of his presence as a researcher. His position as a middle-class, privately educated, classical music playing, art-loving university researcher is vital both to his gaining access to the research site and in generating data. The students clearly liked Khan, and were willing to talk to him both as a teacher and as a researcher because of his own ease in that context. He fitted in with their ideal of a brilliant teacher, and they spread rumours about his greatness in the recital room and the squash court. Khan's ability to speak the language of St. Paul's, to be able to get these elite kids on his side through his shared history and biography, is clearly not just advantageous to him as a researcher but shapes the entire research process. Yet he avoids offering reflective comment on *whether anyone else would have been able to do this research*, and does not offer the reader any insight into whether he would have been able to generate the quality of data he does if he were not an alumnus of St. Paul's, or if he were someone without an excellent education, whom the school might not recognise as having the potential to be a stimulating temporary addition to the their teaching staff.

Khan's reflective conclusion is useful for us though in adding further weight to the rationale for reflexivity. Reasoning that 'objectivity is often a false mark that researchers hide behind in order to assert their scientific authority' (Khan, 2011: 201), he tells us his initial research strategy, to stay detached, separate, without a social 'position', failed. 'I found that from my attempts at an objective stance I could see almost nothing' (Khan, 2011: 202). In taking a position through making a strident intervention with the school's administrators (discussed in chapter seven), Khan sacrifices his supposed 'objectivity', that 'was never possible in the first place' (Khan, 2011: 202), for a deeply embedded subjective position, to generate *understanding*. This places greater pressure on the researcher. Khan highlights how friendships are created but need to be managed, with friends often gossiping about details which cannot be mentioned in a book for public consumption, while the continued awkwardness of having to remind confidantes of one's position as a researcher is a necessary and unavoidable discomfort.

As a counterpoint, Khan (2013) has written elsewhere that issues in ethnography arising from the insider/outsider dichotomy can be made irrelevant through the internalisation of scientific logic, particularly that of negation. Negation requires researchers to seek disconfirmation, to sceptically try to undercut their own findings (an interviewee's description of the schooling perhaps, or a particular social event). This moving beyond reportage of people's words to a critical analysis of them is what gives the findings of ethnography validity, rather than any hypothetical objectivity. It is a criticism Jerolmack and Khan (2014) make of the interview method, positing that, unlike ethnography, interview-based research is rarely concerned with examining the disjuncture between words and actions. In the studies examined in this chapter, it is interesting to note that Khan and Duneier both make a big deal of their efforts to corroborate their data, but the reporting of efforts at triangulation and confirmation are less obvious in the work of Jones and Mckenzie. Van Maanen (1979) artfully argues that we should try to 'explode' the theoretical constructions we build, metaphorically testing them to destruction. As the next chapter will show in detail, doing this methodologically is just as important.

As someone deeply sympathetic to Khan's motivation for wanting to do this research – that studies of inequality must focus on all levels of the social scale – one could argue that Khan had a responsibility to do this research. Being reflexive requires an honest appraisal of a researcher's skills and position: in this case, Khan had an *in* with a significant elite body in the American social system, which is hard to gain access to. He had to take the opportunity, just as Lisa Mckenzie and Hannah Jones (but not Mitchell Duneier), through the very nature of who they were and what experiences they had, had opportunities to study their sites and populations. Balancing what needs to be researched and what it is possible to research is something my colleagues and I stress when teaching research methods. Realising what you are best placed to do, and why the stories that may be common to you need telling to everyone else, is at the core of good reflexive practice.

Conclusions

This chapter has presented four studies – of the elite, the managerial class, the working class, and those on the extreme margins – in relation to which each author has had to tackle different issues of positionality in their relationship to the research and their participants, and they have all employed varying reflexive strategies to show how they managed these issues. While Duneier's reflexive practice is the most all-encompassing, it is perhaps not the one that we can take the most from. Asking research participants to fly 3,000 miles to join an elite university's staff as a visiting lecturer in order to completely remodel your research project is not a realistic avenue open to most early-career researchers. Nor is conducting one's research over eight years usually compatible with today's three-year (read, research, write) model of doctoral inquiry.[2] But, on a smaller scale, Duneier does reveal how the ethics of accurate representation and reflexive practice (asking 'Is it because I'm me that I found this out?') can intersect. Ultimately it is Jones' approach which feels the most suitable for new researchers in the twenty-first-century

---

[2]   Taylor and Reisz (2014) have recently argued that the Research Excellence Framework (REF) in UK academia, where each academic must submit four pieces of research within a five-year period in order to obtain grant funding, precludes the longer-term commitment required for ethnographic studies because they are seen as more work for less reward.

neoliberal academy to follow, as she openly engages with reflexive questions early on in her published material, but is clearly not oppressed by this. Jones' (2013: 27) argument is compelling and possibly the most important lesson for being reflexive: researchers are not that special. They are not perfect, have as many faults as their participants, and will always be engaged in messy personal politics in the pursuit of new knowledge. The good news is that the reflexive turn and the increasing inclusion of reflexivity as a legitimate tool in all research agendas, whether micro individual-level self-analysis or macro 'state-of-the-field' style analysis, is becoming the new normal. The hesitancy or fear of losing legitimacy, as Blackman (2007) warns, have almost been replaced with the fear of not being adequately reflexive. Looking in detail at how others have tackled this issue is the best way of thinking it through in one's own research. The importance of researchers reflecting on their own uniqueness, abilities, and interpretations has been a theme here, and is one that sits at the heart of the next chapter as well.

Doing reflexivity: reading research and personal skills

Take one of your favourite empirical social science studies. Reread it, focusing on the role of reflexivity, subjectivity and bias, and positioning within it. Write a review of it solely in these terms:

- How do you see the study now?
- Has the review made you appreciate it more, or do you see flaws in the methodology and data collection, or data interpretation and conclusions?
- Are theoretical, methodological, or policy claims made in the study reinforced or undermined by your new reading of it?
- Consider ways in which the author could have incorporated reflexive work or approached the issue of subjectivity differently to improve the study.

In this chapter, Mitch Duneier's commitment to ethical research standards was recounted. Assess the work he did to meet this commitment: were his actions reasonable and necessary, or overkill?

Think about the key quotes emanating from your research, and why you have deemed them 'key' quotes. Are they challenging your prior ideas about your findings, or confirming what you already thought? Make sure they are representative of the totality of the data.

Any researcher's skills are varied and multifarious. Listening, thinking on your feet, being empathic, challenging assertions, melting into the background, smelling or tasting, and gossiping, are all skills which qualitative researchers may have to employ from time to time. Think about which of these or similar skills you feel have. Do you focus on researching certain subjects or applying certain methodologies because of personal (dis)comfort in certain fields, or your strengths or weaknesses identified in this skills audit? And consider whether these choices are having an impact on research findings as a result: are there different ways of doing what you're doing?

SIX

Desert Island discourses: doing a parallel analysis

In a recent study from fivethirtyeight.com, the analytical news website founded by the American statistician and election pollster Nate Silver (who famously correctly predicted the winner in 50 out of 50 states in the US Presidential election of 2012), the major discrepancies which can be found in *quantitative* research are made apparent. The study was part of a concerted effort by the science writer Christie Aschwanden (2015) to show how difficult science can be, but also to defend the choices of rational yet subjective actors against accusations of scientific fraud.

In the study, website users are given the opportunity to explore whether the US economy does better under Republican or Democratic leadership. The site first unpicks the two obvious problems with such a research question: how is 'better' measured, and what counts as 'leadership'? An online tool gives users the opportunity to play around with the statistics. By ticking various boxes on economic measurement – GDP growth, level of employment, levels of inflation, or stock market success – and choosing whether leadership should be measured through holding the presidency, or being in control of the Senate, the House of Representatives, or a majority of state governorships, or a combination of all four, users are able to input a huge variety of data, and *draw a wide variety of conclusions*. To put it simply, you can get whatever result you want. It is possible to propose through statistical probability, with the common probability measure of $p<0.05$ (i.e. that there is less than a 1 in 20 chance of this variable relationship being a coincidence or of your hypothesis being wrong),[1] that the US economy does 'better' under Republican leadership and badly under Democratic leadership *and vice versa*. Through a supposedly objective choice of measurements, none of which are unreasonable in themselves, any politician would be able to construct a sympathetic argument to further their cause. The statistics are not wrong, but political phraseology such as 'economic strength' and 'leadership' are so broad as to be emptied of meaning. The online tool helps to illustrate how the choices

---

[1] The article criticises the use of p-values, and especially the relatively 'easy' threshold of $p<0.05$, as certification of publishable quantitative research. Studies have shown that researchers, who need to get published for advancement in employment, frequently participate in p-hacking – changing their questions and measures in order to generate statistically significant results of $p<0.05$ around which a lot of results coalesce. As journals have been shown less likely to publish material which shows no relationship between variables – known as 'publication bias' (Franco et al., 2014) – there is no reward for scientists who produce such research, even though in a neutral and logical scientific community surely we can see how proving a relationship does not exist between variables can be as important as demonstrating that there is one.

researchers (and lay users of statistics) make to collate their data and draw their conclusions exist in a politicised social world, and not in a vacuum.

Similarly, Aschwanden (2015) reports on a second study from the Centre for Open Science (2014) which published a single dataset about football on its Open Science Framework website and invited researchers to analyse the data. Overall, 29 research teams took the same set of statistical data, concerning football and ethnicity and the probability of being sent off if you were a dark-skinned player. Each of the research teams was asked to test the hypothesis that 'dark-skinned players are more likely to be sent off than non-dark-skinned players', using whatever statistical methodology they saw fit. When the work was completed the teams found that nine studies showed no relationship between skin colour and being sent off, and twenty studies did show a statistically significant relationship between the two variables. All the teams made their analyses available on a shared public forum for their colleagues to pick over and dissect – a limited practice within the social sciences and one that, given the pressures to publish and the sheer volume of literature published, is terrifyingly uncommon. This culminated recently with the publication of the Open Science Collaboration's (2015) attempt to replicate the findings of 100 psychological experiments using the same methodology as the original studies. In their report, the original results were replicated in only 36% of cases (although since publication significant critiques have been made of the accuracy of those replications [Gilbert et al., 2016]).

In medicine, the academic and writer Ben Goldacre (2015) has made similar calls for both research data and analytic code to be shared, so methodological choices can be understood and important interventions tested in a more open and rigorous democratic fashion than is often the case. This is because, as Bourdieu and Wacquant (1992: 35) put it, '[e]ven the most minute empirical operation – the choice of a scale of measurement, a coding decision, the construction of an indicator, or the inclusion of an item in a questionnaire – involves theoretical choices, conscious or unconscious', while data and facts remain the constructions or results of interpretation (Alvesson and Sköldberg, 2000: 1). Such an issue is vital for science, especially at a time when cynicism about information seems at an all-time high in society. No one likes to see the sausage made, as the old saying goes, but in the development of methodology, it is a necessity:

> The false paths, the endless labors, the turns now this way and now that, the theories abandoned, and the data collected but never presented – all lie concealed behind the finished product. The article, the book, the text is evaluated on its own merits, independent of how it emerged. We are taught not to confound the process of discovery with the process of justification. (Burawoy, 1991: 8)

The central point to the above debates is that different researchers can see the same research differently or arrive at the same point through different approaches (see, for example, Morison, 1986: 56; Alvesson and Sköldberg, 2000; Brunt, 2001: 84;

Burnham et al., 2004: 218–19; Massey et al., 2006; Frost et al., 2010). Following in this vein, but tailoring the ideas to the issue of reflexivity this chapter presents a *parallel analysis* of a small qualitative dataset. Whereas *secondary analysis*, studying the same data again, is a common methodological approach within the social sciences (see Heaton, 2004; Bishop, 2007; Hammersley, 2010; Goodwin, 2012; Haynes and Jones, 2012), the idea of different researchers studying the same data in parallel is relatively and surprisingly untested, with few accounts of reflexive work in qualitative data analysis (Mauthner and Doucet, 2003). While a research team may go away and study the results of their research separately before coming together to compare notes and draw up a set of commonly agreed findings, the idea that the findings may not be commonly agreed is rarely made public. What this chapter will show is that there are many reasons for this variety in analysis, while also demonstrating how researchers reflexively account for these differences, and what it means to them when these differences are made apparent. The results from this small investigation will show that parallel analysis could provide a fruitful methodological tool for (social) scientists wanting to understand empirically how positionality and biography work in (research) practice, and how reflexive thinking and discussion can bridge the gap between these differences.

The project

> [D]ata analysis techniques are not just neutral techniques. They reflect, and are imbued with, theoretical, epistemological and ontological assumptions ... (Mauthner and Doucet, 2003: 413)

In 2015, I invited a team of my colleagues – Cinnamon, Penny, Henry, Stephen, and Diarmuid – to collaborate on a project examining how researcher differences play out in the process of research. We come from varying methodological, philosophical, and disciplinary backgrounds within the social sciences, as well as obviously being different people with different experiences and possessing the multitude of personal characteristics such difference creates. To examine the impact this has on research practice I devised an experiment. Each of us would analyse three transcripts from the popular BBC Radio 4 programme *Desert Island Discs* (henceforth known as *DID*), interviews with Ricky Gervais, Frank Skinner, and Johnny Vegas, all three male, working-class, British comedians. The six of us completed this analysis separately and on our own terms, and then came together to discuss our different interpretations of and approaches to the data. Central to this later discussion were the following questions:

- Why do you think you chose to explore the data in the way that you did?
    - Epistemological and ontological approaches brought to the task;
    - methodological approaches;
    - personal and/or emotional connections to the data.
- How do you think these altered how you did your analysis?

- Did knowing that you were working with colleagues on this task affect you? How?
- Were you nervous or apprehensive about presenting back today?

While 'Why do you think you have analysed the data in the way that you have?' is a seemingly simple question, there is a value to asking it in such plain terms: it is rarely put as pointedly as this.

The resultant discussions brought up issues such as the difference between being trained as a psychologist or a sociologist, the theoretical underpinning a researcher has to their previous work, and more personal issues, such as how an individual's age and gender affected their focus and interpretation, and mundane and practical questions of how much time one has to devote to research can alter one's understanding. This is a simple idea, but it has rarely been examined before (for an overview, see Dean et al., 2015).

The research team

Table 6.1: Research team on the *Desert Island Discs* project

Name	Discipline	Job position	Age	Gender	Research approach and main focus
Cinnamon	Sociology	Principal Lecturer	44	F	Qualitative sociology; gender inequality; work
Jon	Sociology	Lecturer	28	M	Qualitative sociology, class inequality, charity; method
Penny	Psychology	Senior Lecturer	47	F	Qualitative psychology; health
Henry	Psychology	Doctoral researcher	23	M	Discursive psychology; immigration
Stephen	Sociology	Senior Lecturer	59	M	Ethnography; cultural studies; race and ethnicity
Diarmuid	Psychology	Senior Lecturer	33	M	Quantitative psychology; individual differences; religion

As Table 6.1 shows, the six of us came from a relatively narrow set of positions within the academic field (undertaking the same task with architects, physicists, historians, and musicians is perhaps the next step), though there were quite significant differences within the range. Three sociologists and three psychologists led to a varying mix of approaches, as do our different ages and our varying positions in the academic hierarchy.

The dataset

In trying to identify the best way to test this methodological problem, certain choices had to be made. As the project is ultimately about asking researchers to reflect on the variables which may affect their analysis, including more variables within the dataset seemed a distraction. Therefore choosing a set of interviews from the same source, with the same interviewer, pattern of questions, and length and style of interview seemed a useful way to engage with the methodological issue. Selecting interview transcripts which could be used in such an experiment was in many ways a personal issue which requires some reflection. Ideas of sampling go out of the window, as do ideas of representativeness, with the centre of the task boiling down to 'What will people want to listen to and think about?' In asking my colleagues to do an extra ten hours work on top of their regular workloads I wanted to avoid being too burdensome. Further, rather than using a semi-random set of transcripts from a discrete research project, taking a widely known cultural phenomenon as the source of our material would not only allow us to reflect on our own understanding of that phenomenon and our relationship to it, it might also be more fun as well.

And *DID* is a British cultural phenomenon. First broadcast in 1942, over 3000 programmes have since been recorded, and it is a much-loved and discussed socio-cultural artefact, described by the music journalist David Hepworth (2014) as a perfect format for great radio. The premise of each programme is pretty simple, and has stayed relatively constant since the show's inception. Each week a guest is asked by the presenter (currently former newsreader Kirsty Young) to name eight tracks (usually music tracks but occasionally spoken word pieces or sounds) that they would like to be stranded with on a desert island. These eight tracks intersperse a 45-minute life-history-style interview, where key events in the guest's life, such as their upbringing, schooling, career, and current status are discussed, generally in what could be seen as an open and revealing manner. At the end of the interview, the guest is asked which one of the tracks they would most like to save if their box of records is threatened by the encroaching sea, and what book and luxury item they would like to take with them in order to make life more liveable on the island.

With *DID*'s 70th anniversary in 2012, a significant proportion of the show's back-catalogue of interviews was placed online.[2] This made it relatively easy to identify interviews which could be considered together as part of a research project, so as to avoid the narratives being too disparate. This easily accessible digitised archive will be increasingly useful for researchers looking to document the change in cultural tastes and methods of public presentation undertaken by this social, cultural, or political elite: for example, Ruth McDonald (2014) has used a sample of 17 elite doctors who appeared on the show to map their tastes and music choices, and to examine the link between class and professional prestige. Equally, Laurie Cohen (2015) argues that *DID* provides a 'treasure trove' of data for her work examining scientific careers.

---

[2] The *Desert Island Discs* archive of castaways can be found online at: http://www.bbc.co.uk/radio4/features/desert-island-discs/find-a-castaway.

This project also hopefully serves as a useful case study or teaching example for helping researchers think and work through the nature of interpretivism when analysing data, and will provide an example of how the issue of personal affect influences the research process.[3] All three of the transcripts from *DID* are available to read, alongside links to the programme pages for each of the comedians. Also available is the transcript from the focus group held between the six of us, which has received very minimal editing.

The results

Table 6.2: Overview of analytical approaches on the *Desert Island Discs* project

Researcher	Main analysis on *Desert Island Discs* project
Penny	Took a holistic thematic approach. Catalogued instances of anecdotes and stories from the interviews to identify five main themes (career success through a working-class lens; alcohol as muse and monster; art, life, and creativity; grounding of friends and family; humour in the darkest places).
Diarmuid	Took a holistic thematic approach. Catalogued instances of anecdotes and stories from the interviews into four broader themes (conflict between lofty art and commercialism; money; religion; the role of the interviewer), and focused on finding similarities between the interviewees.
Stephen	Took a macro-cultural studies approach. Focused on the role of *DID* as a media institution, the social and political positioning of the guests, and interrogated the 'authenticity' of the conversations under analysis.
Henry	Took a discursive psychological approach. Focused on the introductions to each interviewee by the presenter Kirsty Young, and carried out a granular analysis of the language to show how each of the comedians was presented as an individual with dichotomous experiences.
Cinnamon	Took a specific thematic approach. Initially focused solely on the role of gender in the interviews, but moved to examine social class and age, and the meaning of being a successful middle-aged man from a working-class background.
Jon	Took a specific thematic approach. Collated the stories in which the uneasiness of being from a working-class background in the celebrity world was discussed; used the Bourdieusian theory of hysteresis to analyse how interviewees dealt with the 'fish out of water' syndrome.

The results in Table 6.2 provide a brief overview of what everyone did. They are presented chronologically, in the order of who presented their findings back to the group first, second, and so on.

As Table 6.2 shows, there were definite links in the 'what' and 'how' of our analyses, but also some striking differences, in method, theory, and conclusions.

---

[3] If you would like the raw materials to test reflexivity, interpretation, and researcher positionality for yourself, you can find them at http://desertislanddata.wordpress.com.

Some social cleavages such as class and age were examined in detail, whereas others like 'race' and ethnicity or nationality were not. The rest of this chapter explores in detail how Stephen, Henry, and myself looked at the data; the problems that Diarmuid felt he had in examining the data and doing the task; how Penny and Cinnamon reflect on the different ways they approached the task practically; whether listening to interviews and reading the transcripts can provide different interpretations; and finally there is some examination of the success of the task itself and what we can learn about some of the potential impacts of positionality from it.

In what she described as a traditional thematic analysis, Penny catalogued the instances in which stories and anecdotes from the three interviewees arose, and grouped them together under loose headings. She did not apply any particular theories, but instead it followed a precise ordering of the narratives. Diarmuid followed a similar thematic approach, but grouped the themes slightly differently. In particular, he focused on how the comedians discussed their relationship with their parents, with some focus on class and how the role of comedian may not live up to the value standards of a 'working-class job', and how all three mentioned the importance of religion at a young age, but with little clarity or pattern as to how this had affected each of them through their careers. Cinnamon's style of analysis was again similar, pulling out common themes and patterns around class background, education, and family. But Cinnamon told us how she had gone into the task with the specific aim of exploring themes of masculinity, but this developed into the more specific question of what it means to be a middle-aged man. The interviewees' professional successes in Cinnamon's analysis were moderated by a sense of uneasiness with their success that stemmed from their working-class origins. This sense of uneasiness was at the heart of my own analysis as well.

Class and comedy: my analysis

Why did I write what I wrote? Throughout my academic work, hysteresis has played a significant role. While sociologists are well aware of the 'fish out of water' syndrome and, as chapter two demonstrated, it is a particularly relevant theory for understanding Bourdieu and his academic work, it is not much studied or written about. While I try to be a Bourdieusian scholar, neither dogmatic nor wilfully abusive of his theoretical frameworks or terms (Atkinson, 2013), his is the toolbox I feel most comfortable using, and the one I have most interest in applying and developing as I move forward academically and professionally. I think the desire to focus more on the hysteresis effect comes from a long-standing interest in it as a social problem. How do people make sense of/account for being or feeling out of place? When people experience massive change and, in the case of the three comedians in this project, become successful, entering worlds unlike to their own, that they do not seem to be ready for, how does this make them feel? How does it change their relationship to the people around them? How do coping measures develop, and when and how are these put in place? Surprisingly, for such a common issue, the word 'hysteresis' arises only infrequently within the academic literature, even the Bourdieusian literature. But in the three transcripts, after my listening and re-listening, it quickly becomes apparent that all three men have faced and continue to face feeling like 'fish out of water' at various points. All three seem to make sense of their lives, at some point, through telling stories where the overwhelming feeling is 'I can't believe this is happening to me', or 'I can't cope with this change.'

Early in his interview, Frank Skinner recounts the story of his first visit to the Royal Opera House, and of moving from boredom to enchantment very quickly during the first half. He speaks of how on a later visit, he falls into conversation during the interval with 'a very posh guy in an evening suit', and was worried that a technical inquisition was about to begin, as if the gentleman was about to start questioning Skinner's very right to be at the opera. Instead the man asks, 'Did you get the tingle?', referencing the shiver down the spine Skinner felt when the tenor Placido Domingo hit a top C in the first half. Skinner continues:

> I said, 'Did you get that as well?' He said, 'Oh yes, I think most of the people in here would have got that.' It is a bit magical. I can't think of anything else like that. I haven't explained that very well, but it blew me away.

There is a class tension here, with Skinner automatically assuming that this 'posh' gentleman will want to display superior knowledge and establish a social hierarchy. However, his presumptions are displaced, by the use of the everyday word 'tingle'. It's such a simple, colloquial word, unexpected from this bow-tied stranger, and serves to break down the barriers of the field, easing the hysteresis that Skinner feels. It must be awkward for successful celebrities, who are used to reigning over their domain, to be plunged into a situation where they are not comfortable. For these men especially, who have come from ordinary, working-class backgrounds, one gets the impression that they still feel as if it could be whisked away from them at any moment. This is the 'imposter syndrome', recognised by any (young) academic, where someone grabs you by the collar and says 'I'm sorry, there's been a terrible mistake; you don't belong here after all.'

This story comes from Skinner's recent past, after his stage and televisual success. Ricky Gervais tells a similar anecdote in this vein, which comes from a time when he was less well known and his success less concrete. He tells the story of how initially came to know music legend David Bowie:

Gervais: I remember the first time I met him. It was soon after *The Office* broke. I went along to see one of those VIP concerts for radio or something. I went along with my girlfriend. Afterwards we went in the green room, and Greg Dyke, then the head of the BBC, bounced over and said, 'You're a Bowie fan, aren't you?' I went, 'Yes.' He went, 'Do you want to meet him?' I went, 'Isn't he just chilling out?' 'No, come on. We're going to meet him.' So me, my girlfriend, and Greg Dyke, went down to Bowie's dressing room. On the way Greg Dyke shouts, 'Salman!' So now …

Young: That will be Rushdie?! (Laughter)

Gervais: That will be Salman Rushdie. So we were in his dressing room, and we met him, and he said, 'Hello,' and was chatting to us. The next day in the pub my mate went, 'What did you do last night?' I went, 'Nothing.' What could I say?! 'I hung out with Salman Rushdie, David Bowie, and Greg Dyke. Why, what did you do?!'

This story is very human and touching: funny and warm, it shows Gervais in a thoughtful mood with an eye for the ridiculousness of the whole encounter, but also sad, because he clearly understands the move away from his friends that is taking place, the disconnect that he'll feel with them if he tells the truth. A lot of this interview is about how Gervais copes with fame (a subject explored in his second sitcom, *Extras*) and how he actually feels relatively untroubled by it, with the great majority of people either leaving him alone or being very polite when asking for a photograph or signature. He also explains how his routine is very ordinary, in his pyjamas at 6 p.m., slumped in front of the television. But given the increased number of press appearances that must have taken place since this incident, his hosting of award ceremonies, plus a social media which documents his every move, Gervais probably won't feel the need – or be able – to lie to his friends about his celebrity encounters any more. The way he talks in the interview, he seems to have managed his field transition, and the development of his habitus well, but this story demonstrates the torn discomfort at managing the realities that came with his situational hysteresis.

As someone deeply interested in social class, it is stories like these that led me to choose these interviews as data for the project. These three men have different ways of reporting class inequalities and what these mean to them now. Skinner tells the story of never playing, nor even considering *walking* on the other side of the road, because that side were privately owned and his side was council housing, giving him 'a very early sense of the class war'. He goes on to recount the difficulties he has had reconciling his upbringing, and particularly his relationship with his loving but difficult and occasionally violent father, with his celebrity status. In explaining how his father always made the family watch 'Abide With Me' when it was sung at the FA Cup football final, he says:

I cannot watch that now without crying. Even, when I've been to the FA Cup Final, and I'm in company, often at some celebrity jolly, I think, 'How on earth am I going to get through "Abide With Me"?' Because I just know I will think of my dad watching it and I will think of when he used to talk to me about football, when he used to tell me jokes, when he used to sing.

The disconnect between the 'celebrity jolly' lifestyle and a relatively meagre childhood also arises in Gervais's discussion of how his newfound fame brought him opportunities to earn money through advertising products or doing comedy gigs at corporate events:

> I remember I was offered a couple of adverts and a couple of corporates, and the reason I did it was because the first one I was offered was my dad's salary, for 20 minutes.

Through describing how they have brought their habitus to new fields, Skinner and Gervais articulate how they have not been able to align their established doxa and values with those of their new surroundings and colleagues. Uncommonly for working-class white men, but not for British comedians, all three interviewees went to university, Skinner to Birmingham Polytechnic, Gervais to University College London, and Vegas to Middlesex University. As Gervais tells us: 'I didn't know that we were poor until I went to university and people spoke like the Queen.'

Johnny Vegas struggles to use humour to deal with his hysteresis as easily as the other two interviewees do. He talks of the discomfort he found at university and of the resentment towards his family this elicited in him, as his failure to fit in was predicated on his father's inability to afford to help him out financially:

> My dad had warned me before I'd left to try and save some money … there was a lot of people there from far better off backgrounds than us and I was quite blasé about that until I got there. I ran up a lot of debt in my first year, but then in the second year, the party was over, there was no money. My family couldn't afford to send me that money and suddenly a friend in need is a pest. God forbid, it was a very bad time when I started to resent my parents. When I first went there, I resented my parents for not being able to support me.

The downwards-directed anger Vegas recounts here came mixed with anger directed upwards, as he talks explicitly about the 'inverted snobbery' of class violence which he felt at university, as he selected Pulp's 'Common People' as one of his records:

> When I was at college, there was a lot of resentment building up.… One of them was inverted snobbery and it was a resentment of these people who just had everything. If you called, your daddy could stop it all and my daddy couldn't. This song came along and just said it perfectly. Thank you Pulp, thank you Jarvis.

When Vegas's career moved on from his deranged on-stage comedy, his sense of discomfort translated to his experiences of being an actor without any classical training or experience, again feeling the sense that he may not belong (Friedman et al., 2016), or that the people he was working with felt he may not belong:

Vegas: [Acting] was something I quietly wanted to do, but without having the formal training, I didn't really feel very confident about putting myself out there and saying, 'I want to act,' because I thought, 'If you can't do it …'

Young: Did you feel quite self-conscious to be in groups of serious, proper actors?

Vegas: I always have and it's something I've never really got to grips with.

Young: You still do?

Vegas: Yes. I always felt like I was never fully doing justice to something that somebody else had written.

Henry's granular approach and the value of a research team

Henry was the youngest researcher in the team and also the only doctoral candidate. Yet his approach to the data was the clearest application of a method, and he was more certain of the conclusions that he was able to draw than many of us. This was similar to how, in Frost and colleagues' (2010: 457) study, the issue of experience arose in a counter-intuitive way in that the researchers 'with more experience of qualitative research used more tentative language than those with relatively less experience who had a more authoritative voice in their written accounts'. Applying a discursive psychological approach, Henry's attention centred on the ways in which the presenter, Kirsty Young, introduced the three guests. Examining how she 'pressed the levers' at the edges of each man's experience, Henry drew attention to the ways in which Young would situate the achievement of the comedians using dichotomous examples to intrigue the listener and 'set up' the conversation for the Radio 4 audience. This pattern is obvious throughout the three introductions:

Young [on Vegas]: As a stand-up comic, he made his name as one of the most unpredictable and brilliant acts on the circuit; his stage persona a self-pitying drunk, belligerently heckling an audience, who at times were unclear if they were watching a well-honed comedy act, or witnessing a genuine breakdown. These days, with his stand-up work behind him and after a good degree of success as an actor, he describes himself as an entertainer. He's also consigned his heavy drinking to the past and lost a third of his body weight, both part of a plan to ensure he reaches the ripe old age of 40 and can be a proper father to his young son.

Young [on Gervais]: With seven BAFTAs, two Golden Globes, sell-out stand-up tours, and now a thriving Hollywood career, his place in the British comedy hall of fame is guaranteed. Whether he will want to be there, is another question. He is notably scathing about the celebrity culture of our time, and uncommonly forthright in his views of fellow performers.

Young [on Skinner]: Comedian, writer, TV host and, it would seem, walking contradiction. He was expelled from school as a teenager, yet he went on to get a Master's degree in English. A staunch Catholic, he's unmarried and childless, sharing with audiences the most intimate details of his many sexual adventures. An opera buff, he once paid £11,000 at auction for a shirt worn by Elvis Presley. He was 30 when he realised where his future lay. 'I was an unemployed drunk going nowhere,' he says, 'and then comedy turned up, comedy saved my life.'

By drawing out the most extreme personal experiences of the interviewees, as a media interview is wont to do, Young is able to draw crude oppositional caricatures which can then flesh out a more-rounded figure over the next 40 minutes of the interview. This oppositional approach is most clear in Skinner's introduction: 'walking contradiction', expelled 'yet' a Master's, Catholic, but unmarried and sexual, opera buff fan of Elvis, they in Henry's terms 'prime' the listener to receive certain stories in a certain order, which is at once an accepted part of the interviewer's art of directing the conversation and 'doing the work' of the genre, and also moralistic and symbolically loaded: 'we want to know that yes, he's now on that path, he's on the right path' (Henry).

There are several things that are interesting for us to consider here. First, Henry's training in deep linguistic and discourse analysis (and the fact that he is still doing the training), led him to focus on a quite small element of the data, the first 30 or 40 seconds of the shows' introductions, which in his analysis reveal most, if not all, of the content of the interviews, mapping out both the subjects to be covered but also the overall narrative Kirsty Young and her production team have chosen to shape the programme; listeners can anticipate the course of the interviews to come from these short sections, where the person in control of the ship tells you of the course they are going to take. Second, his age led him, he felt, to ask different questions of these men's answers due to his subjective position towards their cultural significance:

Henry: I suppose that links to how I saw it, being my age. I'm only 22 and a lot of these comedians would have made their name when I was a child. Like *The Office* thing came out in the early 2000s when I was about 10, so it's something I've grown up with. Equally I don't accept that they just exist as – they've had a career and when they talk about history

	and Bob Monkhouse, those type of references don't resonate with me in the same way.
Steve:	That's a good point.
Henry:	So a lot of it can sometimes go past me, or I might just completely misinterpret it. But I don't accept they just exist as people in history because they must have come from somewhere. It's that sort of process thing that makes me more critical when I do read it, how does – what makes you this or that?
Steve:	It's true, whereas for me, these are somewhat youngsters. They're not really my contemporaries. I mean, I was brought up with Tommy Cooper and Les Dawson and that sort of comedian. So, yes, perhaps that's got something to do with it as well. Maybe it's a life-stage thing going on there too, in terms of how I look at this strand.

Mauthner and Doucet (2008) argue that research done in teams must prioritise the relational work done between members rather than extending potential epistemological divisions. Doing parallel research or data analysis gives the research team equal weight. In Bourdieu and de Saint Martin's (1979: 8, my translation) concept of disciplines as social and research censorship, the authors examine the hierarchies in which research is produced, addressing how '[t]his censorship by the division of labor and skills is carried out within the same discipline, through the task hierarchy that prevails in most major scientific production units and also in the minds of researchers'.

Stephen's analysis changed as he worked through the task. He came to think about the context of *DID* in greater detail, positioning it within the hierarchies of celebrity culture, and British society. While originally he felt that the speakers were 'genuine' and had 'the sense that the interviewer had enabled a very searching exploration of their personas', he became more sceptical about this, and Stephen found himself more annoyed at the conversations, as he struggled to take the interviews as authentic. He saw it as: 'a ritual, rites of passage type of thing … one of those shows that [shows] you're now a consecrated celebrity, a consecrated person in the Pantheon, and it did make me wonder how much of this was rehearsed and how much of it was [true] …' He was the only one of the six researchers who could be said to have brought a media or cultural studies element to his analysis, focusing on the positioning of the guests and the show's role as a cultural institution. Looking back on our six interpretations, even though in our discussion we came to the conclusion that Stephen's was probably the most *useful*, this did not mean the others were worth less, merely they contributed different elements that would be equally necessary in constructing a 'proper' research project. In fact Stephen's was the simplest analysis in many ways, as he made little effort to theme the stories the comedians told, or try and aggregate issues raised across the transcripts. He noticed this himself:

I think in many ways mine was a sort of lazy approach because I didn't engage properly, fully with the task, I have to admit. I came to it, looked at it, and it seemed to me – I think my ideas, they do tend to circulate around ideas of validity and truth in terms of cultural sphere, ideas and representation. But listening to many of the things that you've said, I think those other techniques brought out different facets to the things I did.

But because we were glad Stephen had brought to the surface underlying themes of validity and truth, and because we are genuinely nice people, the other researchers refuted Stephen's analysis of his own work. While one would hope that during a research project both micro and macro elements would be examined, there emerged here a clear demarcation of who had contributed what. If we were solving an empirical problem rather than exploring a methodological one, *all* of the analyses would contribute to the overall findings. But in a reflective session such as the one we held together, it is the uniqueness and difference of the approaches (particularly Henry's and Stephen's) which garnered most of the attention.

The positivist's dilemma

Diarmuid was the only member of the group who explicitly stated he came from a quantitative perspective: 'I'm a quantitative psychologist but clearly quantitative methods won't really cut it here.' Epistemologically, he cautioned that an initial problem with doing the task was his preoccupation with 'generalisability':

> You can use stats to make relatively objective, relatively generalisable – in theory – statements from a particular sample to a population. That's the whole idea behind stats. So whether rightly or wrongly, I brought that same kind of approach to this dataset. I wanted to make generalisable statements from these three people to people in general, to make working-class comedians in general, I guess. Then immediately I was worried because there are, in the grand scheme of things, very few working-class forty-something male comedians in the world.

He questioned the idea that people would want to 'research on things like this', but knowing that they obviously do, felt like he was missing a connection with the point of the research:

> So I feel like I'm missing out on something. There's something qualitative researchers know that I don't know about the value of this research.

Diarmuid also reported how he only had a limited amount of training and experience in qualitative work, just an initial exposure to thematic analysis as an undergraduate which he 'fell back on' in this project, and as such found the very principles underlying doing qualitative work a big challenge. What happened throughout the discussion however was that Diarmuid found understanding through the approaches of the other researchers; Stephen's meta-media analysis, for instance, brought home to him the nature of qualitative methods which do not necessarily aim to highlight generalisable patterns:

> Steve, you were placing the programme. You were looking at the cultural *raison d'être* of the programme and where it's situated within a wider culture, what's it doing, what's its function? But those weren't – it didn't even occur to me to look at them, to look at them in that way. Because I'm a psychologist, I was looking at the person.

Asked to reflect on doing the *DID* research a year or so later, Diarmuid still saw the experience as different and stretching, and an example of how important it is to move outside of one's comfort zone, and to work with others with different experiences in order to make the most out of (and see the value of) different forms of data:

> It was a hugely entertaining experience where I had to do work that was at least a little bit stretching (in that it was outside of my comfort zone). I relished playing the role of the confused quantitativist. It was fabulous getting to see how others approached the same material. It was a refreshingly collegiate experience, doing something quite different with colleagues than the normal 'marking, eh'-style interactions. I think at the time I thought of it as a learning experience – a chance to see first-hand how real qualitative research is done, but in retrospect this was probably a very bad example of qualitative analysis – mostly because there were no a priori research questions, and there just wasn't enough data. I was very concerned about what the point of the research was, focusing particularly on the idea of generalisability. At the time, the inability to generalise from this data led to me making the assumption (in my naiveté) that this was generally true of qualitative research. I no longer think that's the case – I think you can talk about general modes of experience or ways of creating narratives with qualitative data and this dataset just didn't enable that.

All researchers also need to be able to make sound judgements about research quality (Hammersley, 2009: 15) but the way one assesses the quality of a piece of research will always be influenced by your own theoretical perspective (Kara, 2015). Diarmuid's response here shows how walls of silence or misunderstanding can be built up in research. Whether it is through working in silos or not collegially, or through regularly taking one disciplinary or methodological approach, it shows how the prior information one takes into a setting or experience can undoubtedly affect how you tackle it. For example, in a similar experiment using visual methods, the photographic company Canon tested how contextual information can affect how a subject is photographed (White, 2015). They asked six different photographers to take a photo of tall, heavily built white man with a shaven head, but told each of them he had a different backstory. The photographer who was told he was a former convict took a dark and moody photo of the man scowling, with lots of shade on his face. Conversely, the photographer who had been told the man had saved someone's life took a more open photo of the man smiling with his face in sunlight. The iconography of saint versus sinner is made obvious, and it is clearly down both to the photographers' preconceived ideas of how society views – and wants to view – such individuals, but also what the orthodoxies within the discipline of photography require of their disciples in presenting different individuals.

Similarly, in Duneier's (1999) work, the use of Jane Jacobs' research on American cities as a theoretical framework through which to understand the data he was collecting was only included due to the suggestion of a research participant. Hakim's reference to himself as a 'public character' – Jacobs' term for someone who was present in the streets and known to a wide variety of people – led Duneier to dwell on the role of public characters in patrolling the life of the sidewalk and keeping the local ecology as it was. The importance of flexibility and attention to new ideas (wherever they come from) is well known, but the extent to which huge pieces of research can be shaped by small, maybe throwaway lines is also perhaps under-reported.

Listening and not listening

Different people interact with the data they collect in different ways, but that doesn't mean there is necessarily an effect. In a study by Gladney et al. (2003) two multidisciplinary teams of researchers were asked to analyse interview transcripts. One group listened to the audio recordings and the other group read the transcripts. The conclusions of the two teams, the themes and typologies they created, were very similar, perhaps a reassuring finding indicating that there may only be so many possible outcomes from data analysis. A butterfly flapping its wings can cause intended consequences, but this doesn't mean every outcome is possible. In our study, for example, Penny chose not to use the comedians' names or initials in her work, instead referring to them by number. She felt this enabled her to have a distance from the (famous) individuals and smooth out some of the inconsistencies between the narratives. While with interview data I would always encourage students to walk around listening to interviewees' answers on their headphones, alongside reading the transcript two or three times in order really to *know* the data inside out, arguably because the more you are on top of your material the better you can understand and communicate it, it is clear that no methodological 'rule' is for everyone, or indeed a rule, perhaps it is more a matter of time and resources.

With these interviews, which have the added bonus of being entertaining and short, I listened to the Skinner and Gervais interviews about five times each and the Vegas interview about three times. This discrepancy probably comes from the fact the Vegas interview is the most serious and the least easy to listen to. The subject matter is physically and symbolically violent and at several times in the discussion Vegas does not sound like he is enjoying it, unlike Gervais and Skinner who seem to revel in being able to tell their anecdotes, and frame their experiences around music choices. They seem to have a bank of stories to fall back on, one to colour any topic, whereas Vegas comes across as more deliberative and unsure. Reading the transcript it becomes clear that Vegas gives shorter answers, with fewer precise, ready-made anecdotes. This perhaps echoes the comedians' differing styles – Johnny Vegas's stage style, of the ramshackle, rambling, anarchic drunk serves as a counterpoint to the more planned segments delivered by the raconteurs Skinner and Gervais. Vegas does not, to my ears, seem to like his music as much, and I feel his (my?) discomfort at the formality of the setting, and his lower, more broken voice is both more emotional and a harder listen. Cinnamon however, who only read the transcripts felt that Vegas was certainly less rehearsed but also 'more lovable or more knowable or more accessible, whatever the word is'.

This led to a split across the research team between those of us who listened to the interviews, and those of us who just read the transcripts:

Cinnamon:	We were saying, weren't we, in the break that I hadn't listened to them, so I'd only got the words on the page. It would have been good to have listened to them and heard the tone and interaction between Kirsty and …
Jon:	Is there a reason that you didn't?
Cinnamon:	No, [well], time, time, time. And I was wondering what I missed because I hadn't heard them.
Penny:	Yes, I didn't listen, but then I'm used to dealing with text you see. That's a normal thing for me.
Stephen:	Exactly.
Cinnamon:	Whether she [Young] got on better with some and not others, just in the kind of banter.
Stephen:	Do you know, I kept thinking up until this morning, 'I really ought to give this a listen,' because there's the sort of Derridian sense here between the word and the voice, isn't there?
Cinnamon:	Yes. It's the meaning you might have lost on this. And the bits of the songs that they particularly chose to play again, that selection of the music.

Stephen:	And dialectical qualities as well, because clearly there's the regional accents as well. Frank Skinner's Brummy, like myself, and Johnny Vegas is …
Jon:	St Helens.
Stephen:	St Helens. So there's some interesting …
Jon:	He has a very broken voice.
Stephen:	Yes.
Jon:	He sounds quite beaten up, and at one point he says, 'Oh, I'm not always this miserable,' but he does have quite a voice that sounds like it's been through the wringer a bit.
Stephen:	It always sounds really strained.

And this difference between reading the words on the page and listening to the research encounters was also discussed by Henry and Cinnamon:

Henry:	When you actually look at theoretical discussions that try and tease apart the difference between written and spoken talk, written text and, you know, it's a lot more stretched out. The meaning you have to try and draw out of it, so it's a lot more interpretative when you speak. I very much change the way I saw the interviews. Because one day I read through them briefly on the train type of thing, and then another day I was listening to them and I very much changed my entire – a lot of the comments looked quite harsh or quite pokey. But then Kirsty's tone to me seemed quite enquiring and softly spoken: 'So, how do you feel about that sort of stereotype?' She's playing the game, isn't she? Obviously because of what she's saying, but how it's said –
Cinnamon:	The words on the paper can look quite brutal, but actually the inflections …
Henry:	Yes. Well, we all tease over it when we send emails, don't we? How is that going to be read? That's the essence of why words on their own can sometimes …
Cinnamon:	I did wonder that.

Penny and Diarmuid's answer to the 'How did you do it?' question reveals something under-discussed and certainly under-theorised in social research, that of how much time and effort can one or is one willing to put into any project:

| Diarmuid: | How did I do it? I didn't listen to it. Why didn't I listen to it? I didn't want to spend more time doing it. Not that I didn't find it enjoyable, but it did take a lot of time. I didn't keep track of how much time exactly. Well, the reflective little bit which we wrote took no time at all. I banged that out in half |

	an hour or something. But the analysis bit, there was a lot of – so I got the transcripts, I went through them making little notes about things that seemed interesting, I guess looking out for what I was thinking of as themes.
Penny:	Then the only other thing I've got is that I spent about a total of five days on this, but normally I would spend much, much longer on analysis and it would be much more polished and thoughtful and contextual than this currently was. So what I've got is a work in progress, and normally it would take me much longer.

There is mundanity to research and work in general that often gets forgotten. A recent Twitter hashtag which caught fire among the online research community was the tongue-in-cheek #overlyhonestmethods, in which researchers from the natural and social sciences addressed the real reasons behind methodological choices, such as leaving tissue samples at cold temperatures for 48 hours because of the researchers' 'refusal to work weekends', rather than any scientific criteria. As Van Maanen (1979: 539) writes, the methods we choose are often 'the best we can do'. The fact that so much of the reality of data collection and analysis goes unwritten or unpublished is both bad science and indicative of the symbolic prestige still at stake in the academic field.

Relating to the data

Penny directly confronted her own subjectivities, feeding back that religion, a theme identified by several participants, did not arise in her work, due, she felt, to her own lack of religious upbringing, an observation I would also say was true of my approach to the analysis. She felt her age was much more vital to her analysis and connection to the data: 'being 46, very similar to the respondents, I identified [with] being middle-aged and some of the crises and some of the achievements and some of the things about the future and that sort of stuff'. Yet Stephen, the only middle-aged man in the group, did not have this connection on a personal level:

Jon:	Steve, I hate to ask, [but] as the middle-aged man in the room; was that ever a thought? Or did that not even come into your head when you were …?
Stephen:	Oh, well, of course. You can relate to them in that respect, I guess.
Jon:	It doesn't seem to have a big bearing on the work that you did?
Stephen:	Not really. Because it seems to me that they are already so well known. In other words, you're not coming to their narratives in a fresh – or at least I couldn't feel that I could look at them

in that way, because the legacy is already there. Which is why I think if it had been an anonymised interview schedule I would have looked at it very differently. In fact, I know that I do, when I see other people's interview transcripts, that I have a very different approach to it. Whereas this seems to me part of the BBC empire in many ways. It's a very self-serving thing within that particular medium, it seems to me; it's stories about BBC people. A lot of the BBC stuff that you hear, I get fed up with it.

So whereas personal connection or shared experience can affect one's approach to the data, it can also be completely bypassed by one's antipathy to the figures being examined. Stephen's dislike of celebrity culture and of artificial and constructed conversations made him highly diffident about seeing Gervais and Skinner, especially, as fellow 'middle-aged men'. This helps show how difficult it is to anticipate which subjectivities or elements of the researcher's personalities will leave the largest mark on research practice.

Asking questions and reaching conclusions

Diarmuid: You asked me was there anything else in my reflective account. Just skimming through it, I found two things; one was that I was unsettled by the lack of research questions or hypothesis when you just presented it to us and said, 'Analyse that.' What do you mean? Then the other one was that I found it very hard to come up with conclusions after reading it, so I found it very hard to…. So I was reading it and finding it interesting and understanding it all, but then actually pulling something out that I could present; 'Here is the conclusion from this data.' I found that very, very hard, and I felt personally that I was underwhelmed with what I was able to come up with.

Cinnamon: I think you're right. When I went at it, I thought, 'Ah, it's going to be straightforward,' and then I came up with all of these [ideas] and thought, 'Ah …' I wanted a conclusion, I wanted a focus, yes, I wanted an end result. I don't think I quite got it. I feel better having talked to everybody and I feel I could shape one better now, but that frustration. Yes, yes.

Stephen: Like I said, I very much felt the same and I felt I didn't do it justice. I don't know what I saw the task to be exactly, but I felt I could have gone further. I wasn't quite sure where to take it either. So what struck me were those things that I pulled out, but I didn't think they were – but I felt they were somewhat superficial.

Henry:	I think I might be the only one then. Because I wrote conclusions, because I feel like I was quite happy with what I did. I suppose it's to do with epistemology really. How are you going to go about getting the knowledge that you want to get? I felt like I got – I then understood how the rest of it was received by looking at the intro – that felt enough for me. Because then everything unfolded, made sense as a listener. Then I just felt like, 'That's shelved then.' It's not neutral, it's been worked up. Maybe that's lazy, I don't know.
Penny:	Were you able to achieve a conclusion because you developed your own question? You developed the question that you were asking of the data.
Henry:	I think because of the approach I take, it's very much a package approach, so it's based on asking a very similar question to a range of different issues; how is this done? And that's basically the question ...
Jon:	Whereas I would want to go away, do more theory work, find out what has been written about hysteresis before; here is how these people make sense of hysteresis or how it's used in this media context. This either supports, changes, alters or opposes what has been written before, and that's how you construct your research arc.
Cinnamon:	And is it because as the disciplines we come from we're trying to be critical? You know, we try to look – you said inequality – but we're trying to look for power relationships, we're trying to look at.... And how do these three texts enable you to fashion something that begins to get you along that line I suppose.
Penny:	I feel that without a question I can't come up with any conclusions. I can come up with some themes, but what those themes mean in relation to my question ...
Cinnamon:	Exactly. It's got to be pegged to a critical ...
Penny:	You have to have that context. Exactly, so.... Yes, I didn't feel I could progress it beyond the purely descriptive because I didn't have the context within which to understand those themes I suppose.
Jon:	That's the problem with nature of the project design?
Penny:	Well not – no!
Cinnamon:	No.
Jon:	No, no, I think that's fine, but if you were going to design a project, you wouldn't design it like this. You would set research questions yes?
Cinnamon:	I'd have a question.

| *Penny*: | I'd have a question, yes. But because you didn't give a question, it's interesting to see that people have asked their own questions, or like us, haven't asked the question at all, have just – or have got a theoretical top down approach … |
| *Cinnamon*: | In order to manage that, yes, a coping mechanism to manage that. |

In research, you are generally driven by guiding principles: aims and goals, methodological guidelines, dates for completion, and perhaps most importantly, key research questions. It is fair to say that the lack of research questions in this task bamboozled a few of the team of researchers. As the above extended extract from our discussions shows, because the task set was ostensibly 'Go away and analyse these', and the key research question was 'How do different researchers analyse the same data?' and not, for instance, 'How can these interviews aid our understanding of the relationship between class and fame?', the project left a few of the research team rather unfulfilled, especially in the stages between doing their analysis and reporting back. The purpose of the task was solely methodological, with an overarching question about research process. Doing an experiment on method itself is rare. The social science journals devoted to research methods are generally full of content stemming from observations drawn from 'regular' research projects, where a population or a policy was being explored and reflections on the process are deemed useful for the wider academic populace to know about. In Frost et al.'s (2010) research, no question was set and it was method that was seen as the driver of enquiry. But to be completely reflective on the social process of research, we must ask whether an abstract task is approached in a different way from a grounded and empirical one? Methods are too important to be left to methodologists (Becker, 1970: 3), and the best way to understand the process of method is to examine it during *actual* research, rather than in the abstract. This task sought, as best as possible and in contravention of what was written in the introduction, to create a laboratory-like space to test individual effects on research findings. But as soon as you tell researchers what they're doing, or include any data for analysis that relates to human life, the illusion of non-social research is shattered. Ergo, is it too self-critical to ask whether this task can ever really work?

Conclusions

The 'choices' we make in our research with regard to ontological and epistemological positioning, methodological and theoretical perspective, and the adoption of particular research methods are bound up not only with our personal or academic biographies, nor are they motivated exclusively by intellectual concerns. The interpersonal, political and institutional contexts in which researchers are embedded also play a key role in shaping these decisions. (Mauthner and Doucet, 2003: 421)

This small, investigative study shows that a synthesis, of research methods, but also of research styles and of researchers themselves, can be invaluable – with the caveat that, in some cases, different research paradigms or methodological lenses may be incommensurable and philosophically contradictory. The example of the *DID* interviews reminds us of the issues raised in different readings of discourse and how each may contribute to a layered and more complex analysis of the text in question. In this case we saw a spectrum of interpretive strategies, from the more micro-textural approaches of Henry, and thematic issue-based approaches of Penny and Diarmuid, to the broader analyses of the power dynamics of Cinnamon and Jon, and a vaguely macro meta-level approach to the function of the text from Stephen. While the case studies presented at the start of this chapter may be concerned with weightier subjects, such as medicine and the direction of the economy, the promulgation of and increased competition within higher education has led to an explosion in scientific output without the same explosion in oversight and reflection. Parallel analysis may be one way of getting more information out of the data we already have, rather than driving for more.

The chapter and project have also served to highlight the realities of research. Les Back (2015b: 821) writes that by focusing our study on everyday life we are forced to 'take the mundane seriously'. Such an increase in focus on everyday life has, as Sarah Pink (2012) has argued, paradoxically meant the hidden, the ordinary, and the mundane behaviours of social life have never been more scrutinised, analysed and generally 'unhidden' (see Neal and Murji, 2015). The aim of reflexive practice, and the open practice of researchers such as Shane Blackman (2007), is to do the same for research. This project hopefully lays open both the nature of interpretation and the mundanity of research practice. As Libby Bishop (2007; see also Oakley, 1981) puts it, reinforcing a central message of this book, 'relatively few methodological studies exist that provide reflection on the actual, not idealised, process'.

Doing reflexivity: why did you do what you did?

Frosh and Emerson (2005) interpret reflexivity as a way for researchers to account for the means by which they arrive at a particular 'reading' of data, or making explicit the process by which they came to know. The question that brought us here – 'Why did you do what you did?' – is vital in providing a rationale that convinces both readers and yourself that your approach to the issue was an appropriate way to answer the research questions you set yourself. Take stock of the seemingly mundane and practical limitations to your research. In the spirit of #overlyhonestmethods be honest with yourself both about why you have made the methodological choices you have, and how the choices may limit your analysis and development of theory.

What would someone else, coming to this data from a different philosophical, disciplinary, or simply different life experiences make of it? Would they focus on the same things that you have? Why not share data with friends and colleagues before starting to write up and finalise your analysis? Whether it's a focus group transcript, a roll of photographs, a week of fieldnotes, or a set of survey responses, doing reflexive work as a group will allow different responses to emerge, just as England (1994) says that a more flexible approach to fieldwork allows researchers to be more open to any challenges to their theoretical position which may emerge from fieldwork.

Visit https://desertislanddata.wordpress.com. Examine the transcripts at the centre of this chapter, including the conclusions we drew. What other themes, theories, or understandings could be brought to this same set of data.

SEVEN

The reflexive me

To find the source of trouble we must look into our own heads. (Saul Bellow)

In Shamus Khan's (2011) research at St. Paul's there was an instant where he went from being a figure of suspicion, to being accepted and rewarded with access. Khan only found himself on the side of his colleagues after several months in the field when he stood up to school management and demanded staff reject a new policy on grounds of academic inadequacy. By chance, it enabled a bond of trust to be built. In one encounter in my own research, I found myself given insider status rather more quickly but in a more public fashion. A youth volunteering worker called Jill had made contact with me, inviting me to speak at a celebration event, as an 'expert' in youth volunteering and as someone who had worked with national volunteering charities. There were many potential interviewees in the room, youth volunteering workers, charity managers, staff from local government, but before I spoke I was having trouble relating to people. They were too busy to talk to me, and perhaps I failed to adequately explain who I was. Eventually, I was invited on the to the stage by Jill as 'Jon Dean from the University of Kent who is going to talk about the national youth volunteering projects' and I got up to indifferent applause from about a hundred people. I spoke about who I was, my own history of volunteering and why I thought it was important, why certain youth volunteering projects such as v (the young volunteers' service) were set up, and the threats they faced from the government cuts and the Big Society policy agenda, which I populistly called 'rubbish' garnering my biggest round of applause and laughter. I stumbled through some extravagant thanks for the organisers and Jill in particular and stood down, again to some very welcome applause.

The reaction I got stepping off the stage was invigorating as a researcher. Everyone wanted to come up to me and talk to me, congratulate me on what I'd said, and ask about my work and offer opinions. As Norman Denzin (2001) says of the reflexive interview, words matter because of the effects they have on people, materially changing the world. I wasn't alone for the next five hours as the event went on, as more and more people came to seek me out. Like Khan, I had done something for my research participants to demonstrate that I was on their side and not to be treated with suspicion. Making that speech in front of a hall full of people was not in my original methodological plan – it couldn't have been. This is the required 'flexibility' of ethnographer, where "'playing it by ear" is an inevitable component of the negotiations, with the researcher frequently having to make instant decisions and think on his or her feet' (Hornsby-Smith, 1993: 54–5).

The ease of access says something about the culture of the thing being studied, 'part of the culture itself' (Carmel, 2011: 552; Burawoy, 1998). After this intervention I found interviewees incredibly straightforward to access, and Jill and her colleagues worked generously hard to get me email addresses and phone numbers for people they felt I should speak to. The culture of the volunteering bodies represented at the event was open and welcoming. As a researcher asking about the relationships that they develop with young people, I could see the skills on display that were vital in the efficacy of volunteer recruitment and placement schemes.

This chapter focuses on me. It details several of the reflexive tasks I undertook during my doctoral research, which drove me towards writing this book. During the process it became apparent the research would have to consider the impacts of my own biography and individual subjectivities upon the research process and findings. These are presented below, with new consideration of their use and wider applicability, and include:

- a substantial critical autobiographical analysis of my own class and political positioning that I wrote after interviewing my parents about my upbringing;
- a discursive section in which I asked fellow doctoral students to examine if the conclusions my research was coming to were *as a result* of the pressures of being a PhD student having to finish within three taut years;
- and a section on the role of emotion in fieldwork and research findings, made up of an extract from my fieldnotes on the day of the volunteering event introduced above, which critiqued my own positioning and resultant relationship with research participants and led me to a change in my academic delivery. This section also includes some consideration of the role of attachment to place in research.

The chapter concludes by addressing the need for researchers to consider the myriad options they have for reflexive work, but maintains that decisions over these choices are intrinsically subjective and context-dependent.

Thinking through who we are

It should have become clear to even the most uninterested reader that I believe that autobiographical reflexivity is a vital part of the production of qualitative research. The subjectivities of the researcher affect their output, both in the research process and in the interpretation of findings, and also in the writing-up process and their chosen approach to dissemination. Therefore doing one's best to inform sociological publics of these subjectivities and their possible implications should be considered a vital part of the methodological process. Second, unlike Bourdieu (2007), I do not want to wait until the end of my career to spell this out to people who may value my own academic contribution. This is not meant as arrogance, but to follow a reflexive approach in a logical fashion involves a constant rethinking of how I believe my subjectivities affect my output. I will not reach the heights that Bourdieu scaled in his career (of little am I more certain), but such methodological approaches should not be reserved for those whose biography the wider public is interested in reading. An egalitarian science cannot prioritise one person's biography over another; it is the biography of the researcher in question that matters, no matter who it is.

From 2009 until 2013 I undertook a PhD at the University of Kent in the UK. The thesis started life as a social policy analysis of the 1997–2010 Labour government's attempts to encourage more young people to participate in volunteering. Having been a youth volunteering worker myself, volunteering with local charities in Liverpool to get young people more engaged in altruistic activities, I was interested in exploring why so many of the young people I managed to recruit were 'the same old faces'. These were young people who would turn up again and again, whereas so many young people I approached, shrugged and moved on, or wouldn't give me a second glance. The thesis aimed to understand why the Labour government had invested so much in youth volunteering (approximately £300 million, at a conservative estimate [Finnegan, 2011]), and to identify which young people were benefiting from such investment.

I collected data through a series of interviews with youth volunteering recruiters, voluntary sector policy officials, and young volunteers, alongside ethnographic research[1] conducted through volunteering alongside young people at numerous charitable events across two areas in England. As I wasn't 26 until 2012, I was able to develop a certain amount of insider status with the young volunteers, furthered both by my experience as a volunteer and a volunteer recruiter, and also the context of the areas in which I carried out research. Data were collected in areas that were anonymised in the thesis and in publications as Croft and Eastwood. Croft is an area in the South of England, a wealthy historic town with good commuter links to London. It has a large tourist trade, several universities, and well-established cultural institutions. Interviewees described it as 'cosmopolitan', 'bohemian', and, overwhelmingly, 'middle-class'. Eastwood is different. A working-class borough in the deindustrialised West Midlands, Eastwood suffers from high levels of unemployment, low levels of health indicators, with a strong reliance on the state: 'uniformly poor' was how one senior director of local government summed it up.

---

[1] I always made the distinction between my *ethnographic* research and *ethnography* – as this seemed important to me. I had not done an ethnography, involving the level of commitment of many of the researchers discussed in chapter five, but had done ethnograph*ic* work. In retrospect, it could be argued, there is little that is ethnographic about the work described either: each instance was merely an individual, short, time-limited opportunity for participant-observation. However the larger frame of policy analysis, which meant I would travel all over the country to attend events and talks, puts them in a wider frame – of a different, non-Chicago School style of ethnographic investigation.

What is interesting for the purposes of this study is my relationship to these areas. I was born and grew up in Wolverhampton, a town bordering Eastwood and an area suffering from very similar problems to the ones outlined above. Yet the culture of Croft is the one to which I found my own middle-class and postgraduate habitus more suited. I felt comfortable researching and interacting in both Croft and Eastwood, because, I believe, of the experiences of my flexible and culturally omnivorous middle-class upbringing, despite knowing little of the area. While my practice suited Croft and the South, my knowledge suited Eastwood and the Midlands. As a researcher, I recognised I could take advantage to some degree of my cleft habitus (Abrahams and Ingram, 2013).

Bourdieu's social project was to uncover and highlight the invisible structures that govern our lives. Therefore, if all science but particularly social science, exists as part of this larger social construction, the choice is not to be either part of this construction or not – a false dichotomy – but to be aware of the construction or not, and to raise awareness of it or not (Bourdieu et al., 1999: 608). In recent examples, Morrin (2016) and Friedman (2016) write personally reflective essays, examining how moments from their childhood and upbringing can be explained through Bourdieusian social theory, and how the sites of research they now find themselves studying (local school systems and elite occupational trajectories respectively) can stimulate critical personal awareness. To examine the link between personal and social history, and how to do so, is a choice the reflexive researcher must make.

The following is an extract from my own personal history written over the course of several weeks. I present to the reader a brief explanation of who the narrator of this book is and how I feel such a biography affected the shape of my enquiry. The potted history of my class and familial background draws on the methodological approaches identified in the narrative sociology of Berger and Quinney (2005), the autoethnographic method developed by Ellis (2004) among others, and the social biography of Walley's (2009) deindustrialised Chicago childhood, but mostly on the biographical vignettes by Michael Humphreys (2005), who used such vignettes to address the call for ethnographers to address their own 'taken-for-granted understandings of the social world under scrutiny' (Van Maanen, 1979: 547). Humphreys grapples with concerns over authenticity, perceptively noting the problem that reflexive research has with authenticity, the fear that one is merely talking about oneself, and thereby not fully applying oneself to research. The personal history below reflects some of these concerns:

> I'm middle-class, yet it's never as simple as that. I was born and grew up in Wolverhampton, a town neighbouring Eastwood, a poor yet safe and secure area, with an ever-increasing population of Sikh and Hindu immigrants from India and Pakistan. My school, the classic easily dismissed as 'bog-standard' comprehensive, with poor average grades but a big heart, sat in the middle of our estate, where my parents worked to build a middle-class oasis for our family. My dad was a

social worker and my mum a health visitor. They had both migrated to Wolverhampton for work, my dad from Stoke-on-Trent, my mum from further north in Rotherham. Their parents had clerical and skilled manufacturing jobs, and had, as mine would for me, worked hard to leave them more than they had before.

My dad was pressured by his work to undertake management qualifications. This involved a Master's course in the evenings when I was seven or eight. I remember him working 7 a.m. till 7 p.m. Monday to Friday, and often all day Sunday. The decision was somewhat against his will and the will of my mum, although in the early retirement they were both able to take in 2011, they are currently reaping the rewards of their investment. When my brother and I were born, my parents took the decisive step that my mum would continue to work, three days a week while we were still at junior school, which increased during our adolescence to four and then four and a half days a week. The extra money these choices brought into the family during the boom years of the 1990s and early 2000s, was invested in me and my brother. While we did not have grand tastes, and were not obsessed with expensive cultural fads such as computer games and football shirts, although I did often ask for these items as birthday and Christmas presents in order to keep up with my friends, it was our cultural capital that was invested in. There was always a computer in our house, first a classic BBC machine, then an Amiga, before moving on to desktops and laptops. We were the first in our peer group to get the internet, and I was the only one of my friends to regularly get taken to the theatre, to see Shakespeare or Miller or Priestley. When we were studying a play in school, we'd travel across the country to see a production. We were encouraged to take up music, and both my brother (violin and trombone) and I (tenor horn and tuba) were shepherded across the Midlands to play in various bands and orchestras. When I was at primary school and I was asked if I wanted to play football after school, I'd reply 'Can't – band.' to which the common reply was 'Why, what have you done?' Participating with children from other schools was not a common experience for many of my friends at school, whose parents, for various reasons sociologists are well aware of, were neither able to nor chose to 'culturally cultivate' their children.[2]

I was taken across town to the well-off suburbs of Tettenhall (Wolverhampton's version of Notting Hill) to play tennis against the boys and girls from the private school. We had regular holidays

---

[2] Especially relevant here would be Annette Lareau's (2000, 2003; see also Metzgar, 2011) theory of the middle-class concerted cultivation approach to childrearing, as opposed to the working-class belief in natural growth.

abroad, driving to relatively low-budget campsites in France, but also flying to America. We ate in up-market restaurants, but only on special occasions, and had both *the Guardian* (twice weekly) and the *Wolverhampton Express and Star* (daily) delivered. The news was constantly playing in the background, and as signalled by having internet access, being involved and informed was actively encouraged. But we never up-scaled our house to Tettenhall, although my parents often thought about it, as they preferred to invest the comfortable amount of money they were making from public sector work in us and themselves, rather than put it in bricks and overwhelming mortgages.

Having progressed to become a social services manager, my dad dealt with local politics on a daily basis, which is perhaps the reason we rarely acted politically as a family. We talked about the issues occasionally, and my dad never missed an opportunity to remind us that he 'knew Tony Blair would be a disaster' and had voted for Arthur Scargill in 1997. But we were not campaigners, or particularly strident. However, for me a political conscience did not arise until nearer age 15. One day on the way home from playing tuba for a brass band in a working-men's club, I happened across a thought and decided to run it by my dad. 'You should get a better quality of health service the more tax you pay,' I opined. My dad said very little, but when we got home he pointedly looked at my mum and said 'Listen to what Jonathan's got to say.' I repeated myself, they both looked at each other, and for 20 minutes proceeded to point out all the flaws in my logic, from its inhumane nature, to its impracticalities. It was the most formative conversation of my political life.

My dad described his father as an 'armchair socialist', and he himself had continued this, reading columns by Polly Toynbee and muttering darkly about 'the bastards'. It is only now, writing this, that I realise he had been actively political for years, but outside of party politics. He worked to fund services for disabled people, winning funding for a special needs health centre in one of the country's most deprived areas. He was an LGBT champion, a relatively thankless task in a town which could so easily be described as illiberal and regressive, but which he knew as welcoming, the bigger issue being the difficulties of being gay or transgender and isolated in a poor area with few support structures. My mum worked tirelessly to help people in some of the most desperate situations, who had resorted to feeding their babies chips from the chip shop mashed with water so the child could imbibe something warm, in flats with neither heating nor electricity. Their politics was not the grand issue of nation-building, global conflict or democracy; it was the vital day-to-day politics of trying to use the 'left-hand' [see chapter 3] of the state make things slightly better for people living in poverty.

My parents pointed out to me that I did not really believe in my nonsensical and unthought through comments about the health service and taxes. I learnt that day and in the days afterwards, when I pondered society and ruminated as only an adolescent can, that deep down I was concerned with inequality, and became more reflexively aware of the fortunate position I was in. I became more active, protesting against the Iraq war for instance, but much more aware of my class. I was middle-class, my parents had been middle-class, and their parents had been middle-class, and I can see some of the omnivorous nature of Khan's (2011) privileged students in myself. Cultural omnivores are taught to absorb everything, and to see the value in high and low cultural formations. But can you truly understand both, or is your apparently confident appearance in a rough working-men's club merely an act? I do not always feel comfortable at the theatre, or in a rough pub. But I feel I can recognise what is going on, and want to understand what may be going on.

I am middle-class, but my middle-class habitus – my 'dispositions – perceptions and appreciations' (Burawoy, 2008a: 4) – has grown out of both middle-class and working-class experience. I was good friends with many of the men and women of that working-men's club and the local brass bands. I went to comprehensive schools in which the social problems of inequality were lived. After university, I took up a full-time volunteering role with Community Service Volunteers (CSV). I worked on social action projects with disadvantaged young people in the poorer areas of Liverpool, such as Toxteth. That I was able to do that, both financially (receiving support from my parents) and personally (feeling confident to go and intervene in a new situation) is a result of the social investment in me as an adolescent and the cultural capital my middle-class upbringing gave me. I was able to volunteer for others without a real concern about the extent to which it would help my future. Reflexively realising how these activities were *also* helping my future employment prospects was second nature to a certain extent. I had the luxury of formally volunteering for others throughout my childhood, adolescence and as a young adult, and many young people, particularly those from more precarious backgrounds, do not have that luxury. I did not *need* these extracurricular additions, and ironically, as a result I was more able to use my intrinsic volunteering experience to get a place on a doctoral programme in a highly respected department in a very good university studying volunteering.

After dwelling on reflexivity for so long, I have come to believe it is vitally important that any reader of my work is aware of these subjectivities before trying to understand my conclusions in order to critique any political judgements I choose to make – about the efficacy of certain volunteering policies, or the impact of class and disadvantage on the ability to be altruistic. In chapter four, we touched on the idea of privilege and accounting for one's positioning in various intersectional social categories. The writer and cultural critic Roxane Gay (2014) writes of the difficulty she has in accepting her privilege. As a woman, a person of colour, and the child of immigrants, all parts of her identity which have caused her hurt, Gay also acknowledges her middle- and upper-middle-class upbringing, her loving parents and family, and her professional success:

> To have privilege in one or more areas does not mean you are wholly privileged. Surrendering to the acceptance of privilege is difficult, but it is really all that is expected.... You need to understand the extent of your privilege, the consequences of your privilege, and remain aware that people who are different from you move through and experience the world in ways you can never know anything about. (Gay, 2014: 17)

Writing as an able-bodied, heterosexual, middle-class, white man working in a social science discipline which, while trying to challenge such hegemonic power internally and externally, still too strongly reflects the unequal world outside, means that I have more critical self-reflection to do than most, especially around the cleavage of class, because, as I saw it, this was a prime division within volunteering (Dean, 2016a). I felt I needed to conduct the self socio-analysis of my class and politics in order to understand the framing I was bringing to the data I was collecting and the resultant conclusions I was drawing. Is it surprising I found that working-class young people were being maligned in the delivery of youth volunteering policies because that's what I believed was happening? Perhaps. But perhaps only someone with that suspicion and with the experience of working in the sector as I did would choose that as a suitable doctoral topic area. The answer to the question of bias is therefore a subjective and interpretive one. But by being willing to pose these critical reflexive questions can we at least provide a deeper, more comprehensive and open base to the findings. Writing and presenting the above extract makes me feel extremely self-conscious, but it is work that I found immensely useful in trying to reassess my own framing of research data.

Practical reflexive issues in research design

Another of the central conclusions of my doctoral work was that young people were being encouraged to volunteer for instrumental reasons (developing their employability) rather than for altruistic or charitable reasons (Dean, 2014). Social forces, the pressures of university applications, employment sanctions, and the tone of government and education policy increasingly pushes young people to think and operate in a more calculating way (Furlong and Cartmel, 2007: 5). Class habitus would suggest that the process of acquiring cultural capital and then utilising it is a subconscious behaviour, one aligned with middle-class behaviours, one that is not explicitly learned or taught. I think this can be seen in my own biography. I thought back to my own volunteering experiences and thought about whether I fitted in to what I was finding. I went to a school which did not particularly push these extracurricular activities. There did not seem to be any pressure to get involved in anything community related, in a school where exam results were average. But I was in the local brass band and the scouts, and played tennis, activities which were beneficial from the perspective of developing social and cultural capital. I've considered that perhaps I felt automatically judgemental, or at least questioning of young people who volunteer for principally instrumental reasons, because I was in the rather luxurious position of being able to volunteer altruistically, while knowing that through those activities I certainly was not doing my own individual biography or employability any harm.

In Khan's (2011) research he critically reflects on his own practice, asking himself whether he is holding his students to higher standards than he himself would have met as a student at St. Paul's. When denouncing his students for failing to do all their suggested reading, and relying on 'cheat' guides on the internet, Khan sternly warns them about the proper ways they should learn and amount of work they should do (much as I do to my students now). However, the students see through this, asking incredulously, 'Don't tell me *you* did all the reading when you were here' (Khan, 2011: 180). Khan continues:

> But Nick and Graham's response eventually led me to be slightly more self-reflective.... How, as a senior, did I do all the twenty-five pages of creative writing assignments that were supposed to be done over the course of a semester? I wrote them in the twenty-four hours before the final assignment was due. (2011: 181)

In order to pronounce on instrumentality in others, it should be part of the reflexive approach to judge instrumentality in oneself. A similar consideration to Khan's must be made regarding my own practice as a volunteer recruiter and the findings of my own later research into volunteer recruitment. I undertook a small reflexive investigation into the concept. My thesis was written inside three years at the University of Kent. This is the standard period for doctoral funding in the UK, but not the standard length of the PhD process, with most theses requiring longer to finish the write-up. I received funding from a studentship to undertake my research, and I knew from day one that the small amount of money it provided would mean I would have no savings left when I eventually finished. This meant that I knew I had to find stable employment from the immediate cessation of the funding, ergo, I had to complete within three years. Having this certainty built into my attitude towards the PhD meant there were certain constraints on how the work developed. I am by nature quite organised and focused, and I don't appreciate misdirection. I am quite sure of myself, and often don't see the need to second-guess decisions I have made already. This meant that once decisions had been made, about theoretical and methodological approaches, these decisions were often treated as final. Distraction, both personal and academic, was treated suspiciously, and it should be acknowledged that this had both positive – structured, clear, certain – and negative – concentrated, formulaic, simplistic – implications for the quality of the final thesis.

I also asked some doctoral colleagues at Kent for their views. On a shared Facebook comment thread, where we bounced ideas around and offered helpful comments and shared events, I asked whether the three-year standard PhD timeframe, and the conditions that PhD students in the UK have to work in (such as low funding, having to teach, and the highly competitive jobs market) affect the output of doctoral theses? Do these conditions mean we have to have a more instrumental focus on our work, limiting what we choose to do? Presented below is a selection of the responses that came in over the next few days. They are from three PhD colleagues approaching the third year of the PhD process:

> There is an argument that what you have just described above is good experience for a life in academia. That said, I don't personally believe that a PhD should necessarily be just that. There should be opportunities (funding flavoured probably) to be more 'blue skies' or abstract in one's research. The issue there would be the 'failure to complete' rate. Not that there is anything inherently 'wrong' with someone failing a PhD. There should be room for that too.

> Yes we are more instrumental because we can't afford not to be. The time/space for the big Thoughts for Thought's sake is a luxury – there might still be some people taking PhDs for the pure love of the subject/desire to contribute to the field/etc but they'd have to have some independent source of income. And even if they are, I bet they are still required to complete progress reports/file meet-with-supervisor forms, etc. as we're accountable to depts [departments] for completion/funders/etc. People grouch about the PhD being inadequate as a training for a research (or academic) career but what is the alternative?… I'm not sure it does *all* come down to funding, but present climate really doesn't allow for the big Thoughts that don't have pretty immediate, demonstrable, measurable Impact. Realistically, you might work on a section with half an eye to publication, as a line on your CV, and a future job. Means to an end. Likewise teaching experience …

> I'm not sure that we can be anything but instrumental. I'm one of the ones lucky enough to have good funding but my funding has a set deadline and once that has passed I am screwed! I feel like my PhD has become a case of just get it done so that I can say I've got it and then start looking for jobs. It has changed considerably from my original proposal (for the better) but also changed to a write what I can with the data I currently have to ensure that it's finished and so could be

considered limited by time constraints, other pressures etc. Although having said that I enjoyed teaching very much …

My colleagues articulated a view that students often have no choice, no opportunity to 'think big thoughts' because the pressure to complete inside three years, pressure which is both self-imposed and comes from institutions, is too great. The implications this has, both for the resulting quality of doctoral theses and for the quality of future academics, should be considered. It has recently been widely cautioned (Taylor and Reisz, 2014) that the current shape of funding for both students and academics precludes the longer-term commitment required for ethnographic studies because they are seen as more work for less reward. Yet ethnographies offer in-depth, longitudinal analysis, providing organisations the ability to account for change over time and space, and to reflect on the causes, symptoms and solutions to problems. The possibility of undertaking ethnographies and longitudinal research will diminish if PhD students are under intense pressure to finish within three years, which may mean that findings do not have as much clarity or be as complete as required. The need to 'write what you can' using the data available, rather than continuing to search for more may be a common problem, along with the likelihood that younger academics would try to hide these 'mistakes' or instances where they feel as if they have not carried out their work to a high enough standard (Blackman, 2007). Of course, such an inward-looking critique can be seen as self-indulgent: taking the path of least resistance to complete a project on time and on budget to a good enough standard is how most of us live our lives.

Feelings in fieldwork

Throughout the ethnographic elements of my research, both the days spent volunteering on youth projects and those spent travelling to and interacting with interviewees, I kept copious fieldnotes. Either written down or spoken into my voice recorder, often in pads or on envelopes, or whatever scrap of paper I had to hand (a collage of inspiration and nonsense), these fieldnotes remain the gateway through which qualitative researchers can remember exactly how they were feeling that day, which is as much a part of ethnographic research as the fieldwork itself (Emerson et al., 1995), becoming part of the researcher (Wolfinger, 2002). Presented here is an extract from my fieldnotes, an extract which became central to my thesis. In it, the reader is made aware of my centrality and yet my complete disposableness during the volunteering event in Croft, where young volunteers and workers were gathering to celebrate the end of their project, referred to at the start of this chapter. The Bourdieusian themes of cultural capital and habitual confidence play large, as does the rather draining yet cheering emotional journey I went on. As the analysis below shows, I chose to exhibit both the personal emotions I was subject to *and* the interventions I made in the behaviour of research subject as a way of honestly detailing the messiness of the research process:

Fieldnote: Volunteering Event, March, 2011

I was there as a volunteer, someone with something to give to the event. As a growing 'expert' in the area of youth volunteering, an advisor to national charities and a PhD student covering the topic, I had been invited to give a short speech on my role in national volunteering, and present some ideas on the future being faced by volunteering organisations due to the budget cuts and a change in political ideology. I obviously also used the time to praise the excellently organised event and encourage rounds of applause for the organisers and the young volunteers who had given their time to make the event work.

I always introduced myself as both a young volunteer and a PhD student writing about youth volunteering, so I feel no ethical quandaries about explaining what I experienced throughout the day. In fact, later on one member of staff asked 'Are you researching now?', and I replied that while it was the interviews that made up the central body of my work, I could not help but be influenced and take notice of what went on around me that day. And instead of my PhD producing wariness or alienation from people mistrustful or uncomfortable at my separateness, I was quickly afforded insider status. The ease with which this happened was staggering. As an older and quieter (due to not being aware of names, interests, and previously established banter) young volunteer, who knew none of the people at the event well and had only met two workers there briefly before, I immediately became a confidante for the emotional issues that were prevalent during the event. It was to be the last big event in which these women, for they were nearly all young women, worked together, and the last time many of the young volunteers could be certain of having full-time professional youth workers and volunteer coordinators to work with and a wide variety of projects to help out at. I was also quickly given a status within the hierarchy of the event, regarded as something special ('Oh, you must speak to Jon – he's doing a PhD and knows sooo much about volunteering'), to the messing about and tongue-in-cheek humorous insults of the young volunteers – the internal jokes that pre-existed between them and developed throughout the day. For example, a local puppetry and theatre project had brought along seven-foot tall robot puppets to be controlled by a small army of volunteers, who could make them walk, wave, clap, and more prominently, pinch and poke. As this was going on, the young volunteers aged 16–20 would comment, 'Oh Joni wants Stan to poke her; she luuurves him – with seven er's' [a joke that works much better said out loud]. It was the confidence and speed with which I, a rather awkward-looking 24-year-old with a notepad semi-prominently on display, was brought inside this pre-university playful flirting. This juxtaposed my experiences of researching in Eastwood – the quiet, the restraint, the difficulty in getting through to people to talk about their volunteering and understand what it means to them. I asked Lorna what she was doing with her volunteering and immediately she rapid-fired her response at me,

'Well, I'm going back to Thailand to teach at the end of April. That's the second time I'm going, just to see everyone you know. And then I'm off to Vietnam to teach because I've always wanted to go and it looks an amazing experience.'

It wasn't the dichotomy of the richness of experience that produced the contrast, but the energy and enthusiasm with which I was told about it. Lorna obviously held masses of self-esteem and pride, and was willing to openly flaunt it in front of an outsider, a stranger who found himself battered by a whirlwind of joy, instead of my frequent 'blood out of a stone' experience of engaging with young volunteers elsewhere. The contrast with the desire to hide volunteering activities as they are uncool could not be starker. It was the certainty in her words and posture than demonstrated that Lorna knew exactly what her volunteering had done for her. This came to the fore as I thanked her and Joni for talking to me.

After mentioning the possibility of conducting some focus groups with young volunteers from around Canterbury, Lorna and Joni jumped at the chance. 'Oh absolutely babes! I'm off to Thailand at the end of April so we'll have to be quick.' They certainly were not made uncomfortable by the request, as clearly a stranger asking questions about their opinions and experiences neither surprised nor disturbed them. They seemed confident in what they had to offer (no asking the self-conscious question 'Why would anyone want to talk to me?'), and they either fully understood my reasons for wanting to speak to them or were willing to enter the unknown and take the risk in finding out what a PhD focus group is all about. Our conversation ended with them having to rush off, as they'd promised to get the two elderly gentlemen from the St John's Ambulance a cup of tea from the buffet ('Can we get you one babes?!'). I said thanks very much, congratulated Lorna on her speech again, and promised I'd be in touch soon. She said 'Oh, great to talk to you', and went in for an affectionate hug. I felt slightly uncomfortable but reciprocated out of politeness and gratitude, even though unsure of the etiquette, both as researcher and as an older male volunteer. Why would a girl who I'd only met four minutes previously be so comfortable in hugging someone who had just demonstrated his instrumental reasons for wanting to talk to her? The confidence on display, the quick ability to judge the situation, and the idea that they were often fulfilling the 'dominant' role in the conversation, were the behaviours on display throughout the event by most of the volunteers, brought home to me by this one hug. Joni immediately went 'Oh, I want a hug too' and so that was that; me slightly taken aback by their brazenness and confidence, and them off to get tea for the St John Ambulance volunteers.[3]

Meeting me and hugging me was an inconsequential moment in their days, yet to me it was probably the most significant instance of the doctoral so far. All day I'd been engaged in conversation with many people regarding budget cuts to youth volunteering services. These young women will probably volunteer and participate for the rest of their lives; they've demonstrated that they don't need the formalised volunteering industry to be a part of the Big Society. But it isn't about them − it's about those who, forget hugging, look uncomfortable when you go for a handshake, and struggle to answer when you ask them why they are volunteering today.

The preceding fieldnote is the part of my doctoral research of which I am proudest and that personally means the most. After it was written I attended the conference referred to at the start of chapter four. At a conference dominated by business studies and economics, instead of giving a detailed Powerpoint presentation about my work, I chose merely to read the above fieldnote out, topped and tailed with some contextual detail about the importance of confidence in youth volunteering and Bourdieusian habitus. And I received very welcome feedback afterwards. I was more nervous delivering academic work with that approach, in terms of both its reception and my delivery, than at previous conferences, when I'd delivered a more standard and recognised form of presentation. In hindsight, it seems strange and disconcerting that I had become programmed by my academic situation to feel more comfortable with the Powerpoint slide show than reading a story, when my interviewees understood their own lives as narrative tales, rather than as Powerpoint slides.[4]

But let's compare the preceding experience with some of the issues that arose from my experience of researching volunteering in Eastwood. Bourdieu (2003a: 292) wrote about conducting his ethnographic work in Béarn, his rural native province and the social milieu in which he was formed, and how it was complicated personally for him to complete it. As he had risen into the academic elite, he had been 'led (or pushed) to despise and renounce' his region and the disadvantaged upbringing it had provided for him. Steve Hanson (2014) held similar internal conflicts as he went back to research his home town of Todmorden.

---

[3]   This may be the archetypal example of Bourdieu's (2008) notion that one must focus on the most trivial data in order to construct valid and formalised models of social conduct.

[4]   Ironically, after my nerves and fear of detachment from standard practice at that conference, I later saw Angela Eikenberry present research on the growth of selling cupcakes as a means of philanthropic endeavour (Nickel and Eikenberry, 2013), utilising a fictionalised and highly emotive narrative to explore the perils of America's addiction to sugary treats.

As someone who grew up in a neighbourhood next to Eastwood, who played sport and participated in the scouts and other activities at various points across the borough, I read much of my analysis of the area glumly. I did not choose to write about Eastwood in terms that stress the negative – these decisions are, in a way, out of my hands. As researcher, I have a duty to stress the significant themes of interviewees' responses, and the culture of despondency arising from chronic poverty, underemployment, and poor local services *were* the dominant themes that arose when I asked 'So, what is Eastwood like?' Presenting Eastwood as a uniform place makes me feel uneasy, even though I personally know what I say to be true, and it is the reality presented in the data. Mills made the call for a 'detailed self-location of social science' (Geary, 2009: 43), aware of the spaces in which knowledge is constructed. While this can produce rigour in the development of social scientific thought, it can also present complications and emotional difficulties for the researcher, forced to rely on their cognitive resources (Kara, 2015: 72), but take account of their emotional resources as well (Jewkes, 2012: 71). I know Eastwood to be a place of joy and good times, and culture – and, frankly, I am sad and feel potentially vulnerable that I produced research which may induce someone who has not been there to assume that it is not such a place.

Emotion may be seen as the 'antithesis of the detached scientific mind and its quest for objectivity' (Bendelow and Williams, 1998: xii). It took me until late in the PhD process to write in personal reflexive narratives, or even to realise that such analysis needed to be written. I feared that this was not what entry to the academy was about. The idea of 'playing it safe' is one that must appeal to young academics, fearful of the risks and costs of not getting it right. Blackman (2007: 700) reiterates Coffey's (1999) suggestion that the 'unwillingness to give a realistic account of fieldwork may be more keenly felt by younger academics', stemming from a fear of losing legitimacy or being discredited (see also Mauthner and Doucet, 2003: 423).[5] Blackman attaches this to controversial episodes in the research process. He draws on cases from ethnographies he has undertaken – giving lifts to heroin users so they can meet their dealers, flirting with and sleeping at the houses of 16-year-old female research participants, accidentally getting young homeless people drunk as a method of sociability – which he kept secret and

---

[5] Age and experience in social research are probably the most under-examined 'social cleavages' when it comes to doing reflexive work. We can see in Jenkins' (2006: 46–7) analysis of Bourdieu's Béarn-centred research a confidence developing with age. The initial research, conducted in 1962, was occluded behind objective description, with none of the emotional atmosphere of pain and treachery present at the time made plain. It was not until the papers' reprint 40 years later (within *The Bachelor's Ball* [Bourdieu, 2008]) that Bourdieu opened up about the realities of the research, fearful as he was at the time of 'ill-intentioned and voyeuristic readings'. In a review of the book, David Swartz (2009) argues that Bourdieu did his participants a great disservice in keeping this research hidden for so long in dusty academic journals, because he failed to help the dominated make sense of their domination, which is indicative of the negative consequences if worry about reflexive work builds up: don't be so precious, would seem the apt advice.

omitted from publication, because he was embarrassed by the incidents, or felt he had let himself or his research subjects down in crossing emotional boundaries.

> When I uncompromisingly examined the world to which I belonged, I could not but be aware that I necessarily fell under the scrutiny of my own analyses, and that I was providing instruments that could be turned against me. The image of the 'biter bit' simply designates one very effective form of reflexivity as I understand it – as a collective enterprise. (Bourdieu, 2000b: 4)

There is a suggestion that confessional authors like Shane Blackman 'give the game away' in research terms, by opening the curtains and letting the light into the murkier elements of data gathering.

A PhD student gets incredibly emotionally attached in their work, particularly as in my case, if the project is one of the researcher's own choice and design, located in spaces familiar to them. So I decided that to not be open in this work is to deny the reader the opportunity to fully understand the work. As Blackman (2007: 712) puts it:

> To advance more 'open' reflexive approaches that explain how research is conducted and written, British sociology needs greater disciplinary understanding and recognition of the real challenges and opportunities faced by qualitative research, which demands emotion.

When Lisa Mckenzie (2015: 191) writes sentences like, 'I still speak to Kath [whose son has been unfairly targeted by the police during the 2011 riots]; we exchange messages on Facebook and text each other', her book stops reading like research and starts feeling like a diary or autobiography. The emotional side of research, through friendship and sensitive support, is laid bare. Kath's turmoil could only have been brought out to the public by Mckenzie's involvement, her passion, and her determination to try to help. Does this activism, where she pushes the story along through her empathy and connection with her participant and friend, invalidate her findings? Of course not. But her insider status, and her deep belief in the political and social necessity of doing what she was doing, meant that she reads as a person rubbed raw and laid bare by her fieldwork and the desire to get it out there.

Conclusion

I for one cannot be objective about the subjects I have researched. My life was transformed by the period I spent volunteering with young people in Liverpool. Attempting to study volunteering without letting my emotion crowd, if not cloud, my judgement, when I have seen the transformative effects it can have in others and have felt in me, is impossible. This does not mean I cannot critique practice, as the youth volunteering charities that I have upset with my analysis of their recruitment techniques will testify, but there is little doubt about whose side I need to represent and, moreover, it is obvious that I have a side that I prioritise for my focus, and I see few problems with such an approach. But with this attitude comes an imperative to explain the process to the reader. Alongside its central aims, the research process and the doctoral thesis itself became an attempt to understand myself and to present that understanding to the reader.

In a similar vein, Jack Metzgar's (2000) book *Striking Steel* covers the 1959 US steel strike, the largest strike in American history in terms of man hours lost, but freely admits that it is his personal relationship with the events that triggered his academic focus on the subject. His dad was a keen union man and his family's life was significantly improved due to the success of the strike: 'if I had grown up in an autoworker's or electrical worker's family in the 1950s, I would have chosen a different event' (Metzgar, 2000: 12). As he says of *Striking Steel*:

> The design of this book, then, allows for a great deal of what is often called subjectivity, and I do not apologize for that. In fact, a rigorous and responsible cultural relativism demands that we abandon the notion that we can have the point of view of God – standing outside our society and observing it – and requires instead that we attempt to place ourselves within the society and history we seek to understand. The undisciplined arbitrariness that most people reject in denigrating 'subjectivity' cannot be overcome simply by pretending that we are not a part of the picture. (Metzgar, 2000: 12)

The thought does run through the reader's head when they interact with Metzgar's defence of labour unions: '*Of course you think that, you did well out of them!*' But Metzgar realises that to remove himself from the picture would be more intellectually dishonest and scientifically inaccurate. Personally, I trust his analysis of the steel strikes and the life of a steel millworker's family *because* he is willing to be so open and critical of himself, especially his scathing analysis of his dad's flaws. Metzgar's research took him on a nostalgic journey into personal history and difficulty, because, as Mills (1959: 225) instructed, he was willing to 'continually work out and revise … [his] views on the problems of history, the problems of biography'.[6] Sociology aims to understand what life is like; it

---

[6] Mills' (1959: 226) eight instructions for intellectual craftsmanship include the conclusion: 'Know that many personal troubles cannot be solved merely as troubles, but must be understood in terms of public issues – and in terms of the problems of history-making.' Metzgar's (2000) attempt to address an event in American history, the importance of which was being washed away by the forces of neoliberalism, was also a jumping off point for the difficult memories he has of his dad.

should not be ashamed of stating that the life a sociologist can understand best is usually their own.

Doing autobiographical self-analysis is not the only way to do reflexive work. It has benefits but it has pitfalls. Luc Pauwels (2012: 260–1) is worth quoting at length on this subject:

> How the various aspects of a reflexive approach should be dealt with more concretely is not always very clear and this often leads to misunderstandings. Closer attention to one's own influence and positioning need not gain the upper hand over the actual topic... While reflexivity should result in more self-relativization and a more modest qualification of the results, some visual researchers do sometimes use it as a means to put themselves to the fore in an almost self-glorifying manner. Such strongly autobiographically orientated explorations can, paradoxically enough, be at the expense of insight into the broader 'meeting of cultures' that they believe themselves to be making a contribution to. The same holds for exaggerated reflexive approaches that in turn degenerate into a repetitive meta-discourse on visual research, against a changing background of given cultural contexts.

Pauwels is right to caution against repetitive meta-discourses and of autobiographical writing gaining an upper hand over the central topic. The problem with such cautionary tales however, is that it is difficult to assess when a piece of reflexive research has descended into such territory. Such a reading is more likely to come from others than the author, and is simply unmeasurable and probably down to personal taste. In a doctoral viva voce, there is the possibility to defend the use of personal narratives, or reflexive vignettes, or meta-discussions about why you may have been structured into asking a certain question. Linda Finlay (2002) offers us a solution to this: celebrate the diversity of reflexive practice and *practise* it, exploring the variety of opportunities and challenges it can offer. Doing the above reflexive work helped me enormously understand who I am, both as a researcher and as an individual, and helped tame the beast of bias that lurks within.

Doing reflexivity: biographical self-critique

In this chapter, I outline several ways in which I undertook reflexive work in order to examine my presence in my research, the intellectual realities that were shaping both me and it, in order to think about how my own class and political dispositions may have been shaping my reading of my data. As Kim England (1994: 82) argues, in a famous piece advocating for a reflexive geography, 'reflexivity is self-critical sympathetic introspection and the self-conscious *analytical* scrutiny of the self as researcher'. You may want to write a biographical statement in which you go through that self-critical introspection. One of my postgraduate students once asked one of her fellow student to interview her about the research she was conducting, asking all the tricky questions about positioning, subjectivity, and political views which may have affected the research process. Bringing in a third party to do this work is quite an invigorating way of honestly appraising one's practice, and can mean the more complicated issues associated with doing reflexivity don't get ducked.

EIGHT

Conclusions

This concluding chapter seeks to do three main things. The issue of narcissism has arisen throughout this book, and it will be tackled head on, offering a stern rebuke to the accusation that at the root of reflexivity sits the researcher keen to do little more than talk about herself or himself. It will then ask how we can build spaces for reflexivity, looking at how the internet and the form and practice of academic writing and publishing can be altered so that reflexive work can be incorporated into our contributions to knowledge. And it will offer some final thoughts on reflexivity as a mindset to embrace, not something to be afraid of. But first, this concluding section wants to examine in detail one final case study, Alice Goffman's (2014) *On the Run: Fugitive Life in an American City*, a story still unfolding at the time of writing, but one it seems will enter the pantheon of teaching and doing reflexivity, for good and bad. While it may seem odd to bring in a new case in the conclusion, I believe that when it comes to thinking about and doing reflexivity and ethics, social researchers are now operating in a post-Goffman environment.

On the Run did that rare thing in social science literature: it started a debate. A vivid and impassioned, yet bleak portrait of a section of black America which is invisible to the vast majority, it details how the constant rotation of encounters with law enforcement, judicial institutions, and social services, intermixed with gang violence and immensely difficult personal lives, merge to exacerbate the difficulties of an already precarious life for poor young black men, who have to combine eking out an existence with avoiding the police. It documents in extraordinary detail both the destruction of drugs and the violence in US urban ghettos, and the racism and class hatred of modern America, detailing how structural and symbolic inequality combine with blinkered social policy and bombastic politics to destroy rather than mend individual lives. It is a powerful indictment of the US criminal justice system, which is shown to take perverted pleasure in entrapping young black men in a pointless and demeaning charade of bureaucracy and violence.

With over 2 million people in jail, and nearly 5 million people on probation or parole, the USA has the highest rate of penal confinement of any democracy in history. One cannot read Goffman's work without feeling ashamed of the waste of it all, especially when such waste emanates from such ingrained institutional racism. The authorities tear apart poor black communities, metaphorically and literally, resulting in a sense of precarity beyond lay comprehension:

> [H]istorically high imprisonment rates and the intensive policing and surveillance that have accompanied them are transforming poor

Black neighbourhoods into communities of suspects and fugitives. A climate of fear and suspicion pervades everyday life, and many residents live with the daily concern that the authorities will seize them and take them away. A new social fabric is emerging under the threat of confinement: one woven in suspicion, distrust, and the paranoiac practices of secrecy, evasion, and unpredictability. (Goffman, 2014: 8)

A book like *On the Run* offers an opportunity for social scientists to grab the public's attention, intervene in political debate, present evidence of the reality of what's going on, and offer solutions to systems which have lost their moral compass. Therefore we must ask what it says about social science and the cynicism of the public sphere in the age of social media, that most of the academic and, ultimately, journalistic debate around Goffman's work came to centre on a frenzied desire to label it as untrue, and, particularly interesting as we come to conclusions as to doing reflexivity, *her right to write it*. This section will first provide a brief overview of Goffman's own attempts to do reflexivity and manage and account for her positionality in *On the Run*, and then move into explaining the critics' critiques, and how the question of who gets to speak for whom is a key one going forward, at a time when calls to 'check one's privilege' have never been so loud.

Doing reflexivity on the run

Goffman stumbled on her research project. After completing an undergraduate assessment on the life of a University of Pennsylvania cafeteria and the relationship between the largely white and privileged student body and the older black women who served them lunch, Goffman asked her boss, a black woman in her sixties called Miss Deena, if she knew of any local students who needed tutoring. Goffman was introduced to Miss Deena's grandchildren who lived in a low-income area of Philadelphia, which Goffman anonymised as 6th Street. From this initial involvement in the community came a series of deeper and more entangling relationships. Goffman came to know the central characters in her book, young men anonymised as Mike, Chuck, Reggie, and Tim, their mothers, occasionally their fathers and grandfathers, the mothers of their children, and the groups of young men they surrounded themselves with.

Her ethnography was all-encompassing. After working as a tutor for several months, she moved into 6th Street, taking an apartment close by, her role 'gradually changing from tutor to friend and resident' (Goffman, 2014: 217).[1] Still an undergraduate, she spent much of every day with Mike, Chuck, and their friends and neighbours, attending meetings with lawyers, court hearings, probation and parole boards, visiting times at jails, halfway houses, local hospitals, as well as taking part in regular ethnographic 'hanging out', on stoops and porches, at parties, playing video games, and regular visits to get takeaway food. In a revelatory yet charming and alarming detail, she agreed to go on a date with her research participant Mike because she was worried members of the community had started to perceive her as a predatory white lesbian with a penchant for younger black girls (Goffman, 2014: 219, 222–3). This date went shockingly badly because, as Mike told Goffman in the car on the way home, 'You ain't ugly.... You just ... you just don't know how to act' (Goffman, 2014: 220). She did not fit in with the embodied habitus of her researcher participants: wrong hair, wrong shoes, wrong way of speaking, and wrong way of holding herself. In personality and look she was out of step. But Goffman used her difference to her advantage: Mike took her under his wing, often referring to her as his godsister or sister. In a sentence which many could view as unethical because of the way it demonstrates a researcher's instrumental (mis)use of a research participant's emotional sentiments, Goffman (2014: 226) reflects on why he did this:

> Sometimes he mentioned that as an only child he'd often wanted a sister.... So maybe he liked having a female friend who wasn't asking for sex.... Whatever his reasons, getting adopted by Mike as a kind of sister was a major stroke of luck.

While it is clear and obvious that Mike and Goffman became very close, this sentence does lay bare the inequalities between them in the research encounter: one wanted a sister and a different relationship with someone of the opposite sex, the other luckily stumbles on access to data.

This leads us to one of the key criticisms of Alice Goffman's work, which concerns positionality and her role as a 'white woman who comes from an educated and well-off family' (Goffman, 2014: 228). Unfortunately, and unfairly, it is difficult to write about Goffman without referring to her heritage. The daughter of famous sociologist Erving Goffman, author of *The Presentation of Self in Everyday Life* (1959) and *Asylums* (1961) and prominent sociolinguist Gillian Sankoff, and adoptive father linguist William Labov after her father died while

---

[1] Ellis (2007) seeks to prioritise ideas about relational ethics in research which recognise and value the relationship between researchers and the people and communities they study. To think of ethics relationally – not just in terms of formal ethics procedures, or the personal values an individual researcher holds themselves to – is to 'seek to deal with the reality and practice of changing relationships with our research participants over time' (Ellis, 2007: 4). If they become our friends, do our ethical responsibilities change, and if so, how? Ellis, as an academic grounded in autoethnography and literary exposition, does not expand on the implications for scientific enquiry of such questions.

she was still young, Goffman's lineage runs through her story as a researcher. No-one should have to live in the shadow of their family, nor have their own successes besmirched by positive association or accusations of nepotism, but Goffman's researcher habitus was forged by her upbringing, her participation in her adopted parent's empirical field studies, and the seemingly constant knowledge of the weight of her name.

She recounts her own lack of knowledge of life in black Philadelphia, having grown up in a 'wealthy white neighbourhood' (Goffman, 2014: xiv), with only vague ideas of the widespread structural inequalities in criminal justice policy. She falls between two stools on occasion: the confident habitus of the researcher, well resourced (culturally and economically) by her parents, but also someone who 'often felt like an idiot, an outsider, and at times a powerless young woman' (Goffman, 2014: 229). On 6th Street she was stuck at the bottom of the micro social hierarchy (if not the macro one) because her lack of knowledge meant 'people would openly express their frustration and bafflement at how slow I was to grasp the meaning of what was going on' (Goffman, 2014: 230).

Goffman recounts developing informal methods for being reflexive in the field, for testing and putting into practice her difference to examine how it affected the data. She worked hard on 'social shrinkage', becoming as small a presence as possible in social situations as to avoid affecting the reality of social life: '[b]lending into the background became an obsession' (Goffman, 2014: 235), as she puts it. She liked it when research participants would tell stories and could not remember whether she'd been present for the incident; equally, when people changed their tone of voice after she'd left the room, Goffman would feel like she had failed to become enough of a piece of furniture. She highlights the problem with such an approach – that it is difficult to tell if you are affecting a scene if you don't know what normal is like – but she also found that her participants often did not want her to fade into the background, and that part of the group's collective practice was to blow off steam and have people interject and calm you down, which they felt Goffman could help with when she was present.

This immersion, while leading to incredibly deep and rich data, also led to significant instability in Goffman's own behaviour. She came to find herself unable to cope in white society, fearing being in the presence of young white men, unable to remember to attend or care about organised meetings with senior academics at her university, and tensing and panicking at loud bangs and sudden movements (Goffman, 2014: 244–8). Hammersley (1997) writes of the 'cultural habitus' developed by researchers, especially those doing ethnographic work, where immersion in the field changes perceptions and outlook (Bornat, 2014). While this can be read as the researcher embodying the behaviour and smarts required for endurance in the particular field of 6th Street, it can also be seen as 'going native', of Goffman's developing inability to cope *outside* of the research field, and of losing her sense of proportion of the realities of being a student researcher.

The reaction to On the Run

There is an argument that researchers can turn their difference into a positive benefit to the experience of gathering data, seeing their different race, background, or gender as a foreign identity, which enables them to see what locals may not be able to or open doors to public officials and issues that are otherwise closed off (Merton, 1972; Phillips and Earle, 2010). As Goffman (2015) put it in one public lecture, 'You use what you've got and make up for what you haven't.' Equally, many researchers see this difference as almost insurmountable, with patronising white middle-class researchers partaking in a voyeurism of lives that they can never truly understand and can go home from at the end of the day. After the publication of *On the Run* the black female Buzzfeed writer Tracy Clayton (2014) stated that we should 'ban outsider ethnographies' for just this reason. Similarly, Lisa Mckenzie (quoted in Dabrowski, 2015), the working-class ethnographer who wrote *Getting By*, was stinging in her rebuke of academia's continued acceptance of allowing 'the middle class to pruriently watch us, write about us, and lie about us'. Mckenzie goes on:

> This is the reality of class inequality – it's deep and pervasive and it never fucking goes away. I suppose this is why I am angry and often uncomfortable in academia as I know if my name was Goffman and I was ignorant and self-righteous enough to think it's okay to live and watch poor black people, and write a dubious book 'about them' I might be more successful.... I'm self-aware, reflexive, and critical and I know if I hurt my community or people that I have real connections with, it hurts me and my family.

The efficacy of such arguments is thin, although they come from the right place. The lack of access for working-class and ethnic minority individuals to higher education and to research roles is real, and the racism, classism, and sexism of academia can be crippling. The lack of black professors in UK universities for instance (85 out of 18,510) is appalling (Shilliam, 2015: 32), with similarly shameful records in US institutions (Strauss, 2015). But telling students or researchers of any background that they cannot study a social group because they do not belong to it seems a pointless and illiberal attack on intellectual freedom. Bourgois and Schonberg's (2009) epidemiological ethnography among homeless heroin addicts in San Francisco would be one vital and mesmerising study absent from our shelves if we banned outsider ethnography, and others are too numerous to mention. Drawing lines about who is allowed to research what community is a dead end, because of the personal vagaries and multifaceted identities we all have. While clearly both insider and outsider perspectives have assets and liabilities, automatically privileging one to exclude the other is damaging and limiting, especially if such reasoning is done before any analysis of research quality. It is best to therefore to think of the insider–outsider relationship as a spectrum rather than a dichotomy (Bridges, 2001).

Asking how a researcher's position may have affected or diminished their findings and analysis is obviously a vital critical question, and one that we need to ask more often. The key, as Mckenzie rightly highlights, is to be reflexive, which Alice Goffman *is* to a greater extent that can be expected. She devotes nearly a fifth of the book to explaining her positioning, how this affected her access, and the difficulties she faced and the necessary amendments she made in her practice as an outsider.[2] As Singal (2016) writes, after visiting 6th Street to examine for herself the accuracy of *On the Run*:

> These concerns come from a valid place: There is a long, unpleasant history of white ethnographers tromping into unfamiliar terrain and writing condescending, inaccurate, stereotype-reinforcing things about the inhabitants they encounter. But there's a wide chasm between acknowledging this and arguing that Goffman's whiteness was *inherently* problematic. Scholars who agree to devote huge amounts of time to understanding the nuances of a given subject should be given the benefit of the doubt, regardless of their own group-identity status.

What this may mean is that, while the book's future as a must-read social science text is assured, the controversy surrounding its publication and review means it is more likely to be filed alongside Laud Humphrey's (1970) *Tearoom Trade* and Carolyn Ellis's (1986) *Fisher Folk* as a study in the complicated world of research ethics. A profusion of critical articles lamenting inaccuracies and inconsistencies in *On the Run* (Campos, 2015), attacking Goffman's perceived lack of reflexivity (Sharpe, 2014), and ultimately accusing her of the crime of conspiracy to commit murder while undertaking her research (Lubet, 2015) appeared soon after publication. These were seen by some as an overblown attempt to discredit a young researcher (Fernandez-Kelly, 2015; Singal, 2015, 2016), and by others as the necessary challenge and rigorous unpicking of controversial social science.

In a long, detailed, and coruscating article in *The Chronicle of Higher Education*, the legal scholar Paul Campos (2015) dissects what he labels Goffman's 'implausible ethnography'. Going through her book with a fine toothcomb, Campos highlights many examples in which the dates Goffman provides for events and issues do not match up with reality (for example, a participant refers to the 'Obama era' [Goffman, 2014: 180] in an extract dated 2007, over a year before Obama became US President). Some of these mistakes were accepted by Goffman as sloppiness emanating from confusion due to the many notes she took, and the amount of ethnographic fieldwork on which the book was based. Goffman attributed much of this inconsistency and purposeful 'scrambling' of facts to prioritising anonymisation for her participants (Nayfakh, 2015). The pressure increased due

---

[2]   Of course this debate can go on *ad infinitum*: as a middle-class white academic of course I am defending the rights of middle-class white academics to research the lives of working-class or black communities. I *would* say that.

to the fact that Goffman burned the thousands of pages of fieldnotes she collected during the research process, again out of a desire for anonymity and to protect her participants, reasoning that upon publication of the book law enforcement officials would seek out extra information about the illegal activity she documented so rigorously. Shamus Khan (quoted in Campos, 2015) was one social scientist who felt this didn't pass muster: if the brutality and the extent of police control documented in the book is true, it is arguable how much the confused and yet easy-to-bypass anonymisation process was necessary.[3]

In an angry response to Campos' article, Princeton University sociologist Patricia Fernandez-Kelly (2015) refuted his main claims, arguing that not only did the article fail to present any persuasive evidence, it was merely part of wider witch hunt against Goffman because of the success of her book and the hard work she had put into researching it. In particularly strident terms, Fernandez-Kelly posits that it is sexism, not presumed flaws in her research, which is driving the critique of *On the Run*: 'she is being persecuted for who she is: a young white woman of exceptional talent determined to unearth realities concealed to most Americans', with Fernandez-Kelly asking 'Would she be enduring the same treatment if she were a man?' Fernandez-Kelly's argument did not receive much sympathy, reinforced by her failure to point out that she is credited in the acknowledgements section of Goffman's book.

In a similar vein to Campos's work, Lubet's (2015) forensic critique was the first to accuse Goffman of articulating her participation in a conspiracy to murder after she joined Mike in driving around searching for Chuck's killer.[4] In the final pages, Goffman clearly states that driving with Mike did not emerge out of ethnographic curiosity, but because she had grown so close to her participants she wanted vengeance for one of their deaths. Lubet (2015) considers the role of reflexivity in this scene:

> Viewed in that context, Goffman's reflection on her desire for 'Chuck's killer to die' [Goffman, 2014: 260] and her satisfaction with the experience, comprises a meaningful part of the whole story. But expressing a bone-deep emotion is one thing, acting on it is quite another, and impulse control would seem to be an indispensable tool for the ethical ethnographer.

---

[3] As Campos (2015) writes: 'It took me 10 minutes of Internet research to find Chuck's real name, date of birth, home address, and criminal record. It took just a little more time to identify many of the book's other central characters, as well as the precise location of the Philadelphia neighborhood – Goffman calls it "6th Street" – where the narrative takes place.'

[4] Space does not allow for a full discussion of this extraordinary issue, but see Goffman (2014: 251–61) for an overview of the events, Lubet (2015) and Campos (2015) for articulations of the accused criminality, and Lewis-Kraus (2016) for a sympathetic explanation and defence against the accusations.

This section of *On the Run* is so short and abrupt that the reader cannot help but feel it is included for journalistic impact rather than sociological explanation. It is natural that Goffman had taken sides in her research, and that her bias was deep and intense: it would have been impossible for this not to be the case. But this passage became so explosive and difficult for Goffman legally after publication, that her publisher and supervisory team could easily be seen as guilty of a lack of care and forethought.

Michaela Benson (2015) argues strongly that it is Goffman's supervisors and teachers who failed, through their lack of attention to the researcher they were meant to be training and guiding: there was little acknowledgement of the ethic of responsibility regarding the 'potential harm that could be done to a local community by an inexperienced researcher, but also the potential harm to the researcher'. This lack of good guidance, Benson feels, seeps into the naivety and mistakes in research practice which are obvious in *On the Run*. A young undergraduate, learning 'on the job', did not have 'the critical skills to conduct and analyse ethnographic research in a way that deconstructed, among others things, her own position in relation to her research subjects and the ethical practice relating to this encounter' (2015). Carolyn Ellis (2007), reflecting on her work in *Fisher Folk*, revealed a similar lack of ethics training and oversight.

In his critique, Paul Campos (2015) encourages us to address how social science is evaluated and rewarded. Concerns about the efficacy of peer review are numerous, especially given the proliferation of academic journals, and the seemingly increasing pressure to publish in order to establish an academic career. What, in effect, Campos is doing is asking us to take a Bourdieusian approach to framing Goffman's work, to consider the intellectual environment which has affected (distorted? corrupted?) her academic output. He writes:

> to focus exclusively on Goffman's individual conduct misses the larger point. Alice Goffman is a product of a system that uncritically rewards the kind of things she was doing, even when those things may have included engaging in serious crimes, or serious academic misconduct.

In effect Campos is arguing that in Goffman's politics, her immersion in siding with poor black men, her 'flamboyantly nonjudgmental' lack of moral questioning of the violent criminals she surrounded herself with, and her desperation to explain the horror in which many of the people of 6th Street lived, she was so caught up in the unfairness and injustice of it all, and her publisher so keen to tell liberal America of her findings, that basic research standards were allowed to slip.

What did this entire, occasionally dispiriting, episode tell us about reflexivity, researcher positionality, and the ethics of good research? First, that there is no model for how to do reflexivity. Goffman's extensive and detailed methodological appendix, in which she explains how she gained access to her research site, the practicalities of gathering and recording data, and the emotional impact on her of the research, would be enough for some readers and reviewers, but was clearly not enough for many others. It seems that in the case of some authors, such as Sharpe (2014) and Mckenzie, the only reasonable approach would have been for Goffman to be so reflexive about her project that she would have chosen not to do it. To read interviews with Goffman since the publication of *On the Run* (Singal, 2015; Lewis-Kraus, 2016) is to read several acknowledgements of and apologies for oversights and absences in the production of the book, for missing appendices, for a lack of clarity of detail, and for an anonymisation process that seemingly led to a confused author, a questioning and disbelieving public, and, it would appear, a lazy and absent publisher. Nayfakh (2015), in particular, expresses frustration that *On the Run* is 'a work that can't be trusted to reflect any reality, let alone a general one, and cannot be effectively defended against skeptics', with controversy blinding us to the more important issues at stake. In being made the story, Alice Goffman tarnished her endeavour to explain new facets of the structural racism and inequality on 6th Street.

Second, we can also conclude that research is rarely finished and the need for reflexive practice never ceases. While publication of a book or article or submitting a thesis may feel quite final, the highly diverse public of scholars out there will have different hurdles and standards for reflexive practice: some will not care about it or focus on it; others may perceive your inability to do it the way they would as a personal insult and an example of the reproduction of the continuing inequalities within academia and society. As with most things in social sciences, there are few right answers. And, third, reflexive practice has never been so important in the sociological imagination, and those who fail to examine it properly, even if they produce work that is prescient and (initially) acclaimed like Alice Goffman, may be heading for a fall. In a social media world of instant gut reaction, it often seems that taking account of one's own positionality as a researcher is no longer enough; you may have to think about everyone else's as well. As Bourdieu (1969: 107) remarked, 'the existence of what I call cultural legitimacy lies in every individual whether he [sic] wants to or not, whether he admits it or not': the anticipated reception of a piece of research must be internalised as part of the process of production (Robbins, 2007).

Narcissism

> Reflexivity requires an 'I' and no apologies are needed. (Berger, 1981: 220–1)

As has been seen throughout this book, it is an unavoidable truth that reflexivity involves the researcher talking or writing about themselves. The key criticisms of reflexivity as Bourdieu and Wacquant (1992: 43–4, n77) spell them out are narcissism, futility, and meaningless regression, and there often remains the worry, particularly among younger researchers, that reflexive practice may come across as self-absorbed, with the writer promoting their voice over those of their participants. Kenway and McLeod (2004: 527) posit that the mere recounting of biographical details is little more than self-indulgence and 'vanity reflexivity' of behalf of the researcher. But there is a valid argument that the researcher should be 'promoted', if you will, as an expert: as Hannah Jones (2013: 27) points out, they have likely had specialised training, often have broader contextual experience than research participants (who have deeper, particular experiences), and have frankly thought (or obsessed) about the issues at stake for a lot longer than anyone else. One could argue that being professionally required to apply research methods and skills rigorously is a bulwark against vain indulgence.

But dwelling on one's experience in doing the research, and the rationale for thinking about how you may have affected it, can get lost in wider public debates about academics as navel-gazers who have never done a proper day's work in their lives: a 'copout', as one non-academic puts it to Anjali Forber-Pratt (2015: 822), and visible in Moore's (2004) concerns about engaging with participatory action research outside of hegemonic research paradigms. Nowhere is this more apparent in methodological discussions than in autoethnography. Autoethnography has been popularised by writers such as Carolyn Ellis (2004, 2009), Norman Denzin (2003, 2006) and other academics from fields as diverse as education, communication and media studies, organisation and management, much of whose published output can be found in journals which experiment with form, such as *Qualitative Inquiry*. In her work, Forber-Pratt (2015: 821) autoethnographically studies the process of doing an autoethnographic piece of research at a prestigious university and the problems this causes, in finding her voice as an author, in getting such a piece of work through the university's bureaucratic review panels (see also Tolich, 2010), and in validating the work as a 'proper' piece of research:

> When I started down this path, I made a commitment to myself that I would finish writing knowing that I was true to myself and to not hide behind any façades through this process.

Such a commitment to a certain level of personal emancipation is at the heart of much of the sociological project developed by writers like Denzin, but it is easy to see how such an approach can rub people up the wrong way. It is certainly at the very fringes of scientific research and can be very difficult to evaluate in a systematic way (Holt, 2003), and has received trenchant critique, such as that of Sara Delamont (2009).

In her book, Hannah Jones (2013) offers what we should perhaps take as our guideline in how to do reflexivity in research – don't be held back by the impartiality mafia, but don't allow yourself to narcissistically dominate. Stay smart, stay controlled, but don't feel stifled as a researcher or writer if you have something personal to contribute. As outlined in chapter five, Jones is very upfront about her issues as a researcher. In her initial remarks she argues that 'researchers are *not that special*' (Jones, 2013: 27, original emphasis). While this can be read as getting your excuses in early, or the researcher absolving themselves from their mistakes (Strathern, 2006: 200), by being clear and honest you leave yourself to be judged by others, but give them all the required information to make their own minds up.

While subjectivity and an acceptance of that subjectivity, can offer you insights into the lived experience of difference, it also makes you realise you may be disqualified from offering authoritative insight. It would be hoped that all researchers are constantly questioning the authority of their own analysis, placing it within a history of others' work and the very academic structures in which they sit. As Bourdieu and Wacquant (1992: 40) conclude, 'reflexivity calls less for intellectual introspection than for the permanent sociological analysis and control of sociological practice'. In the final analysis, the best way to consider whether research has become narcissistic, or whether including certain personal reflections is unnecessary, is to ask it as a specific question when others read your work in peer review and when reading others' work.

Building spaces for reflexivity

How much is enough and how much is too much? With reflexivity, as with any good thing, social scientists are unsure. Kara (2015: 72) posits that we need to ensure reflexivity does not become a burdensome task: for reflexivity to permeate the whole research process, 'a researcher would need to stop and consider many questions at every stage of the research, which is clearly impractical.' It may not be the asking of the questions that takes the time, however; it is more likely that writing a daily reflexive journal or having long detailed conversations with fellow researchers or supervisors, which, when time is precious, distract from the analysis of the existing literature, qualitative interviews, or large datasets. As Luc Pauwels (2012: 261) tries to summarise:

> There are no quick or simple procedures for a reflexive approach: occasionally putting oneself or members of the crew into the picture, or a merely verbal acknowledgement of reflexivity, provides little insight into the driving forces behind a researcher and the research value of the product.

Yet Pauwels (2012: 261) moves instantly to counter his assertion by referring to the work of visual anthropologist Jay Ruby:

> Ruby (2000: 155), a fierce advocate of a thoughtful and well-balanced reflexivity, does admit that it is extremely difficult to determine exactly how much knowledge and precisely which aspects of the producer and the production process are needed, and conversely, what should be considered excessive or superfluous and thus detrimental to the end result.

So we are looking for 'well-balanced' reflexive work, but it can be 'extremely difficult to determine exactly how much'. Occasionally, the 'too much' can be made obvious. Here's an extreme example. In summer 2015, the American novelist Jonathan Franzen was met with hostility and ridicule online for comments made during the promotion of his new novel *Purity*. Franzen, a literary star around the world but an occasionally controversial figure, seemed cowed by his own limitations and what these meant for his writing. In one example, where he had received criticism for alleged sexism after writing a positive piece about the novelist Edith Wharton, but in which he had remarked upon her looks, he told the *Guardian* newspaper:

> I am not somebody who goes around saying men are superior, or that male writers are superior.... None of that is ever enough. Because a villain is needed. It's like there's no way to make myself not male. (Franzen, in Brockes, 2015)

Franzen sees the criticism as unavoidable, something that automatically comes with being a successful man in the age of immediate vitriol from social media. But his final rejoinder ('It's like there's no way to make myself not male') raises interesting questions about positionality and the ultimate barriers placed on reflexive practice and empathy. The common phrase may be 'Put yourself in someone else's shoes', but having a positivist-perfect understanding of someone else's point of view is not actually physically or emotionally possible. Empathy as an end goal is a noble aim, but being empathetic is always more a journey than a destination. It is something we strive as best we can to achieve, with the understanding that actually achieving it is beyond us. In empathy, as with reflexivity, *trying* is the point.

How far that effort goes, however, is still up for debate. Jonathan Franzen, it appears, looked to take it too far. Not content with asserting that his 'male-ness' may always hamper his ability to successfully understand or write his female characters, Franzen also worried he lacked any detailed understanding of young people. His initial idea to fill the understanding gap was, he revealed, to adopt an Iraqi war orphan:

> Oh, it was insane, the idea that Kathy [his partner] and I were going to adopt an Iraqi war orphan. The whole idea lasted maybe six weeks.... And my New Yorker editor, Henry Finder, was horrified by the notion ... 'Please don't do that.' And then he paused and said, 'But maybe we can rent you some young people.' (Franzen, in Brockes, 2015)

Franzen's bizarre overcompensation in order to understand something he feels he lacks experience of demonstrates a certain bumbling aloofness, a tragic amorality, and yet also a vaguely understandable (if incompetent) desire to improve himself. He didn't know any young people, so, in order to fully realise a book project centred on a young activist, he sought ways to bridge the age gap through research. The eventual method he found would seem reasonable and sensible to any social scientist: he spoke to a group of recent university graduates and wrote about the experience of working with them. But the idea of adopting a child, of completely overturning your own life and someone else's in order to write better characters is, I hope we can all agree, a totalising step too far for reflexive fulfilment.

When discussing how we build reflexivity into standard academic publications with colleagues, one issue that arises constantly is the problem of 'fitting in' decent reflection: an 8,000 word journal article for example, especially one dealing with qualitative data, just does not have the space for detailed reflexive work. 'Even where reflexive exploration is valued, accounts are invariably strangled by constraining word limits set by academic journals' (Finlay, 2002: 227). Creating blogs, videos, and audio, and effective use of social media (see Carrigan, 2016), which are linked to and supplement the social research outputs, are all ways in which we can make best use of new technologies in this instance. Jon Rainford (2016) has written very openly of the ways in which blogging and social media have enabled him to pursue critical reflection as a doctoral student, and to challenge the limitations of formal academic spaces when facing research difficulties. As the digital spaces for presenting and communicating academic work expand, the 'burden' of reflexivity can be fitted into academia much more easily. Research does not have to be confined to the measured output, and increasingly academia and social research are experienced online. This is also where an awareness of how social researchers interact with new audiences comes in. In my own work, I have found writing a personal blog every time I publish new work a very useful step. These blogs often examine the pitfalls and mistakes I made in the development and conduct of the research, or, as with the anecdote at the start of chapter four, explore the genesis and subjectivities behind the idea of the project. Presenting the work in tandem helps me think through the relationship between the professional and personal questions reflexivity asks of oneself. Have I been adequately reflexive in my published work? No. I have failed to test this thesis but I that believe high-profile journals, particularly those working in social policy analyses, are reluctant to allow authors to spend much of their allotted space on reflexivity – especially when there are so many other items to include (literature review, theoretical reasoning, methodology, detailed presentation of findings, analysis, conclusions, references) that the standard 5,000–8,000-word length of an article gets eaten up pretty quickly. Therefore building less formal spaces to partake in reflexive dialogues may work for some people.

Other researchers take a different approach. Karen Lumsden's (2009, 2013a, 2013b) research on 'boy racers' and car modification culture in Aberdeen is based on a one-year ethnographic study. Spending about 150 hours in field, Lumsden 'hung around' the drivers' and owners' gatherings on Beach Boulevard in Aberdeen, and accompanied the drivers to various car shows across Scotland, and to garages and scrapyards: she also interviewed a range of stakeholders, including the police, local residents, relevant politicians. The focus of her research into the boy racer culture was to explore the value felt by the members who belonged to this subculture, and how it contributed to group and individual identity, but also how, using Stan Cohen's (2002[1972]) framework of 'folk devils and moral panics', the subculture was framed as problematic within the press, and positioned as the villain of the piece. It is a study that achieves great clarity, producing research which speaks to many disciplines and audiences, with great care shown to understanding local history and the relationship between reality and popular myth.

Interesting for our work here, though, is Lumsden's strong contribution to methodological thinking on reflexivity. In her monograph, Lumsden (2013a: 5) sets out her reflexive modus operandi in an early statement: 'A reflexive method was adopted, whereby the researcher acknowledged their role in the research process and the way in which their social position shaped their experiences in the field.' What I find interesting in that statement is that, within the book, there is pretty much a complete absence of reflexive moments. We rarely get a sense of what Lumsden thinks or feels about the interactions she is taking part in, nor reflection on the effect she may be having on her participants, the direction of her research, or her analysis of the data she collects. Apart from one substantial extract from her fieldnotes, where she details her fear at being driven home by one of her participants on a twisting dual carriageway in the rain, Lumsden's personal role is strangely absent from the text. Why? Well, because Lumsden decided to write the reflexive elements of her project into two journal articles focusing on the issues of being a female researcher in a largely male (*boy* racer) world (Lumsden, 2009), and the politicised research issue of ultimately 'siding with the underdog' (Lumsden, 2013b).

Lumsden's approach in splitting her work in this fashion offers a potential way to create spaces for reflexive work. While writers like Mckenzie, Jones, and the others discussed in this book merge their findings with their reflection – with the content making it difficult to separate the two – Lumsden writes a very 'clean' ethnographic work. This may be because of her outsider status: she is neither an insider nor 'boy racer' herself. It is interesting that Lumsden's (2009) first publication was the one that dealt with her gendered interactions in the field, and she has gone on to drive forward the idea of reflexivity within criminological research (Lumsden and Winter, 2014; Lumsden, forthcoming). Her monograph does cite these works, and includes them in the reference list, but there is no signposting that further reflexive output has been conducted.

Lumsden's approach of splitting off reflexive work, potentially into journal articles dealing with specific issues which require reflexivity, points towards one way of incorporating reflexive practice into wider academic work. I would argue that the relationship needs to be much more fluid, but that could easily be judged as hypocritical, given the lack of reflexive work in my own research articles on volunteering (such as Dean, 2013, 2014). Perhaps this indicates the realistic position of reflexivity. In policy-centred research, contract research for the third sector and governmental or private sector organisations' reflexive work is still liable to be viewed as a pointless academic add-on. Form matters. It is the monograph-length work discussed in chapter five that gives researchers the space to develop warm, long-form relationships with their readers. As Finlay (2002: 207) concludes:

> Researchers are, in effect, damned if they do and damned if they don't. It is the task of each researcher, based on their research aims, values and the logic of the methodology involved, to decide how best to exploit the reflexive potential of their research. Each researcher will choose their path – a perilous path, one which will inevitably involve navigating both pleasures and hazards of the marshy swamp.

In this book, I have conceptualised methodological reflexivity as critical analysis of the theoretical, methodological, disciplinary, personal, or practical issues which affect the research process and the subjectivities inherent within it. These five issues have been highlighted at various points to discuss the various ways of being reflective and the ways social scientists need to be reflective. They intersect with each other as well as operating discretely. None of the research studies we have examined in this book gives equal weight to each of these five areas, and would be unwieldy or overly burdensome for every project to do so. It is up to researchers to decide which of these five issues are most important in their work and for them to undertake detailed and scientific reflexive examination of those they feel are the most appropriate to their studies. Reflexivity is both a methodological and scientific concern, to make sure others are aware of the conditions in which data is produced but also, linking back to the role reflexivity increasingly plays in the public service professions, a continued personal compunction for researchers wanting to understand their intellectual curiosity. There is no right way to do it, but as Gay (2014) writes of her supposedly 'bad' feminism, the important thing is to try. We may be hypocritical, inconsistent, messy, or unsure, but the important thing is to try.

Final thoughts

> The trouble with the world is that the stupid are cocksure and the intelligent are full of doubt. (Bertrand Russell)

Thorough reflexive practice is a vital part of conducting social research, especially at a time when the problems of speaking from a position of power are rightly heightened and socially contested. It is important to face outward and to think about 'whose side we are on' (Becker, 1967), but good reflexive practice in itself is not narcissistic; it is methodologically and scientifically necessary, and a lack of reflection on the relationship between researcher and researched can result in unwelcome headlines. Social theories aim to explain social processes, in a shared language, without recourse to example or relativity. These social processes exist and occur whether there is a theory to explain them or not. However, a researcher's attempts to codify those processes into theory are subject to extraneous social processes, the baggage that the researcher brings. These influences include the shared practices of the research collective, the situating and historicity of the discipline, and the habituated biographical experiences of the researcher.

Can we be surprised that Bourdieu, a man who felt out of his comfort zone in the elite schools of the French academy and abashed by his humble upbringings (Bourdieu, 2007), would devote his time to concepts like hysteresis (Bourdieu, 1977, 1990b; Handy, 2008) or the bourgeoisie's battle for cultural distinction (Bourdieu, 2010[1984])? This is not merely a consideration to be made of contemporary work. Durkheim, a far more positivist scholar, was in part inspired to write his most famous work after the early suicide of a close friend, whose death he felt had been influenced by the intensity of his schooling at one of France's *grand écoles* (see Sennett's introduction [2006: xi–xxiv] to Durkheim's *On Suicide*). Diane Reay's biography is clear for the reader to see in much of her work, as her own transition as a working-class woman ascending to one of the grandest offices in the world of British higher education runs parallel to the experiences of the students she studies (Reay 2003; Reay et al., 2010). Tim Strangleman's (2004) research on changes in work identity among British rail workers as privatisation took hold, and his reasons for wanting to conduct the research in the first place, stems from his career working for London Transport, beginning with an apprenticeship at age 16. *White Collar*, C. Wright Mills' study of the middle class, was strongly autobiographical, tracing his family's history at the same time as studying developments in American working life (Eldridge, 1983).

Likewise, I wrote about the volunteering activities of young people under the age of 25, and this was determined by the time I spent volunteering, full-time and part-time, when I was aged between 22 and 25. Politically I am to the left of the governments of the last decade, so is it a surprise to see that my conclusions are dismissive of the impacts made by their policies in encouraging social justice and social mobility through volunteering? I generally get on with people and like talking to people who work for charities, and feel grateful to participants who give up their time to be interviewed – is it a surprise these people are shown in a good light in my research, as everyday heroes battling a inadequate system? As Bourdieu (2007: 102) asserts of his own work:

> How could I fail to recognize myself in Nietzsche when he says, roughly, in *Ecce Homo*, that he has only ever attacked things that he knew well, that he had himself experienced, and that, up to a point, he had himself been?

Accordingly, I believe we have to extend Brewer's (2005) call for the spatial awareness of theory to include a biographical awareness of the roots of the development of thought, and build deeper into our work that self-referential concept – the socio-analysis *of* socio-analysis itself – an often unexplained yet vital component of scientific inquiry. If we are to act truly reflexively, we must apply the theories we are using both to the study itself and to the theory itself. This stems from habitus. What habitus tells us about the apparatus of social science is that to understand and apply a theory we must not only comprehend the theory's technical meaning and scientific application, we must, especially in the social sciences, be extremely aware of a theory's social and biographical origins. We must ask not just whether the behaviours and actions revealed in interviews are the results of or reactions to classed habitus, but what is the habitus of this book, and what is the habitus of habitus, or any other theory? Where has it come from? Why has this knowledge been created, and what are the social circumstances of its creation? As Mills argued early in his career, while the genesis of an idea is deeply social, that genesis does not invalidate the idea (Mills, 1940: 319–20; Geary, 2009: 33–4). Therefore, we can use this biographical approach to buttress the epistemological security of the social sciences (Bourdieu and Wacquant, 1992: 36) rather than see it as a methodological failure of objectivity. We should also deny distinctions between the importance of reflexivity in the positivist and naturalistic contexts. As Hammersley (2003: 344–5) writes, the principle of reflexivity is that:

> throughout the course of inquiry, researchers continually subject their own practice to scrutiny, in terms of why they did what they did and its consequences, both methodological and ethical; and that they make explicit for their readers how their research was done, and their own role in producing the findings.... So, while the principle of reflexivity still requires the researcher to try to monitor any effects of the research process on what is observed, along with any effects of what is observed on the researcher, the purpose is simply to try to identify accurately the social processes operating in the situation, so that we can understand them.

This process must be thorough and total: 'every proposition set forth by the [science of society] can and ought to apply to the sociologist himself [sic]' (Bourdieu and Wacquant, 1992: 202). I, the researcher, and I, the individual, am caught in the problem of reinforcing and challenging certain aspects of volunteering among research participants due to my previous experiences and my political views. This does not necessarily mean that during fieldwork I saw what I wanted to see, or only saw behaviours which I recognised. This means we must entertain the idea that the empirical work could be wrong, or that my interpretation of it may be misplaced: I may have failed to adequately assess the issues at stake, or understand the true processes occurring. This is not second-guessing the research for the sake of it, but a recognition that I, as Bourdieu stated, am a site of research and therefore need analysing. I will continue to try to offer in my academic output reflexive notes on my biography, for, as the biographical explanation that is *Sketch* shows, we need to see where theory is coming from, not just what it says. I could be accused of getting my excuses in early, laying out my subjectivities before I am accused of bias and being 'unscientific'. If that is the accusation, then, yes, I am guilty. But I think we should all plead guilty, a conclusion that won't sit comfortably with everyone. Yet, as Dave Beer (2014: 46) argues in *Punk Sociology*, 'The musicians [of punk] were not afraid to put their limitations on display.' If methodological reflexivity is about anything, it is about this.

Coda: on writing in the social sciences

> Academic writers are often little more than figures of fun. Derided for the opacity of our jargon-filled prose, we swim often unnoticed at the shallow end of the literary pond. (Back, n.d.)

The point of research is not to promote oneself narcissistically, or to further oneself – it is to gather and provide information which others may find interesting or useful. If that information is poorly communicated, in an inaccessible language which hides it from multiple audiences, the research is incomplete. In the social sciences so much investigation is never reported back to those affected by the study (O'Neill, 1995: 149). Reflecting on one's position as a researcher can amount to little if there is no reflection on one's practice as an author and communicator.

Giving due ethical consideration to the undertakings of research is of vital importance. The researcher is required to fill out forms, satisfy the needs of an ethics committee, gain approval, and above all demonstrate reflection regarding the process. Could anybody be hurt either by the research process or by the research conclusions? As a researcher myself at various universities, I have had to go through these procedures. However, there is no form to fill out, or consent to seek, when writing up one's research. Researchers have a duty to endeavour to inform research participants why they were seeking information, and what their conclusions and suggestions are after analysis (see Roberts, 1981b). As Bourdieu (1998: 15) wrote in *On Television*, we must 'make the advances on research available to everyone ... part of our responsibility is to share what we have learned'. Participants may not care, but the endeavour, our moral duty to communicate our knowledge, is an often overlooked element of social research. With its foundations in the public sociology of Burawoy (2004, 2005), this view sees in the social sciences and academia more widely, a tendency to speak down to the subjects of its research. This is why how we write is so crucial. It is why Mills (1959: 221) imagined the test audience for researchers as one-third expert, one-third knowledgeable, and one-third laypeople. It is vital for successful dissemination to be both thorough and relevant, and deliver a convincing argument, but in an engaging way (Smart, 2010).

In *The Sociological Imagination*, Mills (1959) finds himself aghast at the quality of writing within the social sciences. He writes of a 'turgid and polysyllabic prose' prevailing, not for intellectual reasons, but for emotional and personal ones. Most academics, he contends, are fearful of being judged and dismissed by their peers as mere journalists, who believe that to be readable is to be superficial. This is a systemic problem of superiority, perpetuated through generations of academics in social science faculties across the world, rather than a belief in egalitarianism where everyone should have the benefit of being educated or of having access to sociologists' work. How is it that social researchers are so frequently inept at communicating to our publics what we mean that we are increasingly cast into the fetid swamp that is 'Pseuds Corner' in *Private Eye* magazine, a fortnightly column aimed at skewering pretension?

Cowley (1956) coined the term 'socspeak' to describe the impenetrable language of social scientists, rather ironically in an article entitled 'Sociological habit patterns in linguistic transmogrification'. Mills asserts that to use socspeak is to say to the reader, 'You are a layman. I understand something you don't and instead of helping you up to understand my thinking, or simplifying my thinking, you must learn my language.' We may hide behind the need for technical terms, but accurate technicality does not mean jargon. The 'lack of ready intelligibility' (Mills, 1959: 218) so often displayed in sociological writing is insulting to those studied. Our disciplines involve studying society, and therefore, in the vast majority of cases, studying people. People do not speak in 'socspeak' in the everyday, so why should presentation of their conduct be so dehumanised. Mills witnessed a growth in machine-like presentation of sociology, and states that to dehumanise the presentation of sociology is 'pretentiously impersonal' (Mills, 1959: 221). Those who understand it will be inward looking, and those who do not understand will be alienated. As Mills continued: '[a]ny writing … that is not imaginable as human speech is bad writing'. Academics have a responsibility to be a representative of a great linguistic tradition and are expected to 'try and carry on the discourse of civilized man' (Mills, 1959: 222). Unlike the natural sciences, the subjects of social sciences are not indifferent to the research. O'Neill (1995: 159) makes the pressing and urgent argument that social research is ignored by policy makers and those in power due to its opaqueness, which 'threatens to erode civic competence and political responsibility'. Social scientists have important things to say and suggest, and language and presentation are major reasons for 'political ambivalence'.

This inherent responsibility is also a theme picked up by Burawoy (2005), whose concern for the public image of sociology demands findings be presented in an accessible manner. Historically, Schutz had argued for creating an egalitarian approach toward sociology. He felt that the ideas, concepts, and theories discovered and created by social scientists must in themselves be understandable and relevant to all people, and should never be alienated from ordinary human intelligibility and competence (O'Neill, 1995: 149). Schutz (1962: 43–4) termed this 'the postulate of adequacy', one of five principles he felt must govern the construction of scientific research and models of human behaviour. This stated that:

> Each term in a scientific model of human action must be constructed in such a way that a human act performed within the life-world by an individual actor in the way indicated by the typical construct would be understandable for the actor himself as well as for his fellow-men in terms of common-sense interpretation of everyday life. Compliance

with this postulate warrants the consistency of the constructs of the social scientist with the constructs of common-sense experience of the social reality.

Schutz reasoned that if human sciences are the study of human activity and human achievement, then these never can nor should be alienated from 'ordinary human intelligibility and competence' (O'Neill, 1995: 169). The constructs created by the social scientist should be understandable by individual social actors. Compliance with this postulate ensures that scientific constructs are consistent with the constructs of common-sense experience of the social world.

It is one of the most disappointing facets of Bourdieu's work that he rarely complies with the postulate: for despite preaching a form of inquiry and a moral philosophy which put everyday processes of subjugation and violence at its heart, his writing is oftentimes dense and impenetrable. Jenkins (1992: 9) comments that the subversive potential of Bourdieu's work is severely undermined by his writing style, which is laced with:

> Idiosyncratic usages and neologisms, allied to frequently repetitive, long sentences which are burdened down with a host of sub-clauses and discursive detours, combined with complicated diagrams and visual schemes to present the reader with a task that many ... find daunting.

Bourdieu acknowledges this problem and is surely well aware of his failure to break out of the system of inequality and 'polished' language, which he himself is helping to reproduce: 'Academic language is a dead language for the great majority of French people, and is no one's mother tongue, not even that of children of the cultivated classes' (Bourdieu, 1994: 8).

Yet in my view Bourdieu's written analysis[1] can be read in two ways: either as his inability to escape the continuation of standard educational practice; or a bizarre experiment in sociological writing and presentation, a result of his methodological choices, a 'discursive montage' (Bourdieu and Wacquant: 1992: 66) aiming to bridge the gap between quantitative and qualitative approaches. As Burawoy (2008b: 2) writes, Mills 'would probably have little tolerance for Bourdieu's scientific "jargon"'. It has to be the hope of any Bourdieusian scholar that Bourdieu's theories can be successfully utilised without being hampered by his technicality and frequently ugly language. As Les Back (2007: 164) has argued:

> Mills was also clear that sociological imagination meant being self-consciously committed to affecting argument and writing creatively

---

[1] This is his academic output in the middle of his career, and encompasses his most famous works, particularly *Distinction* (2010 [1984]). His final, more polemical works are considerably more mainstream (and less empirical), and are incredibly readable, particularly *On Television* (1998), *Firing Back: Against the Tyranny of the Market 2* (2003b), and *Sketch for a Self-Analysis* (2007).

for a variety of what he called 'reading publics'. The danger he foresaw was that the sociological work might develop a technical language that turns inward on itself.… To avoid this we have to aspire to make sociology more literary.

There are activist and egalitarian reasons to communicate the findings of sociology in such a way as to open it up, not to close it off. 'We teach to change the world,' as Brookfield (1995: 1) wrote. We do not teach to keep the world the same. Encouraging our students to break the academic cycles of writing as others do, and having the confidence to do so ourselves, would be one way of making sure we are free to break out of staid and uninspired disciplines, and to democratise knowledge: 'intellectual life is nothing if it is not addressed to a wider public' (Back, 2015a).

As Back (2002) has contended elsewhere, there is a mistaken correlation between clarity and simplicity: to write clearly and to be clear is to be thought of as a simplistic and naïve fool. Aren't you aware that an enthusiastic use of caveats and subclauses and plenty of portmanteaus is the way to go? Similarly, recounting her own struggles with Bourdieu's writing, Mckenzie (2016) articulates the 'near impossible' task of reading and making sense of Bourdieu's writing, seeing a symbolic value in claiming to 'know' Bourdieu as a young academic, because he is the social theorist *de nos jours*. Mills' writing was accessible without being condescending to the general reader (Eldridge, 1983). Balancing a personally and structurally reflexive social science with a rigorous and analytic application of theory and method *and* a clear and accessible writing style is perhaps the next barrier the social sciences need to overcome.

References

Abrahams, J. and Ingram, N. (2013) The chameleon habitus: Exploring students' negotiations of multiple fields. *Sociological Research Online*, 18(4).

Achen, C. (2014) Why do we need diversity in the Political Methodology Society? *The Political Methodologist*. http://thepoliticalmethodologist.com/2014/04/30/we-dont-just-teach-statistics-we-teach-students.

Adkins, L. and Skeggs, B. (2004) *Feminism after Bourdieu*. London: Wiley-Blackwell.

Alvesson, M. and Sköldberg, K. (2000) *Reflexive Methodology: New Vistas for Qualitative Research*. London: Sage.

Aschwanden, C. (2015) Science isn't broken. *Five Thirty Eight*. http://fivethirtyeight.com/features/science-isnt-broken.

Atkinson, W. (2013) Some further (orthodox?) reflections on the notions of 'institutional habitus' and 'family habitus': A response to Burke, Emmerich, and Ingram. *British Journal of Sociology of Education*, 34(2): 183–9.

Back, L. (2002) Dancing and wrestling with scholarship: Things to do and things to avoid in a PhD career. *Sociological Research Online*, 7(4).

Back, L. (2007) *The Art of Listening*. London: Berg.

Back, L. (2015a) On the side of the powerful: The 'impact agenda' and sociology in public. *The Sociological Review*. http://www.thesociologicalreview.com/information/blog/on-the-side-of-the-powerful-the-impact-agenda-sociology-in-public.html.

Back, L. (2015b) Why everyday life matters: Class, community and making life livable. *Sociology*, 49(5): 820–36.

Back, L. (n.d.) Writing and scholastic style. *Academic Diary*. http://www.academic-diary.co.uk/page.php?entryID=31.

Back, L. and Tate, M. (2015) For a sociological reconstruction: W.E.B. Du Bois, Stuart Hall and segregated sociology. *Sociological Research Online*, 20(3).

Bancroft, A. and Fevre, R. (2016) *Dead White Men and Other Important People*. London: Palgrave.

Baptist Union of Great Britain, Methodist Church, Church of Scotland and United Reformed Church (2013) *The Lies We Tell Ourselves: Ending Comfortable Myths about Poverty*. http://www.irishmethodist.org/sites/default/files/Truth-And-Lies-Report-smaller.pdf.

Barnes, M. and Cotterell, P. (2012) Critical and different perspectives on user involvement. In M. Barnes and P. Cotterell (eds) *Critical Perspectives on User Involvement*. Bristol: Policy Press, pp. 143–7.

Barrett, T. (2015) Storying Bourdieu: Fragments toward a Bourdieusian approach to 'life histories'. *International Journal of Qualitative Methods*, 14(5): 1–10.

Bart, P. (1974) Male views of female sexuality, from Freud's fallacies to Fisher's inexact test. Paper presented at the second national meeting, special section, on Psychosomatic Obstetrics and Gynaecology, Key Biscayne, Florida.

Bartmanski, D. (2012) How to become an iconic social thinker: The intellectual pursuits of Malinowski and Foucault. *European Journal of Social Theory*, 15(4): 427–53.

Becker, H. (1967) Whose side are we on? *Social Problems*, 14(3): 239–47.

Becker, H. (1970) *Sociological Work*. New Brunswick, NJ: Transaction Books.

Becker, H. (2014) How to keep your sociological imagination alive. *The Sociological Imagination*. http://sociologicalimagination.org/archives/16120.

Beer, D. (2014) *Punk Sociology*. Basingstoke: Palgrave.

Bendelow, G. and Williams, S. (1998) *Emotions in Social Life: Critical Themes and Contemporary Issues*. London: Routledge.

Benhabib, S. (1992) *Situating the Self: Gender, Community and Postmodernism in Contemporary Ethics*. Cambridge: Polity.

Benson, M. (2015) On Goffman: Ethnography and the ethics of care. *The Sociological Review*. http://www.thesociologicalreview.com/information/blog/on-goffman-ethnography-and-the-ethics-of-care.html.

Beresford, P. (2016) *All Our Welfare: Towards Participatory Social Policy*. Bristol: Policy Press.

Berger, B. (1981) *The Survival of a Counterculture: Ideological Work and Daily Life Among Rural Communards*. Berkeley: University of California Press.

Berger, R. and Quinney, R. (2005) *Storytelling Sociology: Narrative as Social Inquiry*. Boulder, CO: Lynne Reiner.

Bhatt, C. (2016) White sociology. *Ethnic and Racial Studies*, 39(3): 397–404.

Bishop, L. (2007) A reflexive account of reusing qualitative data: Beyond primary/secondary dualism. *Sociological Research Online*, 12(3).

Blackman, S. (2007) Hidden ethnography: Crossing emotional boundaries in qualitative accounts of young people's lives. *Sociology*, 41(4): 699–716.

Blumer, H. (1999) What is wrong with social theory? In A. Bryman and R. Burgess (eds) *Qualitative Research*, vol. I. London: Sage, pp. 25–33.

Bornat, J. (2014) Epistemology and ethics in data sharing and analysis: A critical overview. In L. Camfield (ed.) *Methodological Challenges and New Approaches to Research in International Development*. Basingstoke: Palgrave Macmillan, pp. 217–37.

Bottero, W. (2004) Class identities and the identity of class. *Sociology*, 38(5): 985–1003.

Bourdieu, P. (1958) *Sociologie de l'Algérie*. Paris: PUF.

Bourdieu, P. (1969) Intellectual field and creative project. *Social Science Information*, 8(2): 89–119.

Bourdieu, P. (1977) *Outline of a Theory of Practice*. Cambridge: Cambridge University Press.

Bourdieu, P. (1979) *Algeria 1960*. Cambridge: Cambridge University Press.

Bourdieu, P. (1980) Sartre. *London Review of Books*, 2(22): 11–12.

Bourdieu, P. (1986) The forms of capital. In J. Richardson (ed.) *Handbook of Theory of Research for the Sociology of Education*. New York: Greenwood Press, pp. 241–58.

Bourdieu, P. (1988) Vive la crise! For heterodoxy in social science. *Theory & Society*, 17(5): 773–87.

Bourdieu, P. (1990a) *In Other Words: Essays Towards a Reflexive Sociology*. Cambridge: Polity.

Bourdieu, P. (1990b) *Sociology in Question*. Cambridge: Polity.

Bourdieu, P. (1990c) *The Logic of Practice*. Cambridge: Polity.

Bourdieu, P. (1990d) *Homo Academicus*. Cambridge: Polity.

Bourdieu, P. (1990e) The scholastic point of view. *Cultural Anthropology*, 5(4): 380–91.

Bourdieu, P. (1993) Concluding remarks: For a sociogenetic understanding of intellectual works. In C. Calhoun, E. LiPuma and M. Postone (eds) *Bourdieu: Critical Perspectives*. Chicago, IL: University of Chicago Press, pp. 263–76.

Bourdieu, P. (1994) *Academic Discourse*. Cambridge: Polity.

Bourdieu, P. (1996) *The State Nobility*. Stanford, CA: Stanford University Press.

Bourdieu, P. (1998) *On Television*. New York: The New Press.

Bourdieu, P. (2000a) Entre amis. *Awal: Cahiers d'études berbères*, 21: 5–10.

Bourdieu, P. (2000b) *Pascalian Meditations*. Cambridge: Polity.

Bourdieu, P. (2001) *Masculine Domination*. Stanford, CA: Stanford University Press.

Bourdieu, P. (2003a) Participant objectivation. *Journal of the Royal Anthropological Institute*, 9: 281–94.

Bourdieu, P. (2003b) *Firing Back: Against the Tyranny of the Market 2*. London: Verso.

Bourdieu, P. (2005) *The Social Structures of the Economy*. Cambridge: Polity.

Bourdieu, P. (2007) *Sketch for a Self-analysis*. Cambridge: Polity.

Bourdieu, P. (2008) *The Bachelor's Ball: The Crisis of Peasant Society in Béarn*. Cambridge: Polity.

Bourdieu, P. (2010 [1984]) *Distinction: A Social Critique of the Judgement of Taste*. London: Routledge.

Bourdieu, P. (2010a) Return to television. In G. Sapiro (ed.) *Sociology Is a Martial Art: The Political Writings of Pierre Bourdieu*. New York: The New Press, pp. 141–6.

Bourdieu, P. (2010b) The intellectual is not ethically neutral. In G. Sapiro (ed.) *Sociology Is a Martial Art: The Political Writings of Pierre Bourdieu*. New York: The New Press, pp. 253–60.

Bourdieu, P. (2010c) A sociologist in the world. In G. Sapiro (ed.) *Sociology Is a Martial Art: The Political Writings of Pierre Bourdieu*. New York: The New Press, pp. 261–78.

Bourdieu, P. (2014) *On the State: Lectures at the Collège de France, 1989–1992*. Cambridge: Polity.

Bourdieu, P. and de Saint Martin, M. (1978) Le patronat. *Actes de la recherche en sciences sociales*, 20/21: 3–82.

Bourdieu, P. and Passeron, J.-C. (1977) *Reproduction in Education, Society and Culture*. London: Sage.

Bourdieu, P. and Wacquant, L. (1992) *An Invitation to Reflexive Sociology*. Cambridge: Polity.

Bourdieu, P. et al. (1999) *The Weight of the World*. Cambridge: Polity.

Bourgois, P. and Schonberg, J. (2009) *Righteous Dopefiend*. London: University of California Press.

Brayton, J. (1997) What makes feminist research feminist? The structure of feminist research within the social sciences. http://www.unb.ca/PAR-L/win/feminmethod.htm.

Breeze, B. and Dean, J. (2012) Pictures of me: User views on their representation in homelessness fundraising appeals. *International Journal of Non-profit and Voluntary Sector Marketing*, 17(2): 132–43.

Breeze, B. and Dean, J. (2013) *User Views of Fundraising: A Study of Charitable Beneficiaries' Opinion of Their Representation in Appeals*. London: Alliance.

Brewer, J. (2004) Imagining *The Sociological Imagination*: The biographical context of a sociological classic. *British Journal of Sociology*, 55(3): 317–33.

Brewer, J. (2005) The public and private in C. Wright Mills' life and work. *Sociology*, 39(4): 661–77.

Bridges, D. (2001) The ethics of outsider research. *Journal of Philosophy of Education*, 35(3): 371–86.

Brockes, E. (2015) Jonathan Franzen interview: 'There is no way to make myself not male'. *The Guardian*. http://www.theguardian.com/global/2015/aug/21/jonathan-franzen-purity-interview

Brookfield, S. (1995) *Becoming a Critically Reflective Teacher*. San Francisco, CA: Jossey-Bass.

Brubaker, R. (1984) *The Limits of Rationality: An Essay on the Social and Moral Thought of Max Weber*. London: HarperCollins.

Brunt, L. (2001) Into the community. In P. Atkinson, A. Coffey, S. Delamont, J. Lofland and L. Lofland (eds) *Handbook of Ethnography*. London: Sage, pp. 80–91.

Bull, A. (2015) Problems with being a person while studying people. *Get Creative Research*. https://getcreativeresearch.wordpress.com/2015/09/09/problems-with-being-a-person-while-studying-people.

Burawoy, M. (1991) Reconstructing social theories. In M. Burawoy, A. Burton, A. Amett Ferguson, K. Fox, J. Gamson, N. Gartrell et al. (eds) *Ethnography Unbound: Power and Resistance in the Modern Metropolis*. Berkeley, CA: University of California Press, pp. 8–27.

Burawoy, M. (1998) The extended case method. *Sociological Theory*, 16(1): 4–33.

Burawoy, M. (2004). For public sociology. *American Sociological Review*, 70(1): 4–28.

Burawoy, M. (2005). Response: Public sociology: populist fad or path to renewal? *British Journal of Sociology*, 56(3): 417–32.

Burawoy, M. (2008a). Cultural domination: Gramsci meets Bourdieu. http://burawoy.berkeley.edu/Bourdieu/4.Gramsci.pdf.

Burawoy, M. (2008b). Intellectuals and their publics: Bourdieu meets Mills. http://burawoy.berkeley.edu/Bourdieu/8.Mills.pdf.

Burgum, S. (2015) The branding of the left: Between spectacle and passivity in an age of cynicism. *Journal for Cultural Research*, 19(3): 306–20.

Burke, C., Emmerich, N. and Ingram, N. (2013) Well-founded social fictions: A defence of the concepts of institutional habitus and family habitus. *British Journal of Sociology of Education*, 34(2): 165–82.

Burnham, P., Gilland, K., Grant, W. and Layton-Henry, Z. (2004) *Research Methods in Politics*. Basingstoke: Palgrave.

Burton, S. (2015) The monstrous 'white theory boy': Symbolic capital, pedagogy and the politics of knowledge. *Sociological Research Online*, 20(3).

Butler, A., Ford, F. and Tregaskis, C. (2007) Who do we think we are? Self and reflexivity in social work practice. *Qualitative Social Work*, 6(3): 281–99.

Butler, R. (1997) Stories and experiments in social inquiry. *Organization Studies*, 18(6): 927–48.

Byrne, D. (2005) Class, culture and identity: A reflection on absences against presences. *Sociology*, 39(5): 807–816.

Calhoun, C. (2002) Pierre Bourdieu in context. New York University. http://www.nyu.edu/classes/bkg/objects/calhoun.doc.

Calhoun, C. (2010) Epilogue: Remembering Pierre Bourdieu. In G. Sapiro (ed.) *Sociology Is a Martial Art: The Political Writings of Pierre Bourdieu*. New York: The New Press, pp. 279–87.

Calhoun, C. (2011) Pierre Bourdieu. In G. Ritzer and J. Stepnisky (eds) *The Wiley-Blackwell Companion to Major Social Theorists*. London: Wiley-Blackwell, pp. 274–309.

Came, H., MacDonald, J. and Humphries, M. (2015) Enhancing activist scholarship in New Zealand and beyond. *Contention: The Multidisciplinary Journal of Social Protest*, 3(1): 37–53.

Campos, P. (2015) Alice Goffman's implausible ethnography: 'On the Run' reveals flaws in how sociology is sometimes produced, evaluated, and rewarded. *Chronicle of Higher Education*. http://chronicle.com/article/Alice-Goffmans-Implausible-/232491.

Carmel, S. (2011) Social access in the workplace: Are ethnographers gossips? *Work, Employment and Society*, 25(3): 551–60.

Carrigan, M. (2016) *Social Media for Academics*. London: Sage.

Centre for Open Science (2014) Many analysts, one dataset: Making transparent how variations in analytical choices affect results. *Open Science Collaboration*. https://osf.io/gvm2z.

Chinoy, E. (1954) *Sociological Perspective*, 2nd edn. New York: Random House.

Clayton, T. (2014) Projects like this make me uncomfortable and angry: Ban outsider ethnographies. https://twitter.com/brokeymcpoverty/status/461881740739739648.

Clegg, S. (1992) Review article: How to become an internationally famous British social theorist. *Sociological Review*, 40(3): 576–98.

Coffey, A. (1999) *The Ethnographic Self*. London: Sage.

Coffey, A. and Atkinson, P. (1996) *Making Sense of Qualitative Data: Complementary Research Strategies*. London: Sage.

Cohen, L. (2015) How *Desert Island Discs* became my treasure trove of research data. *The Guardian*. http://www.theguardian.com/higher-education-network/2015/nov/23/how-desert-island-discs-became-my-treasure-trove-of-research-data.

Cohen, S. (2002 [1972]) *Folk Devils and Moral Panics*, 3rd edn. London: Routledge.

Connell, R.W. (2005) *Masculinities*, 2nd edn. Berkeley, CA: University of California Press.

Cook, K.S. and Levi, M. (1990) *The Limits of Rationality*. Chicago, IL: University of Chicago Press.

Cowley, M. (1956) Sociological habit patterns in linguistic transmogrification. *The Reporter*, 41.

Crouch, M. and McKenzie, H. (2006) The logic of small samples in interview-based qualitative research. *Social Science Information*, 45(4): 483–99.

Dabrowski, V. (2015) Interview with Lisa Mckenzie on *Getting By*: Estates, class and culture in austerity Britain. *Theory, Culture & Society*. http://www.theoryculturesociety.org/interview-with-lisa-mckenzie-on-getting-by-estates-class-and-culture-in-austerity-britain.

D'Cruz, H., Gillingham, P. and Melendez, S. (2007) Reflexivity, its meanings and relevance for social work: A critical review of the literature. *British Journal of Social Work*, 37(1): 73–90.

de Grasse Tyson, N. (2016). In science, when human behavior enters the equation, things go nonlinear. That's why Physics is easy and Sociology is hard. https://twitter.com/neiltyson/status/695759776752496640.

Dean, J. (2013) Manufacturing citizens: The dichotomy between policy and practice in youth volunteering in the UK. *Administrative Theory and Praxis*, 35(1): 46–62.

Dean, J. (2014) The reflexive self in Mailer's protests. *Contention*, 1(2): 11–26.

Dean, J. (2015) Drawing what homelessness looks like: Using creative visual methods as a tool of critical pedagogy. *Sociological Research Online*, 20(1): 2.

Dean, J. (2016a) Class diversity and youth volunteering in the UK: Applying Bourdieu's habitus and cultural capital. *Nonprofit and Voluntary Sector Quarterly*, 45(1S): 95–113.

Dean, J. (2016b) 'Submitting love?' A sensory sociology of Southbourne. *Qualitative Inquiry*, 22(3): 162–8.

Dean, J., Bennett, C., Furness, P., Lennon, H., Spencer, S. and Verrier, D. (2015) Desert Island data: An investigation into researcher positionality. Paper presented at the BSA Annual Conference, Glasgow, 15-17 April.

Deaton, A. (2015) Statistical objectivity is a cloak spun from political yarn. *The Financial Times*, 2 November.

Delamont, S. (2009) The only honest thing: Autoethnography, reflexivity and small crises in fieldwork. *Ethnography and Education*, 4(1): 51–63.

Denzin, N. (1997) *Interpretive Ethnography: Ethnographic Practices for the 21st Century*. London: Sage.

Denzin, N. (2001) The reflexive interview and a performative social science. *Qualitative Research*, 1(1): 23–46.

Denzin, N. (2003) Performing [auto]ethnography politically. *Review of Education, Pedagogy & Cultural Studies*, 25(3): 257–78.

Denzin, N. (2006) Analytic autoethnography, or déjà vu all over again. *Journal of Contemporary Ethnography*, 35(4): 419–28.

Denzin, N. and Lincoln, Y. (1998) *The Landscape of Qualitative Research*. Thousand Oaks, CA: Sage.

Deutsch, S. (1971) Review of *The Coming Crisis of Western Sociology*. *American Sociological Review*, 36(2): 321–6.

DeVault, M. (1996) Talking back to sociology: Distinctive contributions of feminist methodology. *Annual Review of Sociology*, 22: 29–50.

Devine, F. (2002) Qualitative methods. In D. Marsh and G. Stoker (eds) *Theory and Methods in Political Science*. Basingstoke: Palgrave, pp. 197–215.

Dewey, J. (1910) *How We Think*. New York: D.C. Heath and Co.

Dixon, J. and Singleton, R. (2013) *Reading Social Research: Studies in Inequalities and Deviance*. London: Sage.

Dreger, A. (2016) *Galileo's Middle Finger: Heretics, Activists, and One Scholar's Search for Justice*. London: Penguin.

Du Gay, P. (2000) *In Praise of Bureaucracy*. London: Sage.

Duneier, M. (1999) *Sidewalk*. New York: Farrar, Straus and Giroux.

Eldridge, J. (1983) *C. Wright Mills*. London: Tavistock.

Eliasoph, N. (2011) *Making Volunteers: Civic Life after Welfare's End*. Princeton, NJ: Princeton University Press.

Eliasoph, N. (2012) *The Politics of Volunteering*. Cambridge: Polity.

Ellis, C. (1986) *Fisher Folk: Two Communities on Chesapeake Bay*. Lexington, KY: The University Press of Kentucky.

Ellis, C. (2004) *The Ethnographic I: A Methodological Novel about Autoethnography*. Walnut Creek, CA: Altamira Press.

Ellis, C. (2007) Telling secrets, revealing lives: Relational ethics in research with intimate others. *Qualitative Inquiry*, 13(1): 3–29.

Ellis, C. (2009) *Revision: Autoethnographic Reflections on Life and Work*. Walnut Creek, CA: Left Coast Press.

Emerson, R., Fretz, R. and Shaw, L. (1995) *Writing Ethnographic Fieldnotes*. Chicago, IL: University of Chicago Press.

Emslie, M. (2009) Researching reflective practice: A case study of youth work education. *Reflective Practice: International and Multidisciplinary Perspectives*, 10(4): 417–27.

England, K. (1994) Getting personal: Reflexivity, positionality, and feminist research. *The Professional Geographer*, 46(1): 80–89.

Everett, J. (2002) Organizational research and the praxeology of Pierre Bourdieu. *Organizational Research Methods*, 5(1): 56–80.

Fernandez-Kelly, P. (2015) In defense of Alice Goffman. *The Chronicle of Higher Education*. http://chronicle.com/article/In-Defense-of-Alice-Goffman/233680.

Finlay, L. (2002) Negotiating the swamp: The opportunity and challenge of reflexivity in research practice. *Qualitative Research*, 2(2): 209–30.

Finnegan, A. (2011). Did the election of New Labour instigate a significant change in government support of volunteering? Towards a more nuanced account. Paper presented at NCVO/VSSN Researching the Voluntary Sector Conference, London, 7–8 September.

Forber-Pratt, A. (2015) 'You're going to do what?' Challenges of autoethnography in the academy. *Qualitative Inquiry*, 21(9): 821–35.

Forrest, D. (2010) 'The cultivation of gifts in all directions': Thinking about purpose. In T. Jeffs and M. Smith (eds) *Youth Work Practice*. Basingstoke: Palgrave Macmillan, pp. 54–69.

Foucault, M. (1991). Governmentality. In G. Burchell, C. Gordon and P. Miller (eds) *The Foucault Effect: Studies in Governmentality*. Chicago, IL: University of Chicago Press, pp. 87–104.

Foucault, M. (2013) *Lectures on the Will to Know*. Basingstoke: Palgrave Macmillan.

Fowler, B. (2000) *Reading Bourdieu on Society and Culture*. Oxford: Blackwell.

Franco, A., Malhotra, N. and Simonovits, G. (2014) Publication bias in the social sciences: Unlocking the file drawer. *Science*, 345(6203): 1502–5.

Frangie, S. (2009) Bourdieu's reflexive politics: Socio-analysis, biography and self-creation. *European Journal of Social Theory*, 12(2): 213–29.

Friedman, S. (2016) The limits of capital gains: Using Bourdieu to understand mobility into elite occupations. In J. Thatcher, N. Ingram, C. Burke and J. Abrahams (eds) *Bourdieu: The Next Generation: The Development of Bourdieu's Intellectual Heritage in Contemporary UK Sociology*. Abingdon: Routledge, pp. 107–22.

Friedman, S., O'Brien, D. and Laurison, D. (2016) 'Like skydiving without a parachute': How class origin shapes occupational trajectories in British acting. *Sociology*, DOI: 10.1177/0038038516629917.

Frosh, S. and Emerson, P. (2005) Interpretation and over-interpretation: Disputing the meaning of texts. *Qualitative Research*, 5(3): 307–24.

Frost, N., Nolas, S., Brooks-Gordon, B., Esin, C., Holt, A., Mehdizadeh, L. et al. (2010) Pluralism in qualitative research: The impact of different researchers and qualitative approaches on the analysis of qualitative data. *Qualitative Research*, 10(4): 441–60.

Fuller, S. (2005) *The Intellectual*. Cambridge: Icon Books.

Furlong, A. and Cartmel, F. (2007) *Young People and Social Change: New Perspectives*, 2nd edn. Maidenhead: Open University Press.

Gane, N. and Back, L. (2012) C. Wright Mills 50 years on: The promise and craft of sociology revisited. *Theory, Culture & Society* 29(7–8): 399–421.

Garnham, N. and Williams, R. (1996) Pierre Bourdieu and the sociology of culture: An introduction. In J. Palmer and M. Dodson (eds) *Design and Aesthetics: A Reader*. London: Routledge, pp. 49–62.

Gauntlett, D. (2007) *Creative Explorations: New Approaches to Identities and Audiences*. London: Routledge.

Gay, R. (2014) *Bad Feminist*. New York: Harper Perennial.

Geary, D. (2009) *Radical Ambition: C. Wright Mills, the Left, and American Social Thought*. London: University of California Press.

Giddens, A. (1979) *Central Problems in Social Theory: Action, Structure, and Contradiction in Social Analysis*. Los Angeles: University of California Press.

Gilbert, D., King, G., Pettigrew, S. and Wilson, T. (2016) Comment on 'Estimating the reproducibility of psychological science'. *Science*, 351(6277): 1037.

Gladney, A., Ayars, C., Taylor, W., Liehr, P. and Meininger, J. (2003) Consistency of findings produced by two multidisciplinary research teams. *Sociology*, 37(2): 297–313.

Goffman, A. (2014) *On the Run: Fugitive Life in an American City*. London: University of Chicago Press.

Goffman, A. (2015) On the run. British Sociological Association conference 2015. https://vimeo.com/129223947.

Goffman, E. (1959) *The Presentation of Self in Everyday Life*. Harmondsworth: Penguin.

Goffman, E. (1961) *Asylums: Essays on the Social Situation of Mental Patients and Other Inmates*. New York: Anchor Books.

Goldacre, B. (2015) The BMJ should require all papers to share their analytic code. *British Medical Journal*, 351: h4596.

Goodman, J. and Silverstein, P. (2009) *Bourdieu in Algeria: Colonial Politics, Ethnographic Practices, Theoretical Developments*. Lincoln, NE: University of Nebraska Press.

Goodwin, J. (2012) *Sage Secondary Data Analysis*. London: Sage.

Gouldner, A. (1970) *The Coming Crisis of Western Sociology*. London: Heinemann.

Graeber, D. (2004) *Fragments of an Anarchist Anthropology*. Chicago, IL: Prickly Paradigm Press.

Graeber, D. (2015) *The Utopia of Rules: On Technology, Stupidity, and the Secret Joys of Bureaucracy*. London: Melville House.

Grenfell, M. (2004) *Pierre Bourdieu: Agent Provocateur*. London: Continuum.

Grenfell, M. (2008) *Pierre Bourdieu: Key Concepts*. London: Routledge.

Halperin, D. (1996) *Saint Foucault: Towards a Gay Hagiography*. Oxford: Oxford University Press.

Halsey, A. (2004) *A History of British Sociology*. Oxford: Clarendon.

Hammersley, M. (1997) Qualitative data archiving: Its prospects and problems. *Sociology*, 31(1): 131–42.

Hammersley, M. (2003) 'Analytics' are no substitute for methodology: A response to Speer and Hutchby. *Sociology*, 37(2): 339–51.

Hammersley, M. (2009) Challenging relativism: The problem of assessment criteria. *Qualitative Inquiry*, 15(1): 3–29.

Hammersley, M. (2010) Can we re-use qualitative data via secondary analysis? Notes on some terminological and substantive issues. *Sociological Research Online*, 15(1).

Hammersley, M. (2013) *What is Qualitative Research?* London: Bloomsbury.

Hammersley, M. and Atkinson, P. (2007) *Ethnography: Principles in Practice*, 3rd edn. London: Routledge.

Handy, C. (2008). Hysteresis. In M. Grenfell (ed.) *Pierre Bourdieu: Key Concepts*. Stocksfield: Acumen, pp. 131–48.

Hanson, S. (2014) *Small Towns, Austere Times: The Dialectics of Deracinated Localism*. Winchester: Zero Books.

Harding, S. (1986) *The Science Question in Feminism*. Ithaca, NY: Cornell University Press.

Harding, S. (1991) *Whose Science? Whose Knowledge? Thinking from Women's Lives*. Milton Keynes: Open University Press.

Harker, R., Mahar, C. and Wilkes, C. (1990) *An Introduction to the Work of Pierre Bourdieu: The Practice of Theory*. Basingstoke: Palgrave.

Hartsock, N. (1983) *Money, Sex and Power: Toward a Feminist Historical Materialism*. Boston, MA: Northeastern University Press.

Hastings, A. and Matthews, P. (2015) Bourdieu and the big society: Empowering the powerful in public service provision. *Policy & Politics*, 43(4): 545–60.

Hawthorn, G. (1997) Top of the class. *London Review of Books*, 19(9): 19–21.

Hayden, T. (2006) *Radical Nomad: C. Wright Mills and His Times*. Boulder, CO: Paradigm.

Haynes, J. and Jones, D. (2012) A tale of two analyses: The use of archived qualitative data. *Sociological Research Online*, 17(2).

Heaton, J. (2004) *Reworking Qualitative Data*. London: Sage.

Hepworth, D. (2014) Six reasons why *Desert Island Discs* is the perfect radio programme. *The Guardian*. http://www.theguardian.com/commentisfree/2014/nov/14/desert-island-discs-perfect-radio-programme-bbc.

Hoggart, R. (1957) *The Uses of Literacy*. Harmondsworth: Penguin.

Holmwood, J. (2015) Social Science Inc. *Open Democracy*. https://www.opendemocracy.net/ourkingdom/john-holmwood/social-science-inc.

Holt, N. (2003) Representation, legitimation, and autoethnography: An autoethnographic writing story. *International Journal of Qualitative Methods*, 2(1): 18–28.

Hornsby-Smith, M. (1993) Gaining access. In G. Gilbert (ed.) *Researching Social Life*. London: Sage, pp. 52–67.

Humphreys, L. (1970) *Tearoom Trade: Impersonal Sex in Public Places*. London: AldineTransaction.

Humphreys, M. (2005) Getting personal: Reflexivity and autoethnographic vignettes. *Qualitative Inquiry*, 11(6): 840–60.

Jacobsen, M., Drake, M., Keohane, K. and Petersen, A. (2014) *Imaginative Methodologies in the Social Sciences: Creativity, Poetics and Rhetoric in Social Research*. Farnham: Ashgate.

Jeffries, S. (2014) Stuart Hall's cultural legacy: Britain under the microscope. *The Guardian*. http://www.theguardian.com/education/2014/feb/10/stuart-hall-cultural-legacy-britain-godfather-multiculturalism.

Jenkins, R. (1992) *Pierre Bourdieu*. London: Routledge.

Jenkins, T. (2006) Bourdieu's Béarnais ethnography. *Theory, Culture & Society*, 23(6): 45–72.

Jerolmack, C. and Khan, S. (2014) Talk is cheap: Ethnography and the attitudinal fallacy. *Sociological Methods & Research*, 43(2): 178–209.

Jewkes, Y. (2012) Autoethnography and emotion as intellectual resources. *Qualitative Inquiry*, 18(1): 63–75.

Jones, H. (2013) *Negotiating Cohesion, Inequality and Change: Uncomfortable Positions in Local Government*. Bristol: Policy Press.

Jones, J. (2014) Banksy wanted Clacton-on-Sea to confront racism – instead it confronted him. *The Guardian*, http://www.theguardian.com/commentisfree/2014/oct/02/bansky-clacton-on-sea-racism-tendring-district-council-destroyed-immigration.

Jones, O. (2012) *Chavs: The Demonization of the Working Class*. London: Verso.

Kara, H. (2015) *Creative Research Methods in the Social Sciences: A Practical Guide*. Bristol: Policy Press

Kelly, L., Burton, S. and Regan, L. (1994) Researching women's lives or studying women's oppression? Reflections on what constitutes feminist research. In M. Maynard and J. Purvis (eds) *Researching Women's Lives from a Feminist Perspective*. London: Taylor and Francis, pp. 27–48.

Kenway, J. and McLeod, J. (2004) Bourdieu's reflexive sociology and 'spaces of points of view': Whose reflexivity, which perspective? *British Journal of Sociology of Education*, 25(4): 525–44.

Khan, S. (2011) *Privilege: The Making of an Adolescent Elite at St. Paul's School*. Oxford: Princeton University Press.

Khan, S. (2013) Field observation/ethnography: How elite students think about 'the staff'. In S. Khan and D. Fisher (eds) *The Practice of Research: How Social Scientists Answer Their Questions*. Oxford: Oxford University Press, pp. 91–109.

Kim, K.-M. (2010) How objective is Bourdieu's participant objectivation? *Qualitative Inquiry*, 16(9): 747–56.

Kuhn, A. (1995) *Family Secrets: Acts of Memory and Imagination*. London: Verso.

Lafitte, P. (1957) *The Person in Psychology*. London: Routledge.

Lamaison, P. (1986) From rules to strategies: An interview with Pierre Bourdieu. *Cultural Anthropology*, 1(1): 110–20.

Lamont, M. (1987) How to become a dominant French philosopher: The case of Jacques Derrida. *American Journal of Sociology*, 93(3): 584–662.

Lamont, M. (2012) How has Bourdieu been good to think with? The case of the United States. *Sociological Forum*, 27(1): 228–237.

Lareau, A. (2000) *Home Advantage*. Oxford: Rowman and Littlefield.

Lareau, A. (2003) *Unequal Childhoods: Class, Race, and Family Life*. London: University of California Press.

Latour, B. (1999) *Pandora's Hope: Essays on the Reality of Science Studies*. London: Harvard University Press.

Lawler, S. (2005) Introduction: Class, culture and identity. *Sociology*, 39(5): 797–806.

Lemert, C. (1991) Review of *In Other Words: Essays towards a Reflexive Sociology*, by Pierre Bourdieu. *American Journal of Sociology*, 97(1): 276–8.

Letherby, G., Scott, J. and Williams, M. (2013) *Objectivity and Subjectivity in Social Research*. London: Sage.

Lewis-Kraus, G. (2016) The trials of Alice Goffman. *New York Times*. http://www.nytimes.com/2016/01/17/magazine/the-trials-of-alice-goffman.html.

Lovell, T. (2002) Thinking feminism with and against Bourdieu. *Feminist Theory*, 1(1): 11–32.

Lubet, S. (2015) Ethics on the run. *The New Rambler*. http://newramblerreview.com/book-reviews/law/ethics-on-the-run.

Lumsden, K. (2009) 'Don't ask a woman to do another woman's job': Gendered interactions and the emotional ethnographer. *Sociology*, 43(3): 497–513.

Lumsden, K. (2013a) *Boy Racer Culture: Youth, Masculinity and Deviance*. Basingstoke: Routledge.

Lumsden, K. (2013b) 'You are what you research': Researcher partisanship and the sociology of the 'underdog'. *Qualitative Research*, 13(1): 3–18.

Lumsden, K. (forthcoming) *Reflexivity: Theory, Method and Practice*. London: Routledge.

Lumsden, K. and Winter, A. (2014) *Reflexivity in Criminological Research: Experiences with the Powerful and the Powerless*. Basingstoke: Palgrave Macmillan.

Lury, C. and Wakeford, N. (2014) *Inventive Methods: The Happening of the Social*. London: Routledge.

MacDonald, R., Shildrick, T., Webster, C. and Simpson, D. (2005) Growing up in poor neighbourhoods: The significance of class and place in the extended transitions of 'socially excluded' young adults. *Sociology*, 39(5): 873–91.

MacDougall, D. (2011) Anthropological filmmaking: An empirical art. In E. Margolis and L. Pauwels (eds) *The Sage Handbook of Visual Research Methods*. London: Sage, pp. 99–113.

McDonald, R. (2014) 'Bourdieu', medical elites and 'social class': A qualitative study of 'desert island' doctors. *Sociology of Health & Illness*, 36(6): 902–16.

McDowell, L. (1992) Doing gender: Feminism, feminists and research methods in human geography. *Transactions of the Institute of British Geographers*, 17(4): 399–416.

Mckenzie, L. (2015) *Getting By: Estates, Class and Culture in Austerity Britain*. Bristol: Policy Press.

Mckenzie, L. (2016) Narrative, ethnography and class inequality: Taking Bourdieu into a British council estate. In J. Thatcher, N. Ingram, C. Burke and J. Abrahams (eds) *Bourdieu: The Next Generation: The Development of Bourdieu's Intellectual Heritage in Contemporary UK Sociology*. Abingdon: Routledge, pp. 25–36.

McNay, L. (2014) *The Misguided Search for the Political*. Cambridge: Polity.

Maguire, P. (1987) *Doing Participatory Research: A Feminist Approach*. Amherst, MA: Centre for International Education, University of Massachusetts.

Massey, C., Alpass, F., Flett, R., Lewis, K., Morriss, S. and Sligo, F. (2006) Crossing fields: The case of a multi-disciplinary research team. *Qualitative Research*, 6(2): 131–49.

Matthews, P. and Hastings, A. (2013) Middle-class political activism and middle-class advantage in relation to public services: A realist synthesis of the evidence base. *Social Policy & Administration*, 47(1): 72–92.

Mauthner, N. and Doucet, A. (2003) Reflexive accounts and accounts of reflexivity in qualitative data analysis. *Sociology*, 37(3): 413–31.

Mauthner, N. and Doucet, A. (2008) 'Knowledge once divided can be hard to put back together again': An epistemological critique of collaborative and team-based research practices. *Sociology*, 42(5): 971–85.

May, T. (2011) *Social Research and Reflexivity*. London: Sage.

Merrifield, A. (2001). An American aboriginal: A review of *C. Wright Mills: Letters and Autobiographical Writings*. *Antipode*, 33(2): 290–6.

Merton, R. (1972) Insiders and outsiders: A chapter in the sociology of knowledge. *American Journal of Sociology*, 78(1): 9–47.

Metzgar, J. (2000) *Striking Steel: Solidarity Remembered*. Philadelphia, PA: Temple University Press.

Metzgar, J. (2011) Teaching unequal childhoods. The Centre for Working-Class Studies. http://workingclassstudies.wordpress.com/tag/annette-lareau.

Mills, C.W. (1939). Language, logic, and culture. *American Sociological Review*, 4(5): 670–80.

Mills, C.W. (1940) Methodological consequences of the sociology of knowledge. *American Journal of Sociology*, 46(3): 316–30.

Mills, C.W. (1948) *The New Men of Power*. Chicago, IL: University of Illinois Press.

Mills, C.W. (1959) *The Sociological Imagination*. New York: Oxford University Press.

Mills, C.W. (1962) *The Marxists*. New York: Dell.

Mills, C.W. (2008) *The Politics of Truth: Selected Writings of C. Wright Mills*. New York: Oxford University Press, pp. 125–138.

Mills, C.W., Mills, K. and Mills, P. (2000) *C. Wright Mills: Letters and Autobiographical Writings*. London: University of California Press.

Moore, J. (2004) Living in the basement of the ivory tower: A graduate student's perspective of participatory action research within academic institutions. *Educational Action Research*, 12(1): 145–62.

Moore, J. (2012) A personal insight into researcher positionality. *Nurse Researcher*, 19(4): 11–14.

Morison, M. (1986) *Methods in Sociology*. London: Longman.

Morrin, K. (2016) Unresolved reflections: Bourdieu, haunting and struggling with ghosts. In J. Thatcher, N. Ingram, C. Burke and J. Abrahams (eds) *Bourdieu: The Next Generation: The Development of Bourdieu's Intellectual Heritage in Contemporary UK Sociology*. Abingdon: Routledge, pp. 123–39.

Morrison, K. (2006) *Marx, Durkheim, Weber: Formations of Modern Social Thought*. London: Sage.

Moss, R. (2012) Sheffield's Millennium Gallery explores Ruskin's landscapes with absorbing tour of art. http://www.culture24.org.uk/art/painting-and-drawing/art414062.

Museums Sheffield (2012) Force of nature: Picturing Ruskin's landscapes. Museums Sheffield. http://www.museums-sheffield.org.uk/museums/millennium-gallery/exhibitions/past/force-of-nature-picturing-ruskin%E2%80%99s-landscape.

Myrdal, G. (1970) *Objectivity in Social Research*. London: Gerald Duckworth and Co.

Nayfakh, L. (2015) The ethics of ethnography. *Slate*. http://www.slate.com/articles/news_and_politics/crime/2015/06/alice_goffman_s_on_the_run_is_the_sociologist_to_blame_for_the_inconsistencies.html.

Neal, S. and Murji, K. (2015) Sociologies of everyday life: Editor's introduction to the special issue. *Sociology*, 49(5): 811–19.

Nickel, P. and Eikenberry, A. (2013) Gastrophilanthropy: Utopian aspiration and aspirational consumption as political retreat. *Reconstruction*, 12(4).

O'Neill, J. (1995) *The Poverty of Postmodernism*. London: Routledge.

Oakley, A. (1974) *The Sociology of Housework*. London: Martin Robinson.

Oakley, A. (1979) *Becoming a Mother*. Oxford: Martin Robinson.

Oakley, A. (1981) Interviewing women: A contradiction in terms. In H. Roberts (ed.) *Doing Feminist Research*. London: Routledge and Kegan Paul, pp. 30–61.

Oakley, A. (2014) *Father and Daughter: Patriarchy, Gender and Social Science*. Bristol: Policy Press.

Oakley, A. (2016) Interviewing women again: Power, time and the gift. *Sociology*, 50(1): 195–213.

Open Science Collaboration (2015) Estimating the reproducibility of psychological science. *Science*, 349(6521): aac4716.

Owton, H. and Allen-Collinson, J. (2013) Close but not too close: Friendship as method(ology) in ethnographic research encounters. *Journal of Contemporary Ethnography*, 43(3): 283–305.

Pangrazio, L. (2016) Exploring provocation as a research method in the social sciences. *International Journal of Social Research Methodology*, DOI: 10.1080/13645579.2016.1161346.

Pauwels, L. (2012) Contemplating the state of visual research: An assessment of obstacles and opportunities. In S. Pink (ed.) *Advances in Visual Methodology*. London: Sage, pp. 248–64.

Phillips, C. and Earle, R. (2010) Reading difference differently: Identity, epistemology and prison ethnography. *British Journal of Criminology*, 50(2): 360–78.

Phoenix, A. (1994) Practising feminist research: The intersection of gender and 'race' in the research process. In M. Maynard and J. Purvis (eds) *Researching Women's Lives from a Feminist Perspective*. London: Taylor and Francis, pp. 49–71.

Pickering, M. (1997) *History, Experience and Cultural Studies*. London: Macmillan.

Pink, S. (2012) *Situating Everyday Life*. London: Sage.

Piper, D. (2004) *The Illustrated History of Art*. London: Bounty Books.

Presser, H. (1998) Decapitating the U.S. Census Bureau's 'head of household': Feminist mobilization in the 1970s. *Feminist Economics*, 4(3): 145–58.

Prieur, A. and Savage, M. (2013) Emerging forms of cultural capital. *European Societies*, 15(2): 246–67.

Pullen, L. (2012) Force of nature takes shape. Museums Sheffield. http://museums-sheffield.org.uk/blog/2012/12/force-of-nature-takes-shape.

Rainbird, H., Fuller, A. and Munro, A. (2004) *Workplace Learning in Context*. London: Routledge.

Rainford, J. (2016) Making internal conversations public: Reflexivity of the connected doctoral researcher and its transmission beyond the walls of the academy. *Journal of Applied Social Theory*, 1(1): 44–60.

Reay, D. (1998) Rethinking social class: Qualitative perspectives on gender and social class. *Sociology*, 32(2): 259–75.

Reay, D. (2003) A risky business? Mature working-class women students and access to higher education. *Gender and Education*, 15(3): 301–18.

Reay, D. (2004) 'It's all becoming a habitus': Beyond the habitual use of habitus in educational research. *British Journal of Sociology of Education*, 25(4): 431–44.

Reay, D. (2005) Beyond consciousness? The psychic landscape of social class. *Sociology*, 39(5): 911–28.

Reay, D., Crozier, G. and Layton, J. (2010) 'Fitting in' or 'standing out': Working-class students in UK higher education. *British Educational Research Journal*, 36(1): 107–24.

Reed-Danahay, D. (2009) Bourdieu's ethnography in Béarn and Kabylia: The peasant *habitus*. In J. Goodman and P. Silverstein (eds) *Bourdieu in Algeria: Colonial Politics, Ethnographic Practices, Theoretical Developments*. Lincoln, NE: University of Nebraska Press, pp. 133–63.

Remler, D. (2014) Are 90% of academic papers really never cited? Reviewing the literature on academic citations. http://blogs.lse.ac.uk/impactofsocialsciences/2014/04/23/academic-papers-citation-rates-remler.

Rhys-Taylor, A. (2013a) Disgust and distinction: The case of the jellied eel. *The Sociological Review*, 61(2): 227–46.

Rhys-Taylor, A. (2013b) The essences of multiculture: A sensory exploration of an inner-city market. *Identities: Global Studies in Culture and Power*, 20(4): 393–406.

Robbins, D. (2000) *Bourdieu and Culture*. London: Sage.

Robbins, D. (2007) Sociology as reflexive science: Bourdieu's project. *Theory, Culture & Society*, 24(5): 77–98.

Roberts, H. (1981a) *Doing Feminist Research*. London: Routledge and Kegan Paul.

Roberts, H. (1981b) Women and their doctors: Power and powerlessness in the research process. In H. Roberts (ed.) *Doing Feminist Research*. London: Routledge and Kegan Paul, pp. 7–29.

Roberts, K. (1997) Structure and agency: The new youth research agenda. In J. Bynner, L. Chisholm and A. Furlong (eds) *Youth, Citizenship and Social Change in a European Context*. Aldershot: Ashgate, pp. 56–65.

Rogers, C. (1967) *On Becoming a Person: A Therapist's View on Psychotherapy.* London: Constable.

Ruby, J. (2000) *Picturing Culture: Explorations of Film and Anthropology.* Chicago, IL: University of Chicago Press.

Sapiro, G. (2010) Introduction. In G. Sapiro (ed.) *Sociology Is a Martial Art: The Political Writings of Pierre Bourdieu.* New York: The New Press, pp. iv–xxi.

Savage, J. (1991) *England's Dreaming: Sex Pistols and Punk Rock.* London: Faber and Faber.

Savage, M. (2015) Introduction to elites: From the 'problem of the proletariat' to a class analysis of wealth elites. *British Journal of Sociology*, 63(2): 223–39.

Savage, M. and Burrows, R. (2007) The coming crisis of empirical sociology. *Sociology*, 41(5): 885–99.

Savage, M., Devine, F., Cunningham, N., Taylor, M., Li, Y., Hjellbrekke, J. et al. (2013) A new model of social class? Findings from the BBC's Great British Class Survey experiment. *Sociology*, 47(2): 219–50.

Schutz, A. (1962). *Collected Papers*, vol. 1. Leiden: Nijhoff.

Schwandt, T. (2000) Three epistemological stances for qualitative inquiry: Intepretivism, hermeneutics and social constructionism. In N. Denzin and Y. Lincoln (eds) *Handbook of Qualitative Research.* London: Sage, pp. 189–213.

Seidman, S. (1985) Review of *The Limits of Rationality: An Essay on the Social and Moral Thought of Max Weber. Social Forces*, 64(2): 516–18.

Selltiz, C., Jahoda, M., Deutsch, M. and Cook, S. (1964) *Research Methods in Social Relations.* New York: Holt, Rinehart and Winston.

Sennett, R. (2006) Introduction. In E. Durkheim *On Suicide.* London: Penguin, pp. xi–xxiv

Sennett, R. and Cobb, J. (1972) *The Hidden Injuries of Class.* Cambridge: Cambridge University Press.

Sharpe, C. (2014) Black life, annotated. *The New Inquiry.* http://thenewinquiry. com/essays/black-life-annotated/.

Shildrick, T. and MacDonald, R. (2013) Poverty talk: How people experiencing poverty deny their poverty and talk about the poor. *The Sociological Review*, 61(2): 285–303.

Shilliam, R. (2015) Black academia: The doors have been opened but the architecture remains the same. In C. Alexander and J. Arday (eds) *Aiming Higher: Race Inequality and Diversity in the Academy.* London: Runnymede Trust, pp. 32–4.

Shimp, C. (2007) Quantitative behavior analysis and human values. *Behavioral Processes*, 75(2): 146–55.

Silverman, D. (1993) *Interpreting Qualitative Data: Methods for Analysing Talk, Text and Interaction.* London: Sage.

Singal, J. (2015) The internet accused Alice Goffman of faking details in her study of a Black neighborhood. I went to Philadelphia to check. *New York Magazine.* http://nymag.com/scienceofus/2015/06/i-fact-checked-alice-goffman-with-her-subjects.html.

Singal, J. (2016) 3 lingering questions from the Alice Goffman controversy. *New York Magazine*. http://nymag.com/scienceofus/2016/01/3-lingering-questions-about-alice-goffman.html.

Sinha, S. and Back, L. (2014) Making methods sociable: Dialogue, authorship and ethics in qualitative research. *Qualitative Research*, 14(4): 473–87.

Skeggs, B. (1997) *Formations of Class and Gender: Becoming Respectable*. London: Sage.

Skeggs, B. (2004a) *Class, Self, Culture*. London: Routledge.

Skeggs, B. (2004b) Exchange, value and affect: Bourdieu and 'the self'. In L. Adkins and B. Skeggs (eds) *Feminism After Bourdieu*. Oxford: Blackwell, pp. 75–96.

Skeggs, B. (2015) Introduction: Stratification or exploitation, domination, dispossession and devaluation? *The Sociological Review*, 63(2): 205–22.

Smart, C. (2010) Disciplined writing: On the problem of writing sociologically. *ESRC National Centre for Research Methods*. http://www.socialsciences.manchester.ac.uk/realities/publications/workingpapers/13-2010-01-realities-disciplined-writing.pdf.

Smith, D. (1990) *The Conceptual Practices of Power*. Toronto: Toronto University Press.

Sparrow, A. (2015) Election 2015: David Cameron rules out third term – as it happened. *The Guardian*. http://www.theguardian.com/politics/live/2015/mar/23/election-2015-miliband-labour-snp-scottish-seats-live.

Strangleman, T. (2004) *Work Identity at the End of the Line: Privatisation and Culture Change in the UK Rail Industry*. Basingstoke: Palgrave.

Strathern, M. (2006) Bullet-proofing: A tale from the United Kingdom. In A. Riles (ed.) *Documents: Artifacts of Modern Knowledge*, Ann Arbor, MI: University of Michigan, pp. 181–205.

Strauss, V. (2015) It's 2015. Where are all the black college faculty? *The Washington Post*. https://www.washingtonpost.com/news/answer-sheet/wp/2015/11/12/its-2015-where-are-all-the-black-college-faculty.

Summers, J. (2008) New man of power. In C.W. Mills *The Politics of Truth: Selected Writings of C. Wright Mills*. Oxford: Oxford University Press, pp. 3–12.

Susen, S. (2007) *The Foundations of the Social: Between Critical Theory and Reflexive Sociology*. Oxford: The Bardwell Press.

Swartz, D. (2009) Review of *The Batchelor's Ball*. *Contemporary Sociology*, 38(4): 367–9.

Tate (2010) Joseph Mallord William Turner: *Landscape with Water* (c. 1840–5). http://www.tate.org.uk/art/artworks/turner-landscape-with-water-n05513.

Taylor, C. and White, S. (2000) *Practising Reflexivity in Health and Welfare: Making Knowledge*. Buckingham: Open University Press.

Taylor, G., Mellor, L. and McCarter, R. (2016) *Work-related Learning and the Social Sciences*. London: Routledge.

Taylor, L. and Reisz, M. (2014) Laurie Taylor on the endangered art of ethnography. *Times Higher Education*. http://www.timeshighereducation.co.uk/features/laurie-taylor-on-the-endangered-art-of-ethnography/2013946.article.

Thatcher, J., Ingram, N., Burke, C. and Abrahams, J. (2016) *Bourdieu: The Next Generation: The Development of Bourdieu's Intellectual Heritage in Contemporary UK Sociology*. Abingdon: Routledge.

Tillman-Healy, L. (2003) Friendship as method. *Qualitative Inquiry*, 9(5): 729–49.

Tiryakian, E. (1966) A problem for the sociology of knowledge: The mutual unawareness of Emile Durkheim and Max Weber. *European Journal of Sociology*, 7(2): 330–6.

Tolich, M. (2010) A critique of current practice: Ten foundational guidelines for autoethnographers. *Qualitative Health Research*, 20(12): 1599–1610.

Tröger, M. (2012) How can I live with(out) C. Wright Mills? Breaking with the disembodied truth. *Cultural Studies <=> Critical Methodologies*, 12(3): 175–81.

Turner, J., Beeghley, L. and Powers, C. (2012) *The Emergence of Sociological Theory*, 7th edn. London: Sage.

Turner, S. (2014) Mundane theorizing: *Bricolage* and *bildung*. In R. Swedberg (ed.) *Theorizing in Social Science: The Context of Discovery*. Stanford, CA: Stanford University Press, pp. 131–57.

Tyler, I. (2013) *Revolting Subjects: Social Abjection and Resistance in Neoliberal Britain*. London: Zed Books.

Van Maanen, J. (1979) The fact of fiction in organisational ethnography. *Administrative Science Quarterly*, 24(4): 539–49.

Vannini, P., Ahluwalia-Lopez, G., Waskul, D. and Gottschalk, S. (2010) Performing taste at wine festivals: A somatic layered account of material culture. *Qualitative Inquiry*, 16(5): 378–96.

Virag, R. (2001) *The moon is up, and yet it is not night*. Tate. http://www.tate.org.uk/art/artworks/millais-the-moon-is-up-and-yet-it-is-not-night-n05632/text-summary.

Wacquant, L. (1989) For a socio-analysis of intellectuals: On *Homo Academicus*. *Berkeley Journal of Sociology*, 34: 1–29.

Wacquant, L. (2002) The sociological life of Pierre Bourdieu. *International Sociology*, 17(4): 549–56.

Wacquant, L. (2004) Critical thought as solvent of *doxa*. *Constellations: An International Journal of Critical and Democratic Theory*, 11(1): 97–101.

Wacquant, L. (2016) A concise genealogy and anatomy of habitus. *The Sociological Review*, 64(1): 64–72.

Wallace, M. (2003) A disconcerting brevity: Pierre Bourdieu's *Masculine Domination*. *Postmodern Culture*, 13(3). http://pmc.iath.virginia.edu/issue.503/13.3wallace.html.

Walley, C. (2009) Deindustrializing Chicago: A daughter's story. In H. Gusterson and C. Besterman (eds) *The Insecure American: How We Got Here and What We Should Do About It*. Berkeley, CA: University of California Press, pp. 113–39.

Waring, M. (1990) *If Women Counted: A New Feminist Economics*. San Francisco, CA: Harper Collins.

Warren, R. (2014) Eric Hazan responds to David Bell's review of *A People's History of the French Revolution* in *the Guardian*. Verso. http://www.versobooks.com/blogs/1716-eric-hazan-responds-to-david-bell-s-review-of-a-people-s-history-of-the-french-revolution-in-the-guardian.

Welch, P. (2006) Feminist pedagogy revisited. *Learning and Teaching in the Social Sciences*, 3(3): 171–99.

White, A. (2015) Photographers took wildly different pictures of this one guy because of backstory. *BuzzFeed*. http://www.buzzfeed.com/alanwhite/the-camera-never-lies.

White, S. (1997) Beyond retroduction? Hermeneutics, reflexivity and social work practice. *British Journal of Social Work*, 27(5): 739–53.

Williams, J. (2014) In defence of the 'white' curriculum. *Spiked*. http://www.spiked-online.com/newsite/article/in-defence-of-the-white-curriculum.

Wolfinger, N. (2002) On writing fieldnotes: Collection strategies and background expectancies. *Qualitative Research*, 2(1): 85–93.

Woodward, K., Murji, K., Neal, S. and Watson, S. (2014) Class debate. *Sociology*, 48(3): 427–8.

Yallop, J. (2012) Force of nature: Picturing Ruskin's landscapes. Museums Sheffield. http://museums-sheffield.org.uk/assets/PDFs/Force%20of%20Nature%20essay.pdf.

Index